AF474020

PAINTED MYSTERIES

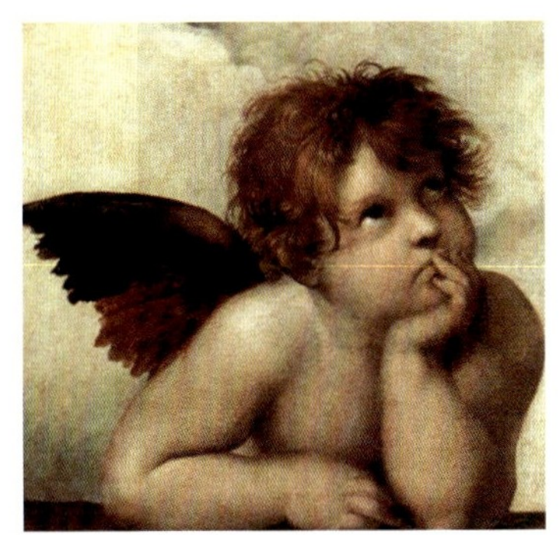

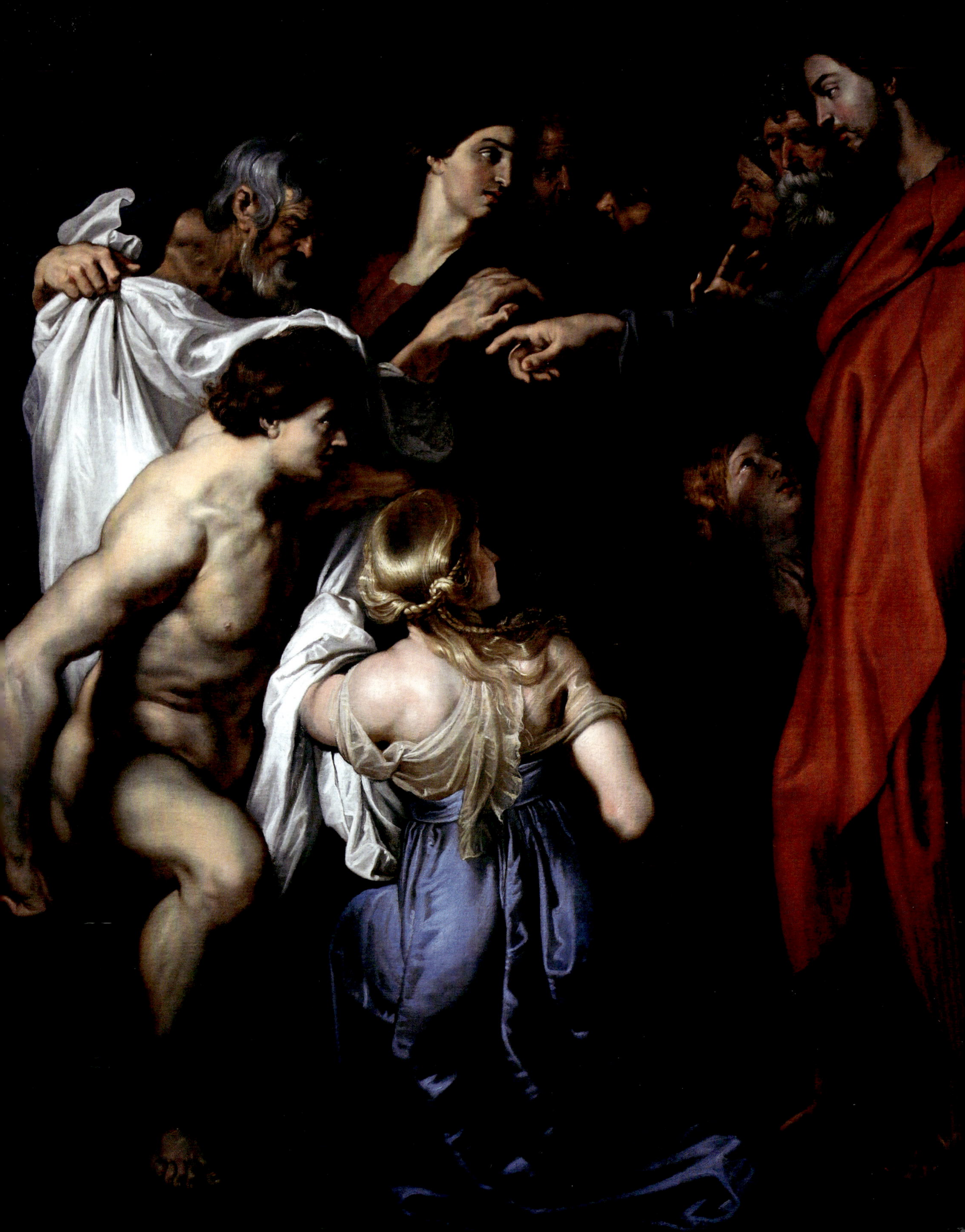

PAINTED MYSTERIES

INTERPRETING GREAT PAINTINGS

Opposite: Peter Paul Rubens, *The Raising of Lazarus*, 1625

Previous page: Raphael, *Sistine Madonna*, 1513–14 (detail)

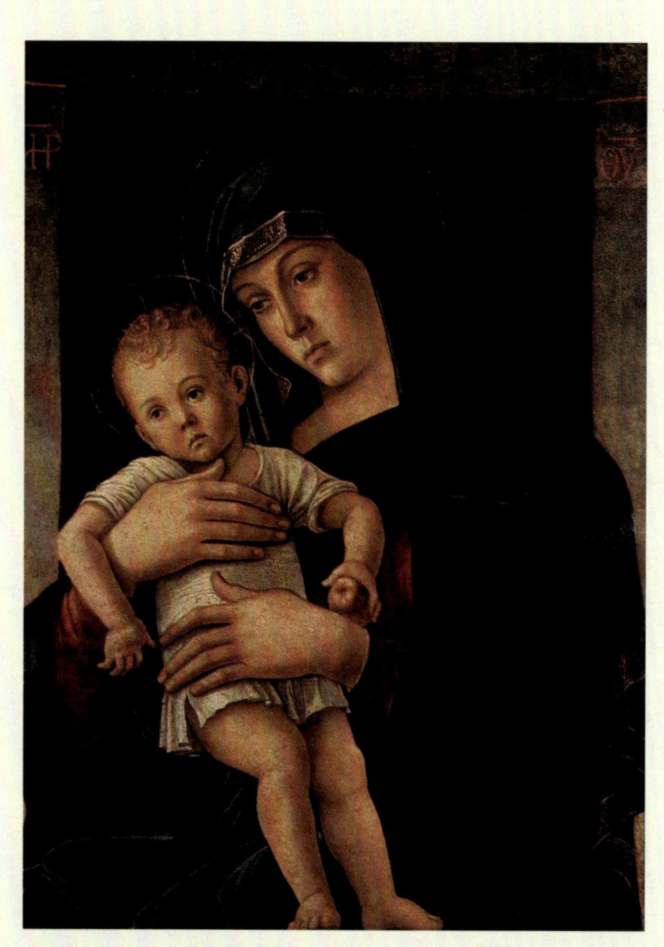

CONTENTS

Opposite: Giovanni Bellini, *Madonna with the Child (Greek Madonna)*, 1460–64

INTRODUCTION

'IT IS PERHAPS NECESSARY THAT THE EYE LEARNS TO SEE AS THE TONGUE LEARNS TO SPEAK.'

Denis Diderot, *Letter on the Blind*, 1749

Today we are so bombarded with images of every kind that we no longer take in fully what we see. We go around museums looking at the exhibits as if we are glancing at the covers of books rather than reading them. In the centuries when most of the works in this book were created, there was no television, cinema, galleries or museums and few books. But there was religion: society was steeped in it. Hell was horribly real; so was the Kingdom of Heaven. The Bible was pre-eminent, its stories a limitless source of inspiration for artists. People were also familiar with the classical world and with mythical and religious iconography. For the illiterate, the works of art within churches and cathedrals were an eloquent illustration of the Church's teachings.

Many European artists perfected a language of symbols, where objects were understood to represent something other than themselves, adding new layers of depth and meaning to their work. Contemporary viewers, even the uneducated, understood this symbolic language. They knew why the Christ Child was holding an apple, a goldfinch or a bunch of grapes. Most symbols had several interpretations and could change their meaning according to context. In the painting on the left by Titian, the rabbit is symbolic of wildly different things: purity or fecundity. To demonstrate how much sources can disagree, the bearded man in the background is said to be Joseph, a shepherd, Titian's patron Federico Gonzaga or Titian himself. Looking back at these works from our own perspective can be a puzzling experience, as we struggle to interpret a multi-faceted world view, which embodies many contradictions and confounds our logical, and linear, preconceptions.

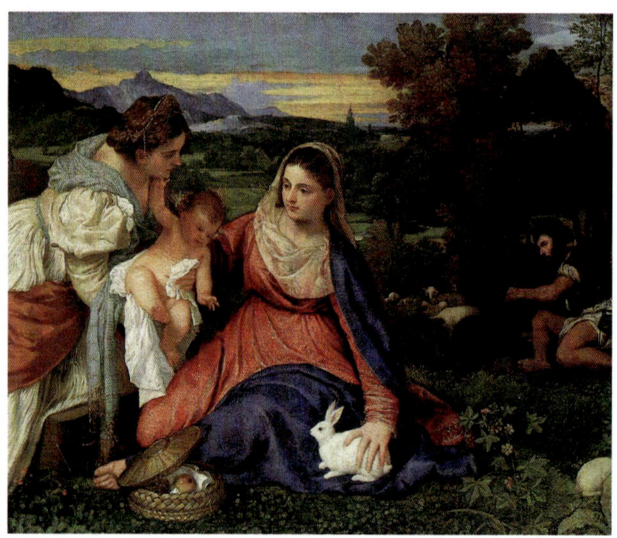

Titian, *The Madonna of the Rabbit*, *c.* 1520–30

Our lives today are full of symbols, but they have not evolved from the same sources as the paintings in this book. A fifteenth-century resident of Florence or Amsterdam would not be able to interpret the meaning of emojis or map symbols or see why a large black Z is the sign for a double bend in the road.

Symbols in a painting should not be confused with attributes. All saints had their attributes (frequently more than one), objects that were connected with their biblical story or legend and that helped to identify them. Thus, people knew why St Catherine was depicted with a wheel, why St Barbara held a palm frond or why St Anthony Abbott was often attended by a pig. Attributes had other functions: in portraits a sitter was often depicted with attributes or possessions that they had chosen to demonstrate or allude to their talents, status, interests, even sentiments.

The paintings in Part Two, 'What's Going On?' have been selected not only for their beauty and fascination but also for their complexity. The accompanying texts explain their meaning and tell the stories behind them. Part Two contains seven chapters. The titles of the first five speak for themselves: Biblical Scenes, Allegory, Classical Mythology, Legend, Classical Antiquity. Contemporary viewers would have instantly recognised the gods and goddesses of Greek and Roman mythology, also the heroes, legendary or otherwise, of ancient history. In the sixth chapter, Life's Rich Tapestry, the images depict various aspects of life at that time, both in urban and rural contexts. The subheading for the last chapter, Enter the Artist, could be Through the Back Door because the images demonstrate how ingeniously the artists smuggled their self-portraits into their paintings, some of them in very unlikely places.

There is still much to confuse and unsettle today's viewers of the paintings, even if they are well versed in the sources. The artists' use of 'modern' (fifteenth- to seventeenth-century) clothes and settings can be anachronistic and perplexing. Sometimes there is so much going on in a painting that the viewer gets lost, and the title is often of no help. Of no help either is the medieval and Renaissance artist's cavalier attitude to timeframes and linear narrative development: several incidents in a character's life can appear simultaneously in one painting. Even though some of the paintings are purely narrative, with not a symbol in sight, they are drawing on a body of knowledge that is no longer possessed by the bewildered twenty-first-century viewer.

It is hoped that the discussions of these paintings on the following pages, and the visual language and world view that was an integral part of their conception, will go some way towards unravelling these mysteries, allowing modern viewers to fully appreciate art from the perspective of a different world and time.

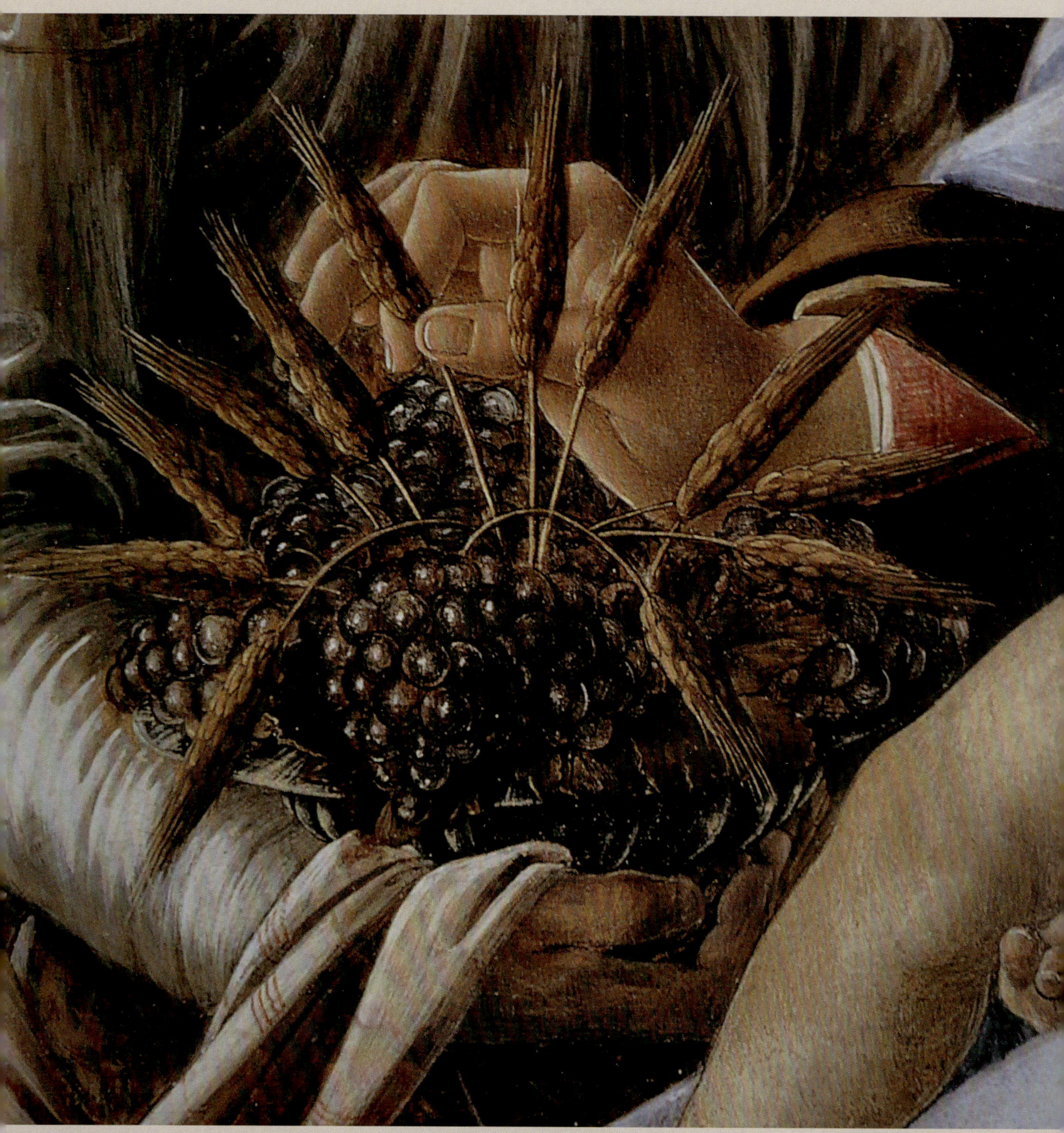

SANDRO BOTTICELLI, *Madonna of the Eucharist*, c. 1470 (detail)

Part One

DECODING THE SYMBOLS

The great art of the past is littered with symbols – a visual language that would have been instantly recognisable to the contemporary viewers but is lost on us today. In societies with low rates of literacy, visual narratives were an essential way of conveying great stories, timeless themes, heightened emotions and, above all, religious sensibilities. The symbols that are discussed on these pages represent some of the most important, and eloquent visual clues that were used by generations of inspired artists to weave new layers of emotion and meaning into their work.

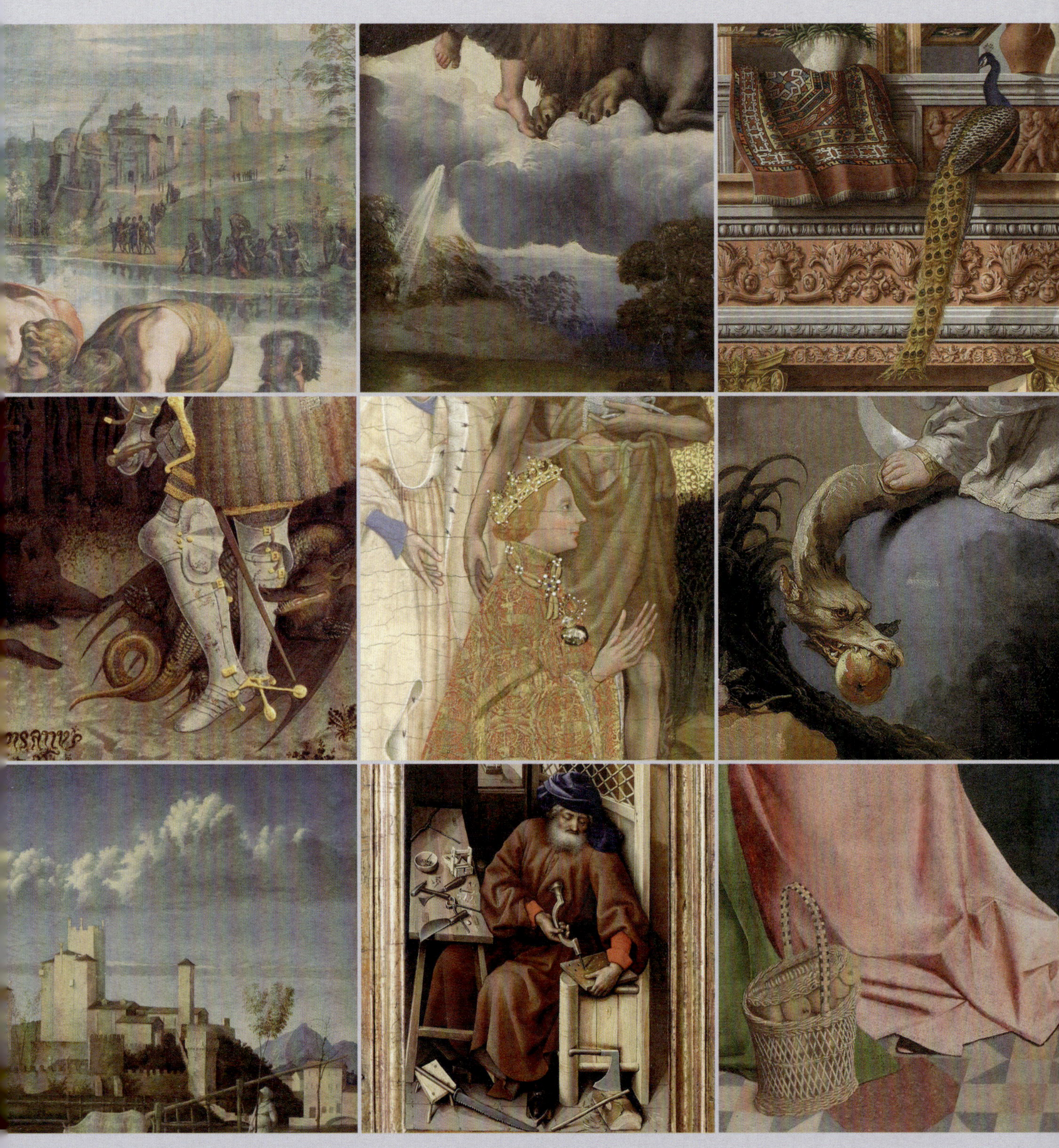

CHAPTER ONE

CHRISTIAN SYMBOLS

ANONYMOUS

The Wilton Diptych

1395–99

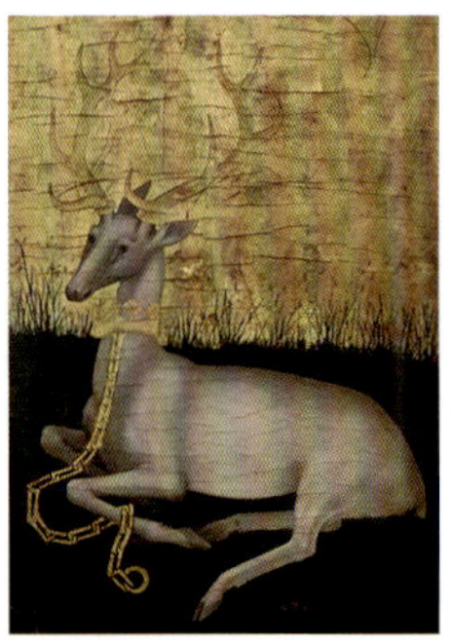

The white hart, which adorns the front of the diptych, lies in a verdant pasture strewn with rosemary, an emblem of Richard's first wife, Anne of Bohemia, as well as irises and pimpernels, emblems of his second wife, Isabelle of France.

The authorship, details and date of this exquisite object have teased art historians for decades. Was the artist French or English? Why is Richard shown as a beardless youth when – if the date of the diptych is roughly correct – he was a grown man? Could it be that he looked like this when he was crowned at the age of ten? Is the Christ Child blessing the king, or the red and white standard? Is the standard a symbol of the Resurrection or is it the flag of St George and thus of England? Is Richard giving the standard to the Virgin and Child or receiving it from them? Why is Mary holding the Child's foot between her thumb and forefinger? And why are there eleven angels when, in medieval iconography, the number eleven has extremely negative symbolism?

The main features of this portable altar are simpler to unravel. Richard II, King of England from 1377 to 1399, kneels in prayer before the Christ Child. Supporting the king are three saints whose attributes reveal their identities. The king's patron saint John the Baptist is on the right. The central saint is Edward the Confessor, former King of England, holding the ring that denotes one of the legends that are associated with him. Edmund, another former (ninth-century) English king, holds the arrow that killed him when he refused to renounce his Christian beliefs.

When viewed on the walls of London's National Gallery, the diptych almost throbs with gold. Gold is everywhere, stamped, punched and incised. The sky is made of it; the Christ Child wears it; Richard's crown and those of two of the saints contain it; there is gold, too, in Richard's robe. All this gold would have come alive as the candlelight glanced off it. But the extravagance in the making of the diptych does not end there: the angels and the Virgin are dressed from head to foot in the fabulously expensive ultramarine blue that was extracted from lapis lazuli, a semi-precious stone mined from a single mountain range in Afghanistan. The red (although faded) of the king's robe is not any old red, but vermilion, another costly pigment, traces of which have been found at Pompeii. Some of the minute details of the diptych are extraordinary: stippled within the Christ Child's halo is a crown of thorns and three nails – symbols of the Passion. During a recent restoration, it was discovered that the tiny orb that surmounts the standard contains a minuscule scene depicting a green island. Could this be England? Around the king's neck hangs a magnificent collar made of gold broomcods – seeds of the broom plant. Known as *planta genista* in Latin, they are a play on his family name of Plantagenet.

The 'front' of the diptych is fairly well preserved and depicts a white hart, chained with a crown around its neck. The back is badly damaged but it is possible to see a heraldic device including the royal arms of England and France impaled (halved vertically) with the supposed arms of Edward the Confessor.

The background and many of the details are inlaid with gold leaf. In places the panels have been tooled or punched beneath the gilding to enhance the decorative quality.

St John the Baptist is easily identified, as he is often portrayed with a lamb and dressed in tattered clothes or animal skins, evidence of his life as a hermit in the wilderness. He puts his arm around the king in a protective gesture.

The Virgin supports the Christ Child as he bends forward as if to bless or welcome the king and assure him that his prayers have been answered.

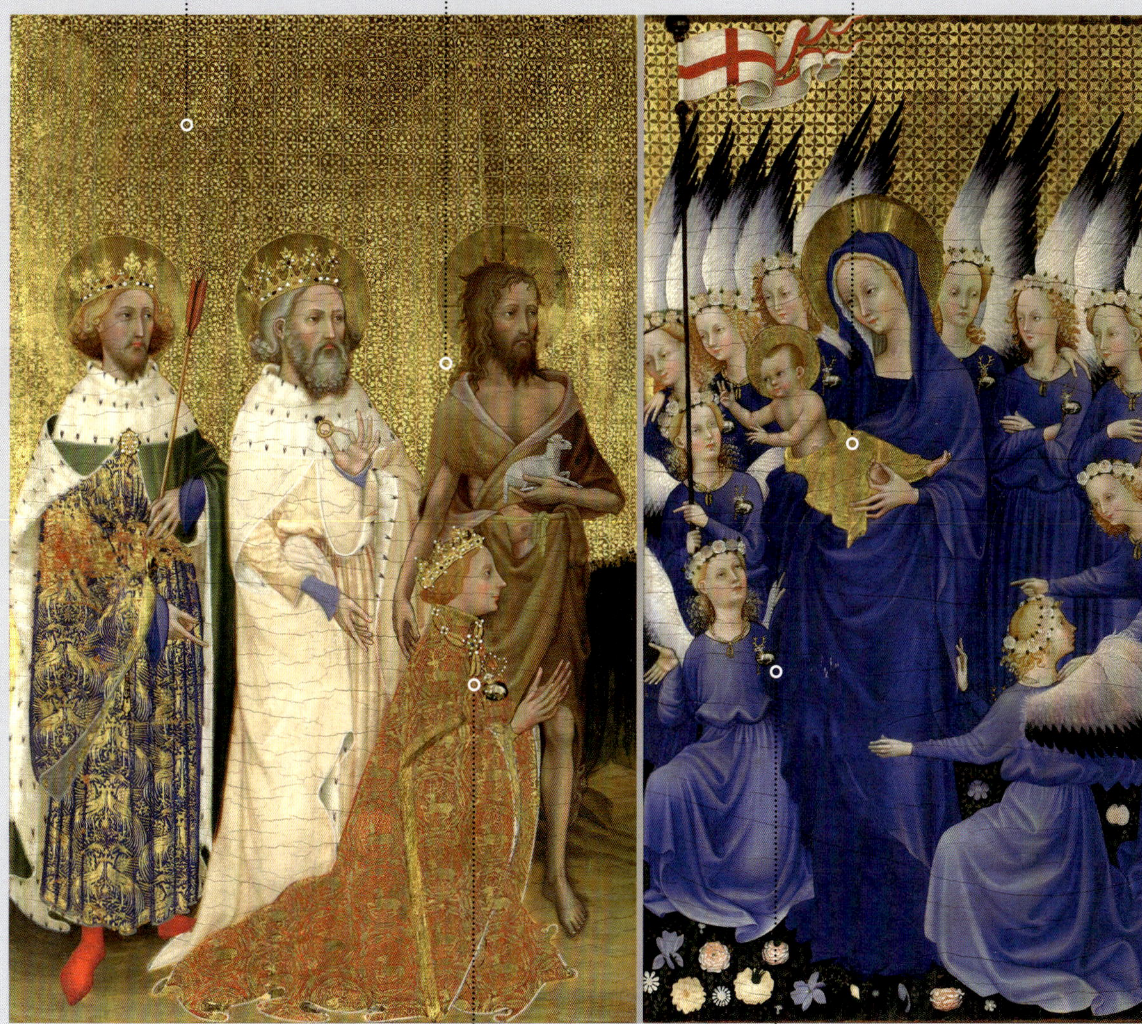

The jewel pinned to Richard's robe depicts his emblem, a white hart or stag. Pearls adorn its gold antlers and a gold crown encircles its throat. The emblem reappears as the principal motif in the king's brocaded robe.

The Virgin and the angels, wearing ultramarine robes, stand in a paradisaical meadow studded with flowers. The angels' heads are crowned with chaplets of roses and all wear the king's emblem.

UPPER RHENISH MASTER

The Little Garden of Paradise

c. 1410

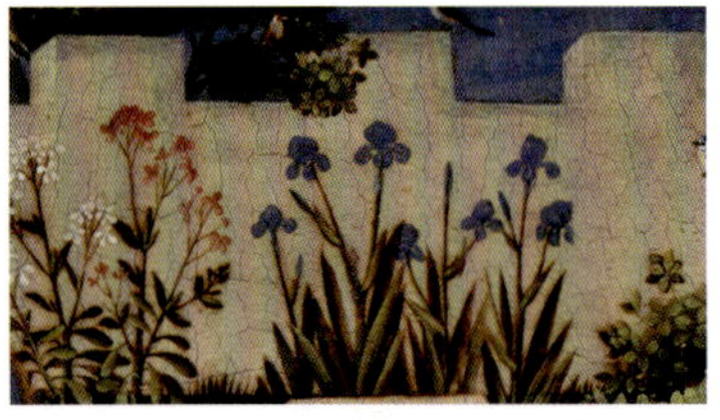

The artist has emphasised the paradisaical character of the garden by filling it with flowers that bloom at different times. Twenty-four plant and twelve bird species are precisely identifiable.

This enchanting painting, smaller than an average chessboard, appears to show a castle garden peopled by graceful figures enjoying a tranquil afternoon in the sunshine. Yet many details in the image stand for something other than themselves. Despite their faces being very similar – small with very dark eyes and tiny rosebud mouths – the contemporary viewer would instantly know that the predominant figure is the Virgin Mary, and that she is surrounded by various saints who are all identifiable by the objects and activities attributed to them in their legends. The garden itself represents a *hortus conclusus* (enclosed garden) that is not only a refuge from the brutish and violent fifteenth-century world beyond the battlements but an allusion to Mary's virginity since, according to Christian belief, she conceived without penetration. There are no shadows in this garden; instead it is illuminated by a bright, unearthly light.

The Virgin wears her heavenly golden crown and a robe painted with the costly ultramarine. She is not seated on a throne, but on a vermilion-coloured cushion below the terraced part of the lawn. On the far left, the lady picking apples is identified by her attribute – a basket – as the martyred St Dorothy. Below St Dorothy is St Barbara, ladling water from a spring with a golden spoon. The Upper Rhenish Master, clearly baffled as how to find a place in his garden for the saint's customary attribute – a tower – compromised by showing another facet of her legend that claimed her bones could work miracles by overcoming periods of drought. Below the Virgin, the Christ Child is playing a psaltery, a medieval stringed instrument. Careful scrutiny reveals the Christ Child's tiny halo, although it risks merging with the stylised grass. (But what does he keep in the little pouch on his belt?) The woman steadying the psaltery is probably St Catherine of Alexandria; throughout the high Middle Ages and the Renaissance she is among the saints most likely to be included in group portraits with the Virgin and Child. The angel with the gossamer wings, golden crown and pensive expression is St Michael, seemingly exhausted after driving Satan and his angels out of heaven. At his feet cowers a token devil in the guise of a monkey. Wearing a skirt and leggings of chain mail and ballooning vermilion sleeves is St George, with the smallest dragon ever vanquished lying dead beside him.

Gardens designed for pleasure were less common in *c.* 1410 than they are today. The Romans cultivated gardens, but they disappeared with the collapse of their empire. The monasteries had gardens, but they grew useful plants like herbs, vegetables and fruit. In the Middle Ages, small gardens could be found within castle walls with lawns and flower borders, places for relaxation and enjoyment. Here, the artist has filled his garden with flowers and birds. Many of them are Christian symbols, but whether he intended them to carry a meaning or just wanted to add to the magic of his paradise is unknown.

According to St Dorothy's legend, she was asked on her way to a martyr's death to send flowers and fruits from heaven. As she prayed, a boy suddenly appeared bearing them in a basket.

The Virgin's head is bowed over her book. Earthly activities such as reading, conversation and picking fruit often feature in the iconography of Paradise.

The white hexagonal table may look innocuous, but it is not there by chance. The apples represent original sin and the wine and bread refer to the Last Supper.

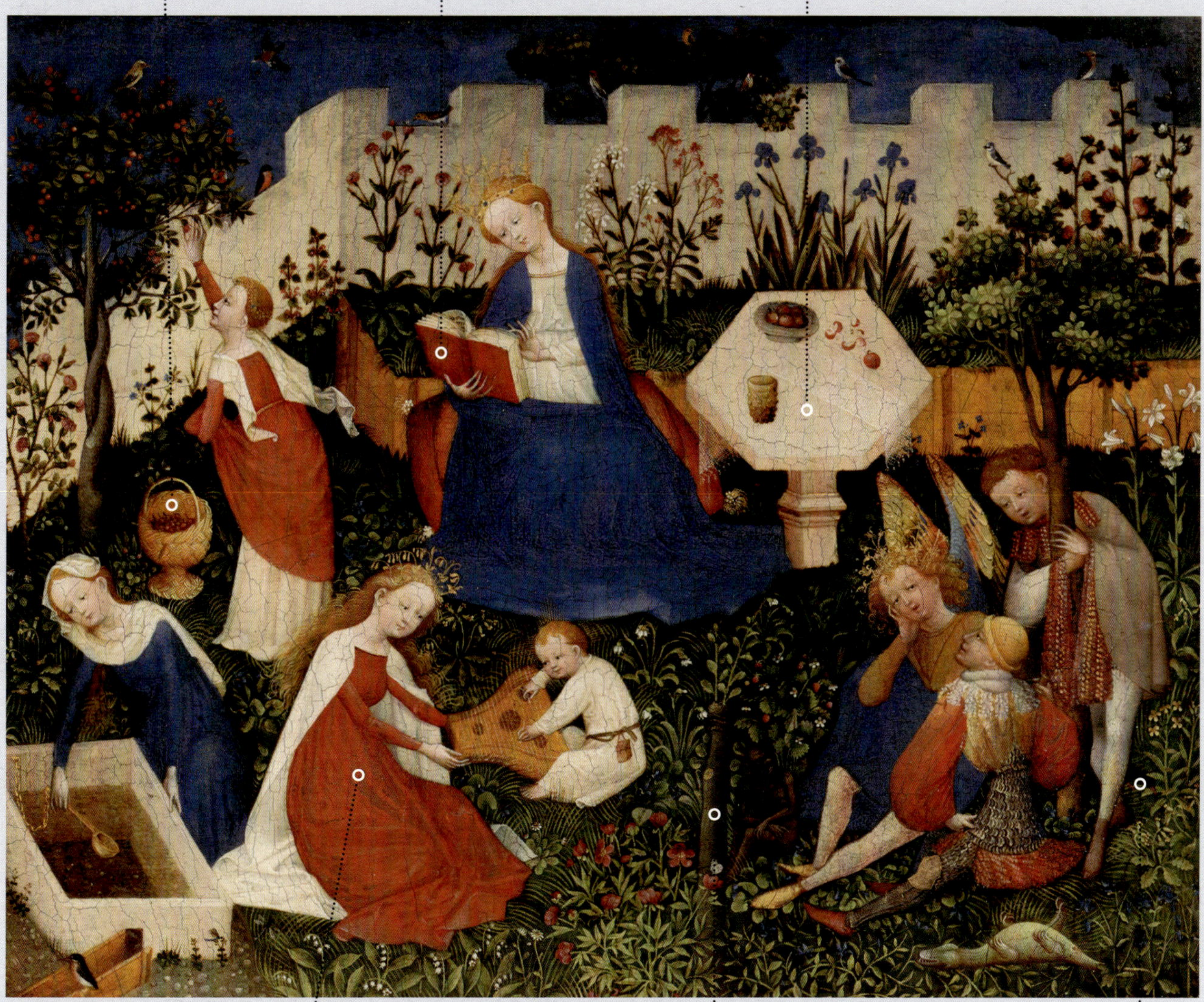

As St Catherine refused to renounce her Christian faith, she was tortured on a wheel. When it was destroyed by a thunderbolt, she was decapitated. Her martyrdom is commemorated by the 'Catherine Wheel' firework.

The tree stump is significant as it stands for sinful humanity, although hope for mankind is indicated by the two new shoots springing from the trunk.

If the black shape by the man holding up the tree is a raven, then he is possibly St Oswald, King of Northumbria, as his legend describes the bird as his constant companion.

ROBERT CAMPIN

The Mérode Triptych

c. 1427–32

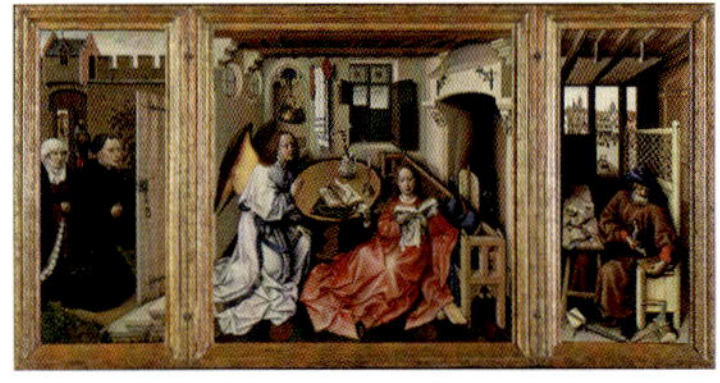

THE ENTIRE TRIPTYCH MEASURES 64 x 120 cm

In this godless age, it is impossible to understand just how important religion was to people at the time when this triptych was painted. It informed everything. Hell was a definite place, as was Heaven. A triptych like this was not intended for a church but served as a house altar, the owners praying before it daily. Campin (1378/79) created it in his large workshop in Tournai in today's Belgium. Unusually at that date, he has set his Annunciation in a typical Netherlandish town, visible through the doors and windows in the left- and right-hand wings. The central panel shows one of the earliest known representations of a room in a bourgeois home, full of commonplace belongings, but Campin has imbued the quiet domestic scene with layers of religious significance.

The Virgin Mary, resplendent in her gorgeous scarlet garment, seems so intent on her book that she is as yet unaware of the arrival of the Angel Gabriel. She is seated not on the bench but in front of it, which signifies her humility. In the left-hand corner of the central panel, the white towel and the brass vessel of water hanging beside it illustrate Mary's immaculate purity.

Despite much research, the city glimpsed through the doors and windows has not been identified. Ghent and Liège have been suggested, but it could be Tournai where Campin had his workshop.

During the Renaissance, patronage played an immeasurable role in the production of all types of art. The husband and wife – the donors or patrons – kneel in reverence of the scene before them.

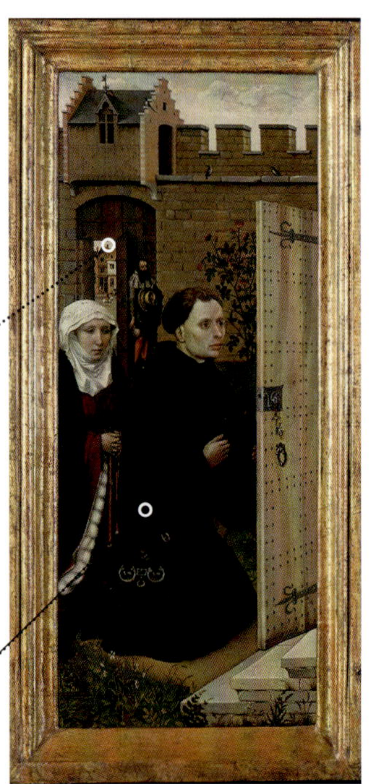

THE LEFT-HAND WING

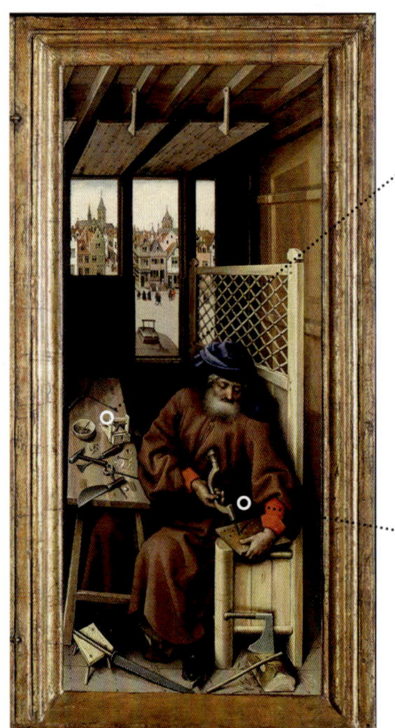

THE RIGHT-HAND WING

After much speculation, it has been decided that this object is a mousetrap. A reconstruction has demonstrated that it actually works. Why it is there is a question that has baffled art historians. Perhaps Joseph has just constructed it?

In his workshop, surrounded by his tools, Joseph is busy drilling a hole in a piece of wood, oblivious that his life is about to undergo a radical change.

The tiny naked figure descending on a beam of light from the round window is Jesus. The wooden cross he carries symbolises Mary's virgin pregnancy and his crucifixion.

The presencee of the Holy Ghost in the room is signalled by the smoking candle on the table. Beside it stands a majolica jug containing the white lily that was almost always present in scenes of the Annunciation as a symbol of the Virgin's purity.

The back rest of the bench has been constructed so that it can be swung over to the other side to enable people to sit cosily by the fire in winter.

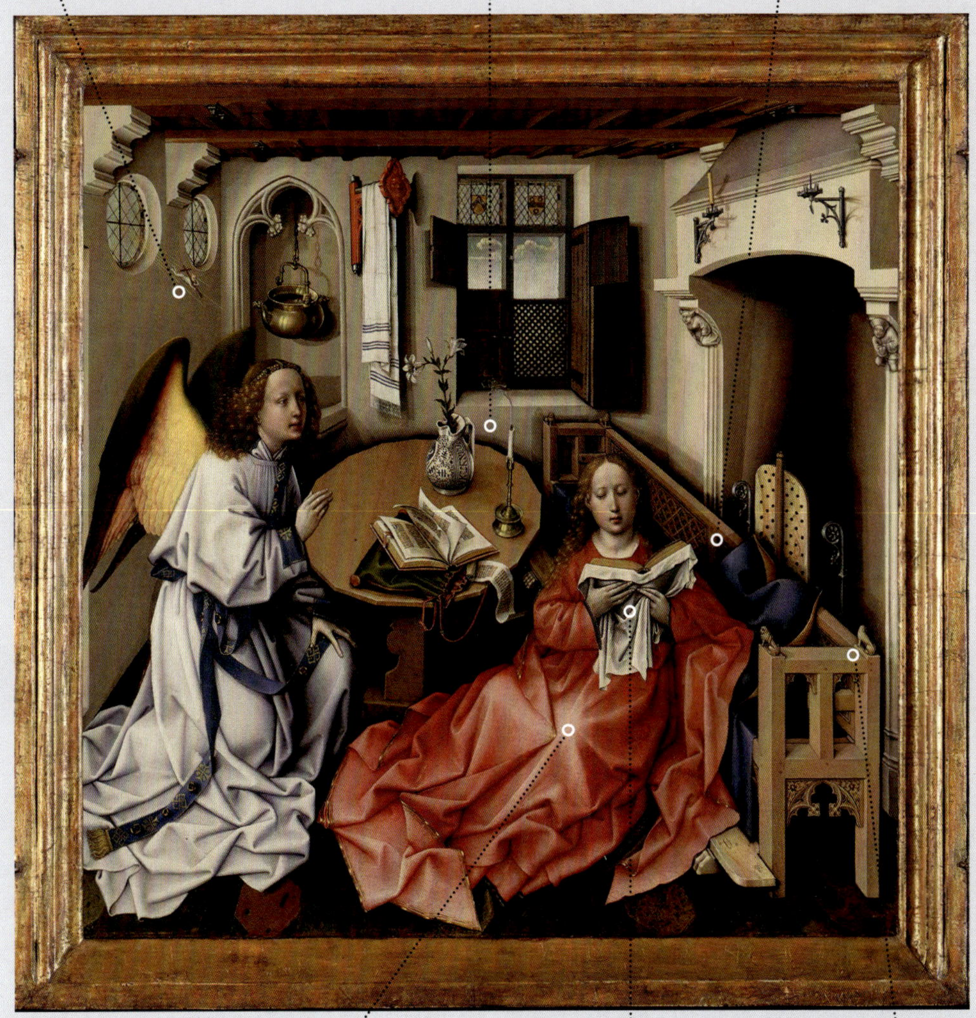

These distinctive angular folds help identify the work of Northern Renaissance artists. The star-shaped light on Mary's knee is thought to be the star of David, a reminder both of her lineage and of the prophecy that the Messiah would come from that line.

Mary is reading a book of hours. Books were very expensive and precious at this date, and she has placed a piece of white cloth between the book and her hands to protect it from grease and dirt and to demonstrate her respect for the sacred text.

The little carved lions on the end of the bench recall the throne of Solomon, and thus the wisdom of the Old Testament.

STEFAN LOCHNER

Madonna of the Rose Bower

c. 1440–42

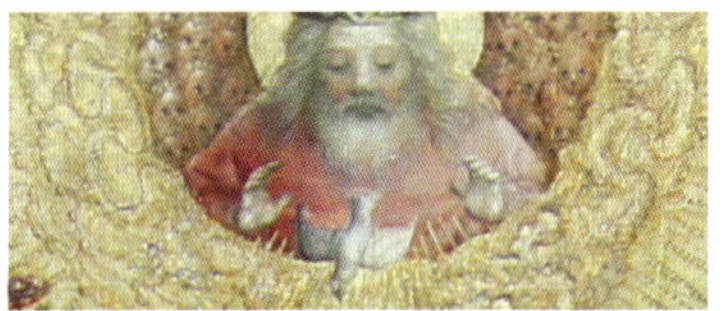

Aloft in the heavens, accompanied by the Holy Ghost disguised as a dove, is God the Father. Together with the Christ Child, they form the Holy Trinity.

This little gem of a painting is heavily infused with symbols. Once again the Madonna is pictured in a *hortus conclusus*, splendidly arrayed in costly ultramarine blue and seated on a vermilion cushion. She is presented as the Queen of Heaven, her large scale and the richness of the gold background emphasising her regal status. The Madonna has a face that radiates sweetness, but the Child wears a thoughtful, almost wise expression as if he knows where his future lies. This acceptance of his fate is underlined by the apple he holds in his left hand, a symbol signifying him as the New Adam, who has assumed his mission to redeem humanity.

Without a magnifying glass, it is difficult to see the exquisite detail woven by Lochner into the Madonna's crown. Every pearl, every jewel, every indentation carved into the precious metal has its own form and theological meaning. The red roses in the bower reference Christ's forthcoming Passion, while the white roses are symbols of her innocence and purity.

Based in Cologne in Germany, Stefan Lochner (1410–51) became one of the city's most famous painters before the advent of Albrecht Dürer. The fact that his painting is in such superb condition after six centuries of wear and tear is a tribute to his skilled craftsmanship and the extraordinary quality of his materials.

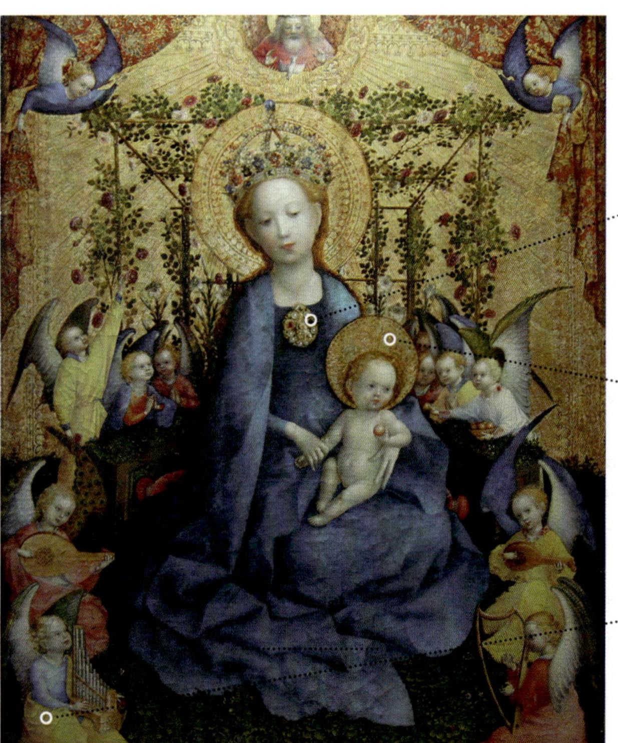

The medallion, encrusted with pearls, shows the Madonna with a unicorn. According to legend, this mythical creature could only be caught by a virgin.

The complex decoration of the Christ Child's halo was achieved by burnishing the layers of gold leaf, then punching and incising them to create a shimmering effect in candlelight.

Some of the angels are playing musical instruments. The angel on the bottom left is playing a portable organ while the others play a harp and two lutes.

ANTONIO PISANELLO

The Virgin and Child with Saints Anthony Abbot and George

c. 1435–41

Pisanello (*c.* 1394–1455) was best known for his superb medals depicting major figures of his day. He was also a consummate draughtsman and watercolourist, his animals and birds minutely accurate and hauntingly alive.

Here is St George as you have never seen him before. He has no need of a saintly halo since he is wearing a spectacular hat that would have turned heads at Ascot, an embroidered cape, shining armour and remarkably long spurs. The dragon lies, miserably crushed, at his feet.

In complete contrast with St George's urban sophistication, a bearded St Anthony Abbot is garbed in a rustic monk's cloak and cowl – fitting apparel for the alleged founder of monasticism. As his legend recounts, at the age of twenty he distributed his property among the poor and retired into the Egyptian desert where he lived the life of a hermit for many years, suffering the torments of countless demons.

Seemingly from another painting entirely, the Virgin and Child are shown in a glorious sunburst in a sky of azure blue. This heavenly event is totally ignored by the two saints below. One of the horses on the right of the picture appears to have noticed, but the other horse, weighed down by his golden bridle, is more interested in St Anthony.

This image of the Virgin and Child comes from the medieval Apocalypse, the illustrated Book of Revelations, in which a woman clothed in the sun gives birth to a child to rule all nations.

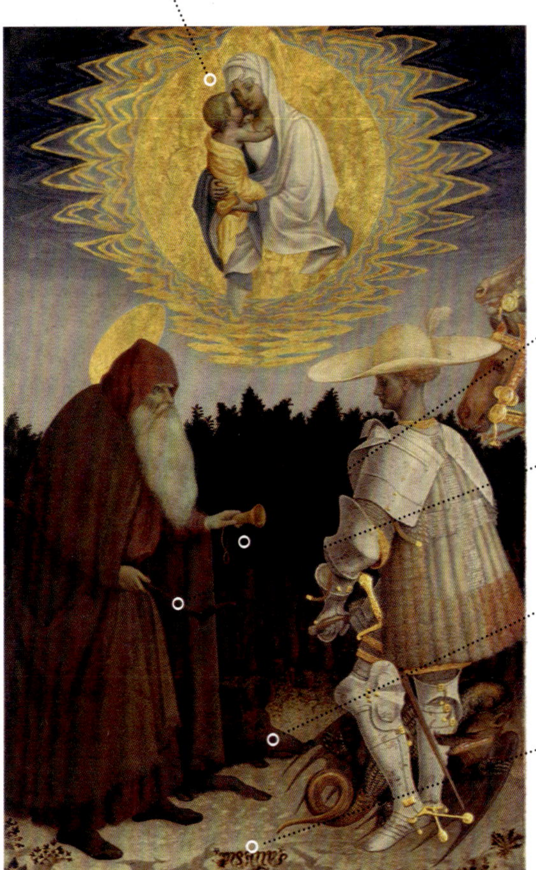

The saint usually carries a bell, which is said to be for exorcising the demons that attacked him in the desert.

This stick, with a bent end like a crutch, is one of St Anthony Abbot's usual attributes.

His main attribute is a pig or boar, seen here sniffing at the dead dragon. The pig may symbolise gluttony.

Made up of curling fronds of greenery and small blue flowers, this is Pisanello's signature: 'Pisanus p[inxi]t' (Pisano painted [this]).

ANDREA MANTEGNA

The Agony in the Garden

c. 1445

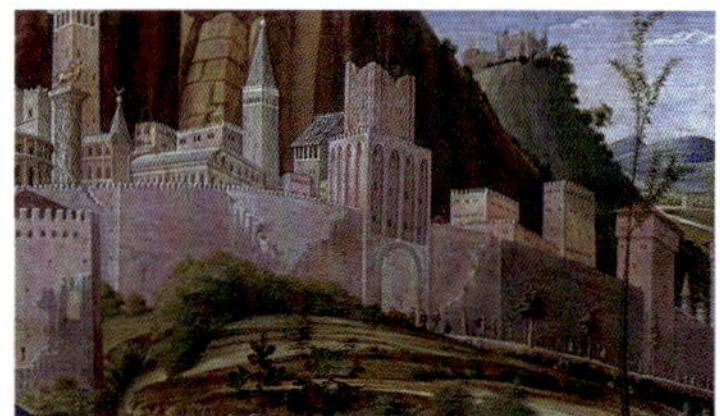

A wild mixture of Roman, Tuscan and Renaissance architecture, Jerusalem is depicted as a fairytale city enclosed by impregnable pink walls and set against a backdrop of improbable mountains.

This mysterious painting, with its harsh, sharp edges and threatening mountains, was painted by Mantegna (*c.* 1431–1506) early in his career while he was still in Padua where he was trained. But the harshness is softened by the humanity: the apostles Peter, James and John, looking like toppled statues, have grown weary of waiting for Jesus and have fallen asleep in a convivial heap. Saints were often colour-coded, so the one dressed in red and green is almost certainly John. As his mouth is open, he is probably snoring.

Aware that his apostle Judas had betrayed him, Jesus left Jerusalem and took refuge in Gethsemane, just outside the city. Kneeling before a rock shaped like an altar, he prays desperately to God on what proves to be the night before his crucifixion: 'My Father, if it be possible, let this cup pass from me.' Bearing down on him, riding on a substantial cloud, are cherubs carrying between them the instruments of Jesus's imminent torture and death: the column to which he will be bound and scourged, the sponge dipped in vinegar that will be offered to quench his thirst, the spear that will pierce his side, and the cross on which he will be crucified.

Both the dead tree and the vulture are harbingers of death.

Led by the apostle Judas Iscariot, Roman soldiers, bristling with spears and shields, march down from the city to arrest Jesus.

Why Mantegna included so many rabbits in his painting is a mystery, as they are generally symbols of fecundity and lust. It has been suggested that they may represent future followers of Jesus who will put their faith in his message.

Although difficult to see, two egrets, symbolic of the purification of baptism, stand in the stream.

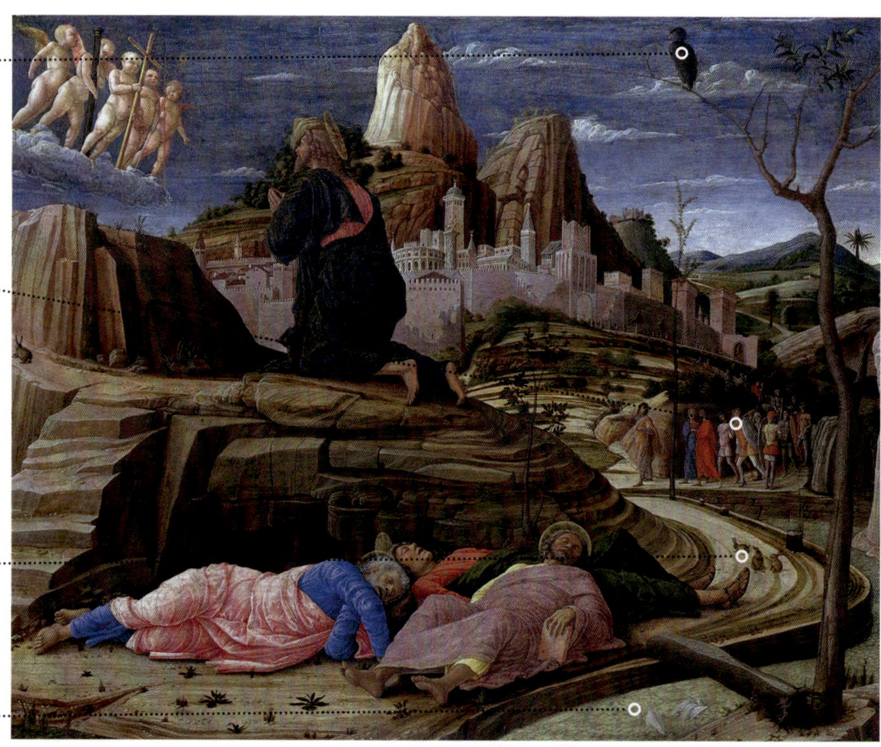

SANDRO BOTTICELLI

The Virgin and Child and Eight Angels

1478

At the height of his fame, the painter and draughtsman Sandro Botticelli (*c.* 1445–1510) was one of the most esteemed artists in Italy. His real name was Alessandro di Mariano Filipepi, but he was nicknamed 'Botticelli', derived from the word '*botticello*' meaning 'small wine cask'. Born in Florence, he was probably a pupil of Fra Filippo Lippi. By the age of twenty-five, he had set up his own workshop. Best known today for his mythological paintings – the most famous being *Spring* (see page 78) – he painted a wide range of religious subjects, including numerous versions of the Madonna and Child. This work is considered to be one of the first great examples of his circular- (or *tondo*-) style Madonnas.

Botticelli has surrounded the Virgin with eight wingless angels who are engaged in antiphonal singing. All the angels hold lilies, emblems of the Madonna's virginity and purity. The angel on the right has propped his lily over his shoulder as he needs two hands to hold the hymnbook. The Madonna gazes into the distance with the same wistful, slightly melancholic expression that was a hallmark of Botticelli's style.

The painting is thought to have been commissioned by the Medici family and is believed to have been painted for the family's private chapel in Florence. During the Second World War, the work was hidden in a monastery in the Alps to protect it from the bombing.

Although difficult to see without a magnifying glass, these two hands are holding a jewelled diadem with which to crown the Madonna Queen of Heaven.

The Christ Child is looking directly at the viewer, thus drawing him or her into the picture.

In order to protect the hymnbook, the angel is holding it with a piece of transparent silk between his hand and the cover.

This arm seems to come from nowhere, but belongs to the second angel from the right who has put it round his fellow angel to give them more space.

HUGO VAN DER GOES

The Portinari Triptych

c. 1476-78

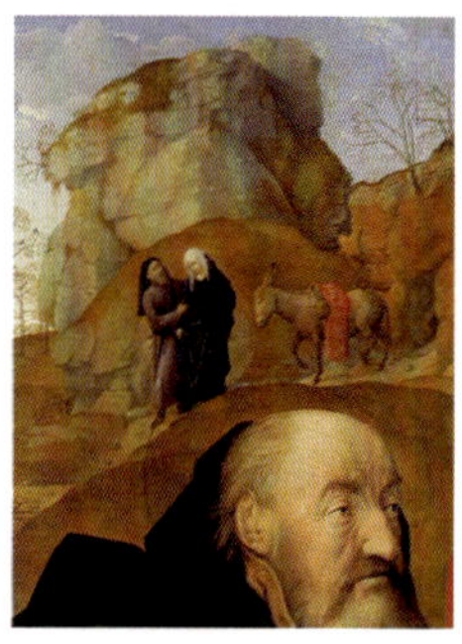

Above St Anthony's head, a touching scene is taking place: amid rocks of an alarming size, Joseph is supporting his pregnant and exhausted wife Mary on their way to Bethlehem.

Tommaso Portinari commissioned the Ghent artist, Hugo van der Goes (*c.* 1440–1482), to produce this great work for his family's chapel in the church of St Egidio in the Santa Maria Nuova hospital in Florence. Portinari, seen kneeling humbly on the left wing of the altar, was an ambitious but luckless Florentine banker who spent many years in Bruges as manager of the Medici Bank, then the biggest banking and trading house in Europe. A measure of his ambition is the sheer size of the altarpiece: when opened, it is an imposing 2.5 x 6 m. As donor of this magnificent gift, Portinari thus ensured his family's inclusion in the daily prayers said in the church.

For the man who paid for the altar to appear as such a diminutive figure seems unfair, but Van der Goes was adhering to the medieval 'hierarchy of scale' whereby size served as a symbolic indication of importance – and saints were more important than mere human beings. Thus Portinari is dwarfed by his name saint, St Thomas the Apostle, who is accompanied by St Anthony Abbott. St Anthony was the name saint of Tomasso's eldest son, Antonio, who kneels behind his father, together with his brother Pigello. This scene is a precursor of the full-blown Nativity of the central panel.

The viewer's immediate reaction to the Nativity scene is that the Christ Child is not even in a manger but lying naked on the cold hard ground. The rays of light emanating from his body signify him as the Light of the World. In her dark blue robe, Mary kneels beside him on the ground, a position that emphasises her humility. She seems too busy worshipping him to bring him any comfort. She is joined in her devotion by numerous angels: some wearing regal robes and crowns, some in startling white, others swirling about in the heavens. In the top right-hand corner, Van der Goes obeys the medieval convention of ignoring the actual sequence of events and bringing together, within one scene, episodes which occurred at different times and in different places. Hence the startled shepherds on the hill hear the angel's announcement that a miraculous birth has taken place and are shown again, in close up, with weathered faces, rough hands, dirty fingernails and homespun clothes.

The area most infused with symbols is the exquisite still life in the foreground. The sheaf of wheat is a reference to Bethlehem – the name means 'house of bread'. The parallels formed by the body of the Christ Child lying on the ground and that of the wheatsheaf correspond to the belief that the one will transform into the other. Thus Van der Goes has incorporated in his Nativity references to the death of Christ, and to Mass and Communion. The Spanish albarello vase on the left traditionally held herbs and ointments and this links it to the altar's eventual location in the church of a hospital. All the flowers in the two vases are symbolic. The clog in the left-hand corner refers to God's Old Testament order to Moses: 'Do not come any closer. Take off your sandals, for you are standing on holy ground.'

THE COMPLETE ALTARPIECE, 2.5 x 6 m

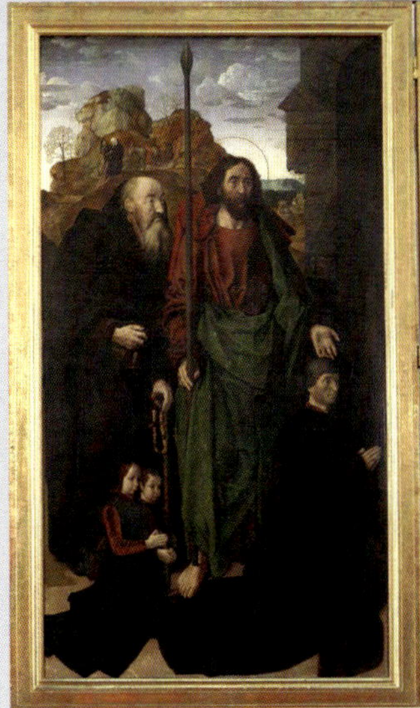

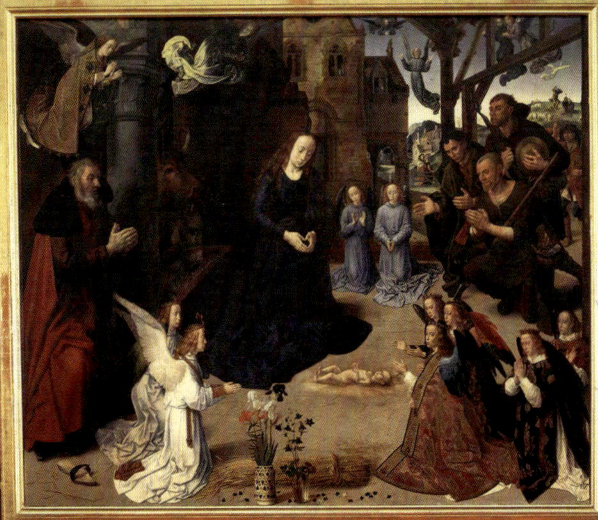

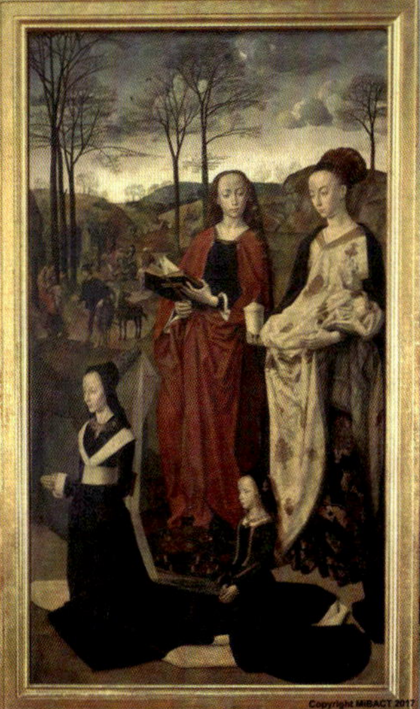

THE LEFT-HAND WING

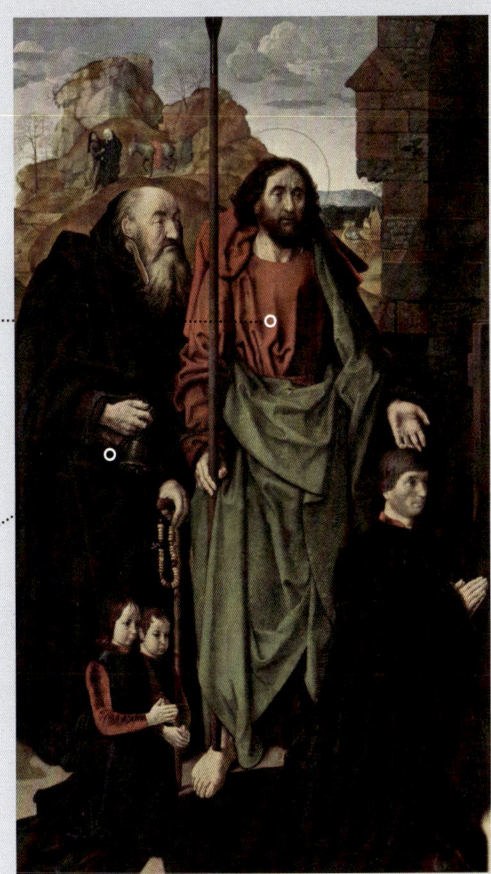

St Thomas was absent when Jesus first appeared to the Apostles after the Resurrection. He is known as 'Doubting Thomas' because he refused to believe Jesus was risen until he touched the wound in his side. He is holding the lance with which he was later killed.

St Anthony Abbot appears here with his bell and stick but not with his usual attribute, a pig or boar.

This angel is dressed in elaborate priestly garments, which reminds viewers that the work hung above an altar at which Communion was celebrated.

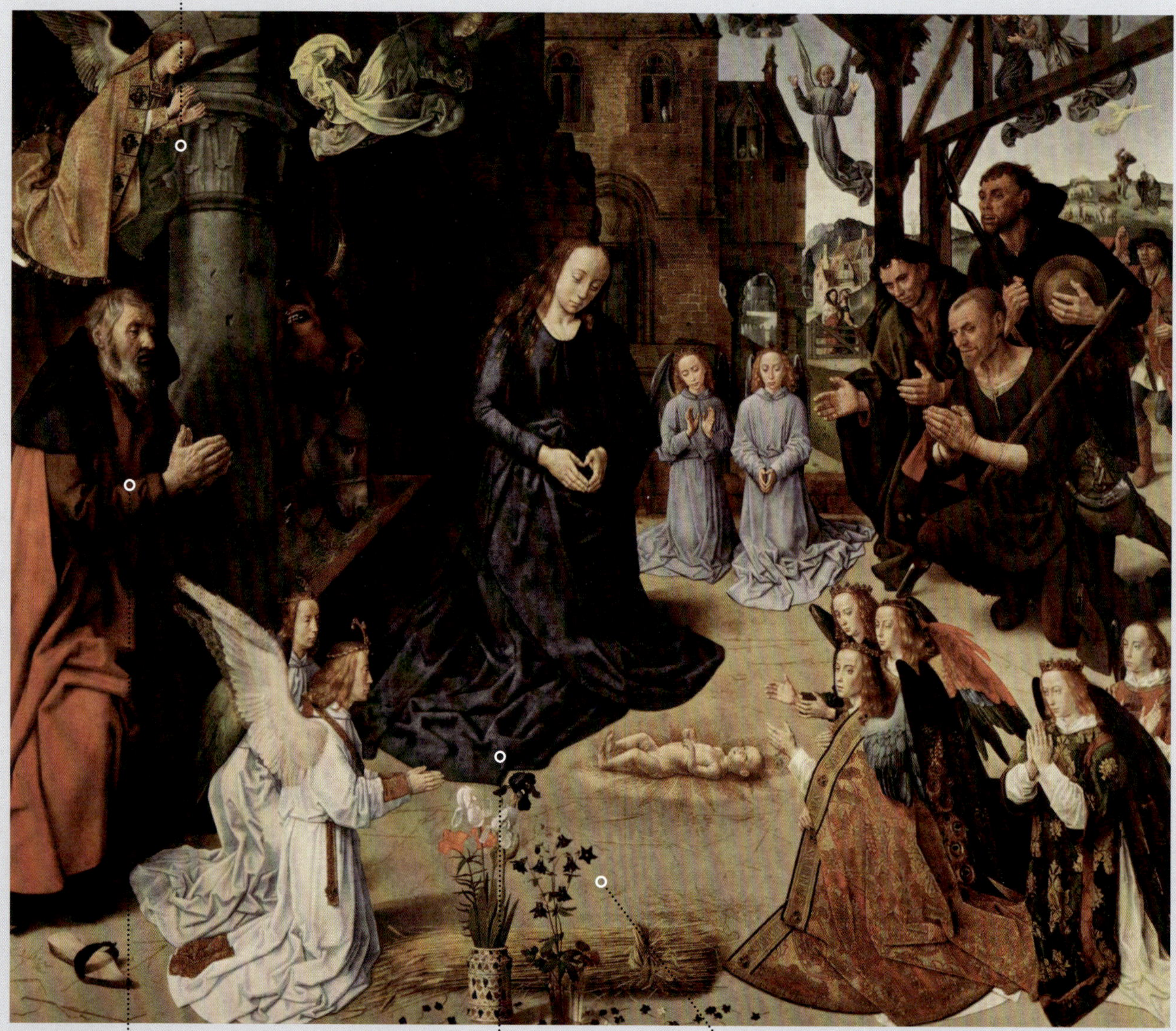

Joseph, who is always depicted by artists as old and marginalised, stands patiently in the shadows, his hands together in a gesture of prayer.

The two white irises represent purity, the purple iris royalty, while the scarlet lily represents the blood of Christ. The violets strewn around the two vases stand for modesty, humility and submission to God's will.

The three red carnations recall the three nails with which Christ was hammered to the cross. The seven blue columbines are symbolic of the Seven Sorrows of Mary.

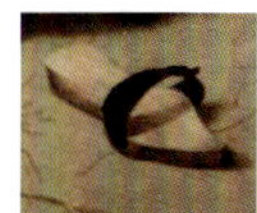

The discarded clog generally indicates that the scene is taking place on holy ground.

Mary Magdalene's bulging figure does not mean that she is pregnant, but like her small, high-laced bosom, illustrates the ideal of beauty held at this date.

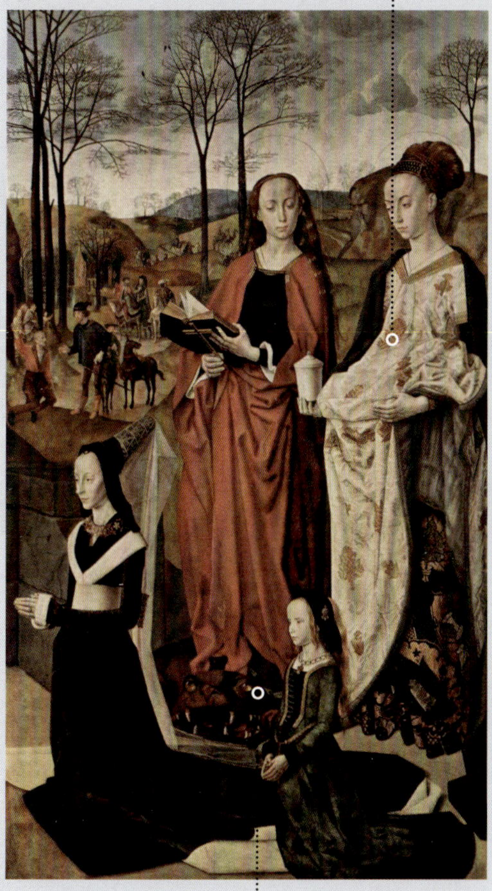

St Margaret's legend describes how she was devoured by Satan disguised as a dragon but emerged unharmed. The dragon, his eyes and teeth glinting, cowers beneath her feet.

In the right-hand wing of the altar, the donor Tommaso's wife Maria kneels in prayer, with her daughter Margarita behind her. Towering over them are their name saints. St Margaret, robed in red, is accompanied by a tall and dignified Mary Magdalene who is holding the attribute that always identifies her: the jar of ointment with which she anointed Christ's feet. In the far distance, beyond the wintry and leafless trees, it is just possible to see the three kings, mounted on camels, approaching the stable. They appear again, closer now, just to the left of the book St Margaret is holding.

In his latter years Van der Goes suffered from depression, and soon after he completed this extraordinary work, he entered a monastery, dying within two years of 'crippling despair'. By then the altar had started its long journey from Ghent to Florence, carried by merchant ship to Pisa via Sicily. From Pisa it was transported by barge up the River Arno to the gates of Florence. Sixteen men carried it from the barge to the church of Sant'Egidio.

The altarpiece's arrival in Florence in May 1483 caused quite a stir. The Florentine painters were impressed by figures that were so true to life, by faces painted with every wrinkle and blemish, and humble shepherds so realistically portrayed and given such a prominent role in a Nativity scene. The work perfectly embodied all the things that northern European painters were thought to do best, and is now considered to have had a direct impact on the art world of late fifteenth-century Florence. In particular, it introduced more individualism in the figures and faces in paintings, and an increased rise in the use of oil paint.

CARLO CRIVELLI

The Annunciation, with Saint Emidius

1486

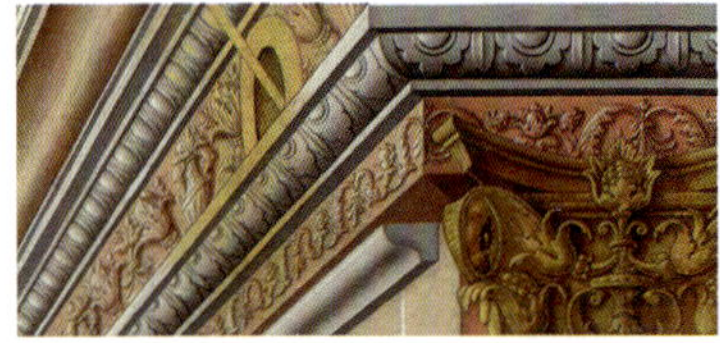

Although born in Venice, Crivelli knew Ascoli well. He has done it justice, with his skilful rendering of stone and brick, decorated pilasters, gilded Corinthian pillars, friezes and panels of yellow marble.

It is unusual for the Annunciation to take place in an urban setting, but Crivelli (*c.* 1430–95) created this painting to commemorate the granting of the right of the town of Ascoli to self-government, news of which reached the town on the day it celebrated the feast of the Annunciation. It is also unusual for a local saint to be, effectively, intervening in a biblical event: balancing a model of the city on his knee, Bishop Emidius, patron saint of Ascoli, accosts the Angel Gabriel as he is about to proclaim to Mary that she will give birth to the son of God.

That Mary appears to live in a Renaissance palace is yet another departure from the norm. Demurely at prayer, she is about to receive the Holy Spirit, disguised as a dove, which has been launched from a mysterious cloud through a handy hole in the palace's facade. She wears a jewelled coronet, a reminder that she is both a virgin and Queen of Heaven. Above her is a peacock, a dove and a birdcage. More doves flutter high above the street, perhaps unsettled by the passing of the Holy Spirit disguised as one of them.

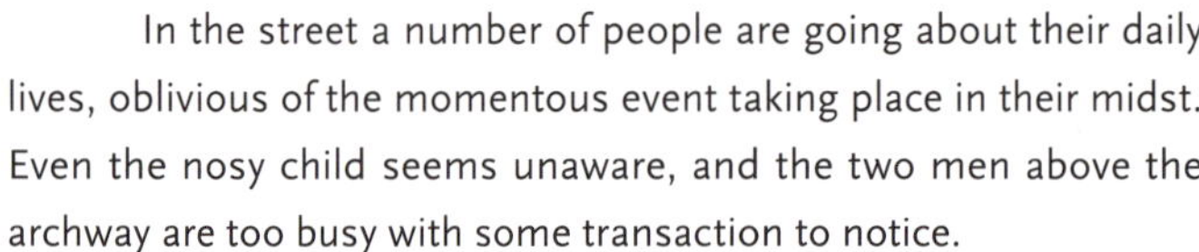

In the street a number of people are going about their daily lives, oblivious of the momentous event taking place in their midst. Even the nosy child seems unaware, and the two men above the archway are too busy with some transaction to notice.

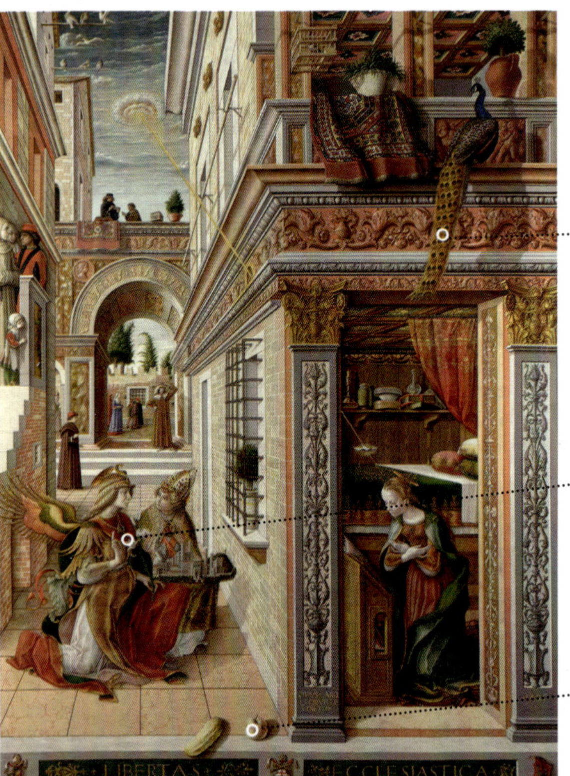

Its glorious tail spread out, the peacock adds another layer to the opulence of the building's decoration. According to an ancient belief that its flesh never decayed, the bird was a symbol of immortality and Christ's Resurrection.

In his spidery fingers, the gold-encrusted Gabriel, with his multi-coloured wings and splendid feathered epaulettes, holds the white lily that symbolises the purity of the Virgin.

Crivelli's paintings are easily identified by his characteristic use of fruit and flowers as decorative and symbolic elements.

GEERTGEN TOT SINT JANS

The Holy Kinship

1495

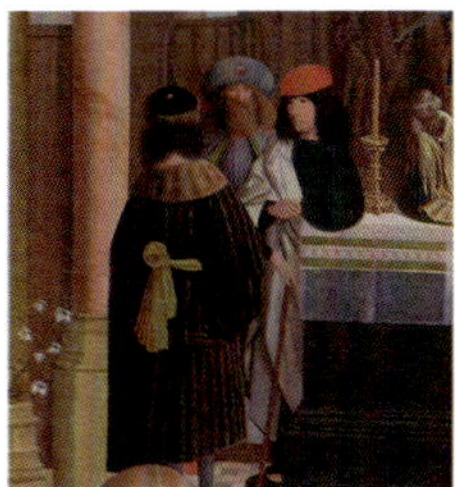

These figures may be St Anne's second and third husbands, and Zebedee, Mary Salome's husband.

All the people gathered in this Gothic church are relatives of Jesus, who is seated on the lap of his mother Mary, his little pink feet thrust out. Mary is the only woman wearing her long hair loose. On her right is her mother and Jesus's grandmother, St Anne. At her feet is a large basket, full of apples. The man in the red cloak behind Mary is Joseph, who holds a lily towards her as a gesture of the immaculate conception. Beside him, wearing gloves, a grey beard and an exotic hat, is Joachim, husband of St Anne and thus Jesus's grandfather. On the right, wearing a quite extraordinary headdress, is St Elisabeth, Mary's cousin. The infant, reaching out to Jesus, is her son John the Baptist. The tall lady with the black and white hat is Mary Salome, mother of John and James, who were to become Jesus's apostles. The artist has given all the women extremely small, rosebud mouths.

Art historians have wrestled for some time over the identity of the artist of this remarkable painting. At one time it was credited to Jan and Hubert van Eyck but the Rijksmuseum, who owns it, have now settled for the short-lived Geertgen tot Sint Jans (*c.* 1460–*c.* 1490) who lived and worked in Haarlem. His appearance on the scene had great significance for fifteenth-century painting in the Netherlands.

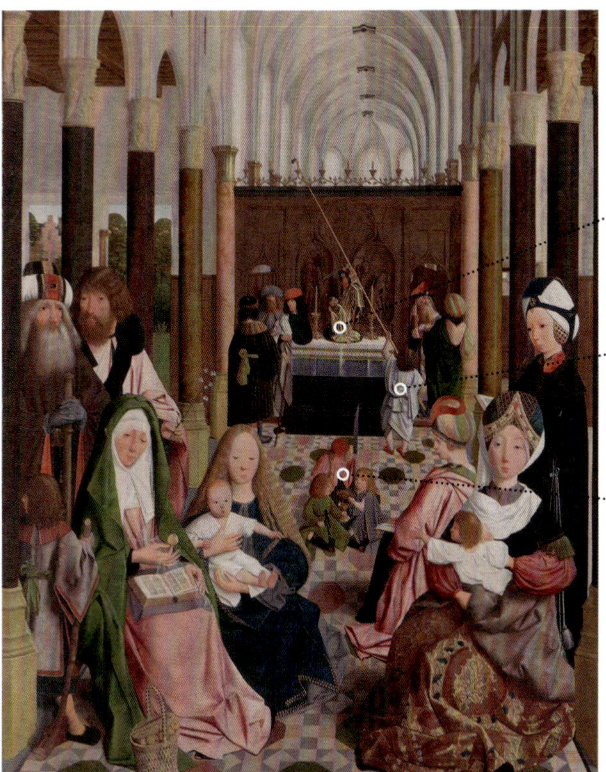

On the altar is a golden sculpture of Abraham sacrificing Isaac. It represents God's sacrifice of his son, Jesus.

The young man with bandy legs, snuffing out the candles, is reputedly young Judas Iscariot.

These boys are Jesus's cousins, his future apostles, and were all martyred. Simon Zelotes was sawn in half; John holds the chalice from which he drank poison; and James the Greater was beheaded. John and James are pouring wine into the chalice, which is a reference to the Eucharist.

GIOVANNI BELLINI

Madonna of the Meadow

c. 1505

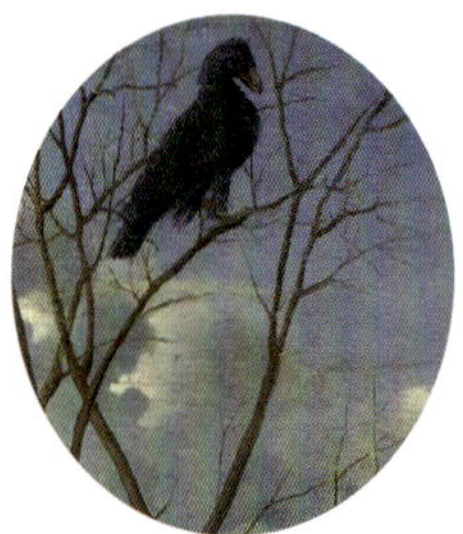

Perched high up in the tree with naked branches, surveying the scene below him, is a large raven, a foreboding symbol of ever-present death.

Bellini (*c.* 1435–1516) was an Italian Renaissance painter, probably the best known of the Bellini family of Venetian artists. He became the greatest of the Venetian Madonna painters, evolving a series of designs and types of unparalleled versatility. During his career of sixty-five years, no fewer than fourteen of the major works that survive are on the Madonna and Child theme. The linear style of his brother-in-law, Andrea Mantegna, was an early influence. Writing from Italy in 1506, Albrecht Dürer observed that Bellini was 'very old, but still the best in painting'. Bellini took on many pupils, including Titian and Giorgione.

The painting is divided in two: death on the left and life on the right. Very much alive are the cows, a lone sheep and a farmer dressed in white. Behind them are the walls and towers of a Venetian town. Creating a sense of serenity and calm, Mary sits on the bare earth: she is not presented as a queen enthroned in majesty but as the Madonna of Humility.

Bellini was one of the first Italian painters to use natural settings not just as a backdrop but to enhance the mood of his paintings. His use of colour and light fills this image with a magical brightness and luminosity that were new at this date.

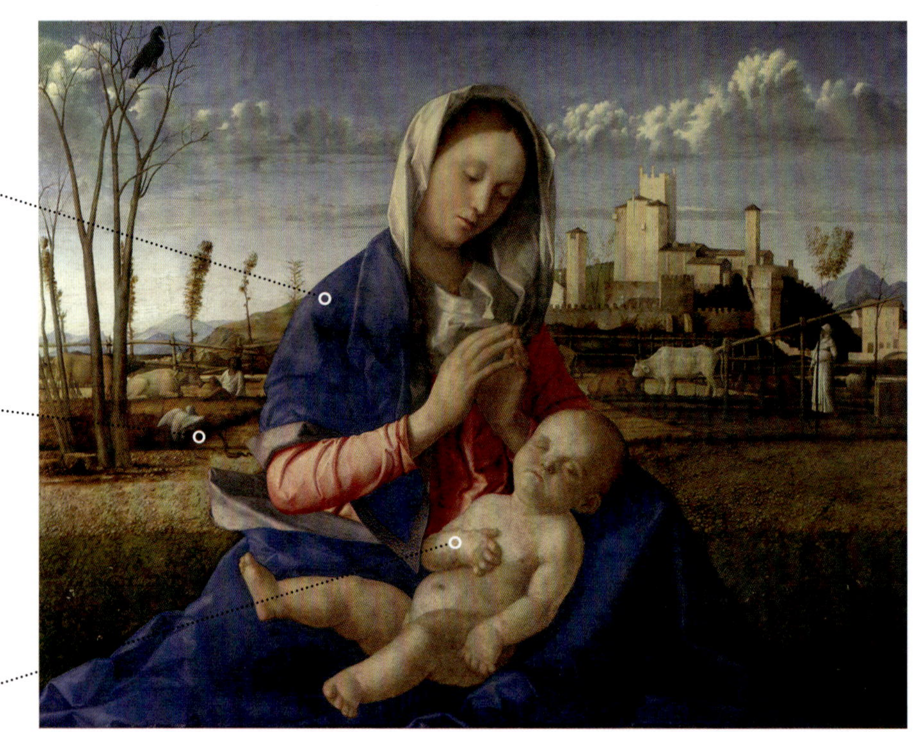

Bellini has not economised on Mary's robe, clothing her in costly ultramarine blue made from the rare stone lapis lazuli.

The white egret, its wings raised in a threatening gesture, is defending itself from an attack by a coiled snake. This combat symbolises the fight between good and evil.

The pose of the Christ Child, his eyes closed and legs stretched out, would have reminded contemporary viewers of a type of picture known as the Lamentation, or pietà, which showed Christ after his death lying across his mother's knees.

RAPHAEL

The Miraculous Draught of Fishes

c. 1515–16

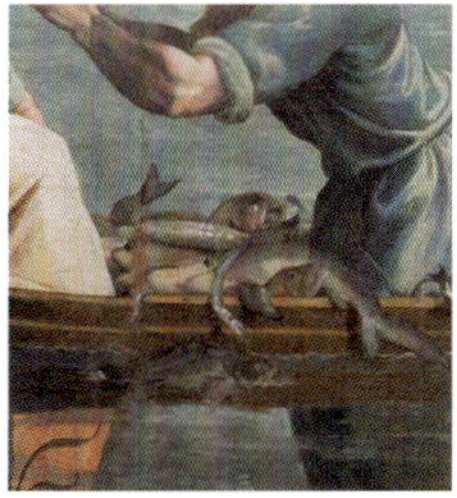

Research has revealed that the catch includes sea eels, sea bream, shark, barbels (also known as John Dory or St Peter fish), sardines, skate and shellfish.

This is one of the full-scale cartoons for ten vast tapestries that were commissioned from Raphael (1483–1520) by Pope Leo X to hang in the Sistine Chapel in Rome. It depicts one of the founding moments of Christianity, when Peter is called by Jesus to be his apostle.

Peter has been fishing unsuccessfully all night on the Sea of Galilee. Jesus tells him to cast his nets into deeper water. Peter obeys, and catches so many fish that the net breaks. He kneels before Jesus, exclaiming that he is unworthy of such a miracle. Jesus, raising his hand in blessing, replies, 'Fear not; from henceforth thou shalt catch men.' To Peter's right, his brother Andrew expresses his astonishment at the amount of fish. The cranes, hoping for a meal, symbolise vigilance. It was believed that in a group of cranes one would keep itself awake by holding a stone in its claw; if it dozed off, it would be woken by the sound of the stone dropping. On the distant shore, people stroll about, oblivious of the momentous events taking place across the water.

The cartoons were made into tapestries by Pieter van Aelst in Brussels. (Seven out of the ten have survived and can be seen in the Victoria and Albert Museum in London.)

The brothers James and John haul in the huge catch. Their father, Zebedee, tries to keep the boat steady as his sons struggle with the overflowing net.

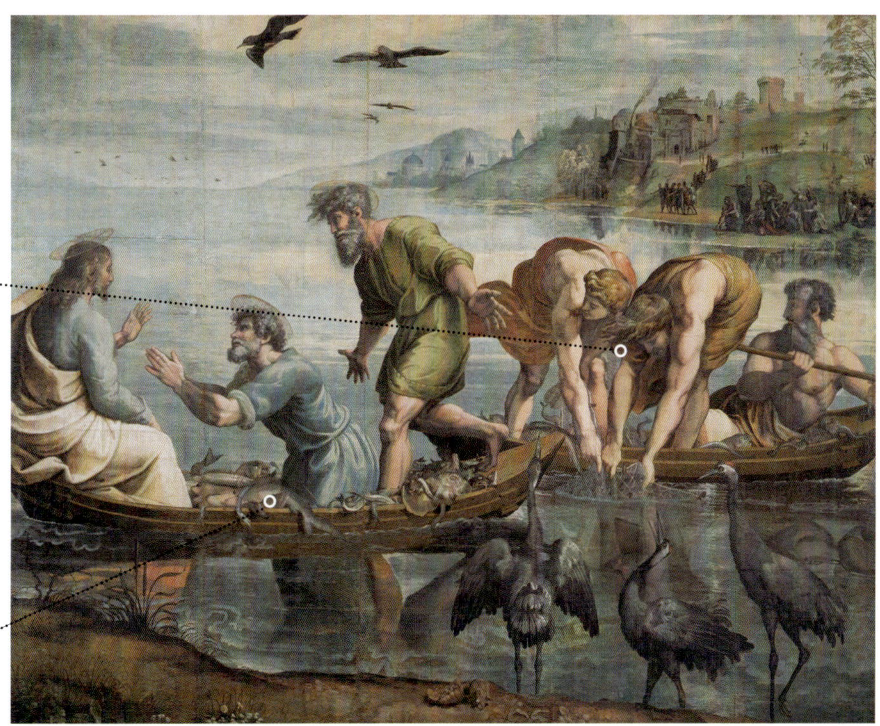

The catch includes a number of saltwater fish. Allegedly, the fish were painted by one of Raphael's many assistants who was either ignorant that the Sea of Galilee is freshwater or decided to ignore the fact.

RAPHAEL

Ezekiel's Vision

c. 1518

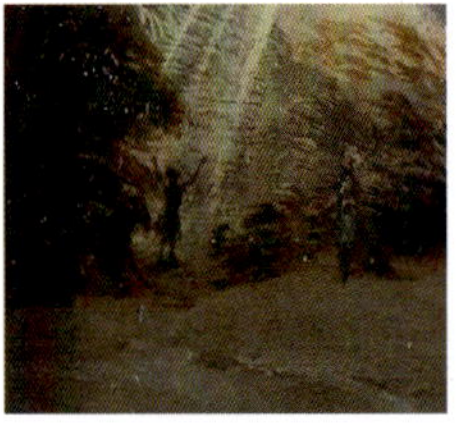

Lit by a brilliant shaft of light from the storm-filled sky is the minute figure of Ezekiel.

Following his apprenticeship to Pietro Perugino in Urbino, the young Raphael Santi arrived in Florence at a time when the reputations of two giants, Michelangelo and Leonardo da Vinci, threatened to engulf any artist who followed in their wake. However, Raphael was not only phenomenally talented but he was also possessed of a willingness to work and a sweetness of temperament that brought influential patrons to his door. In his *Lives of the Artists*, Giorgio Vasari eulogised the young man for his physical beauty, modesty, goodness, gentleness, courtesy, grace and legendary charm.

Raphael painted this work only two years before his tragic early death at the age of thirty-seven. He based it very precisely on the description in the Book of Ezekiel: '... behold, a whirlwind came out of the north, a great cloud, and a fire infolding itself, and a brightness was about it'. The half naked and very vigorous figure of God, bestriding the 'whirlwind', is accompanied by the 'four living creatures' of Ezekiel's vision.

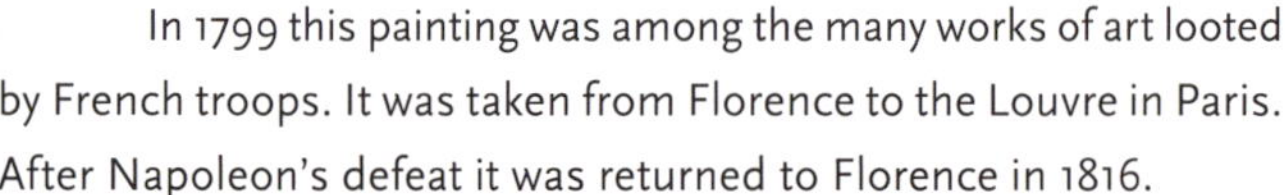

In 1799 this painting was among the many works of art looted by French troops. It was taken from Florence to the Louvre in Paris. After Napoleon's defeat it was returned to Florence in 1816.

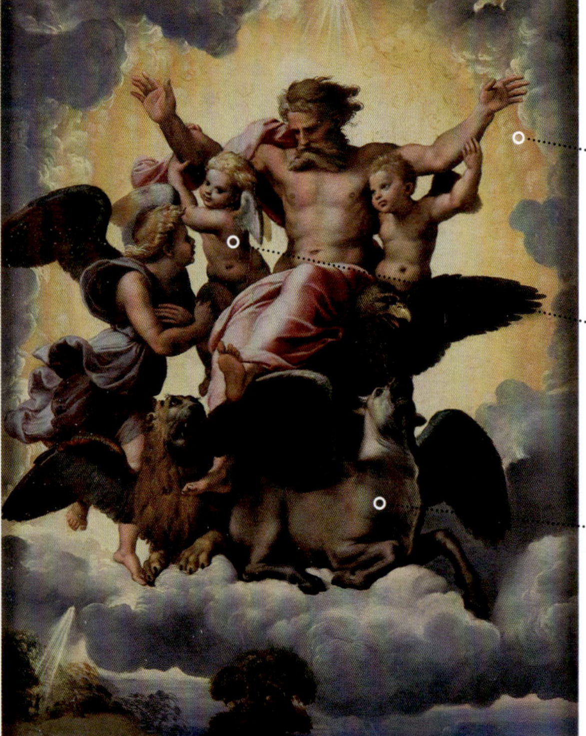

Barely visible – as they are painted in monochrome – a corolla of angelic heads fills the golden opening in the sky and seem to whirl about God's head.

Two plump cherubs support God's outstretched arms. The cherub on the left has extremely short wings: they are about the same length as God's moustache.

The contemporary viewer would instantly identify the 'creatures' by their symbols to be the four Evangelists: the lion is Mark, the ox is Luke and the eagle is John; the angel in the blue-purple gown is Matthew.

GIOVANNI BATTISTA TIEPOLO

The Immaculate Conception

1767

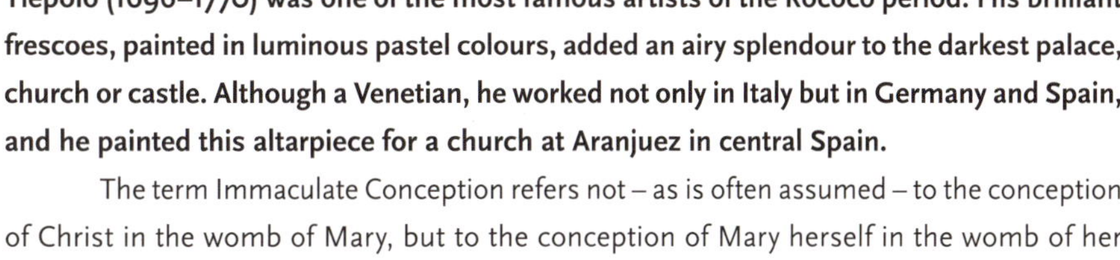

Tiepolo (1696–1770) was one of the most famous artists of the Rococo period. His brilliant frescoes, painted in luminous pastel colours, added an airy splendour to the darkest palace, church or castle. Although a Venetian, he worked not only in Italy but in Germany and Spain, and he painted this altarpiece for a church at Aranjuez in central Spain.

The term Immaculate Conception refers not – as is often assumed – to the conception of Christ in the womb of Mary, but to the conception of Mary herself in the womb of her mother Anne. It was a cult strongly promoted by the Franciscans, and Tiepolo indicates the link with St Francis by encircling the Virgin's waist with the saint's knotted girdle. In the seventeenth century, a specific iconography for the cult developed from what was taken to be a reference to Mary in Revelation 12:1: 'And a great sign appeared in heaven: a woman clothed with the sun, and the moon under her feet, and on her head a crown of twelve stars.' Tiepolo has stuck closely to this text but he has also adhered to Christian iconography for nearly every other feature in this radiant image. Everything has a double meaning: one overt and one hidden.

The Virgin, her hands in an attitude of prayer, is balancing on a globe symbolising the whole world. The dove hovering over her head is the Holy Ghost.

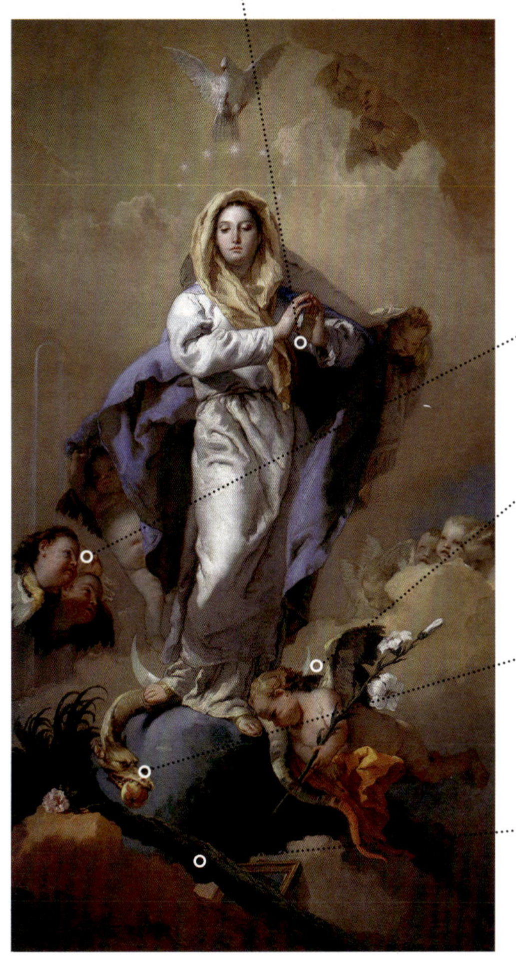

The angels, their curls swept back from their cheeks, look as if they are struggling against a stiff breeze.

The crescent moon, the rose lying on the rock and the Madonna lily held by the cherub in pink symbolise Mary's chastity and purity.

The serpent with an apple in its mouth, crushed beneath Mary's feet, is symbolic of the Garden of Eden and of original sin.

Although often associated with martyrs, here the palm tree symbolises Mary's victory and exaltation while the mirror beneath it symbolises her freedom from all stain.

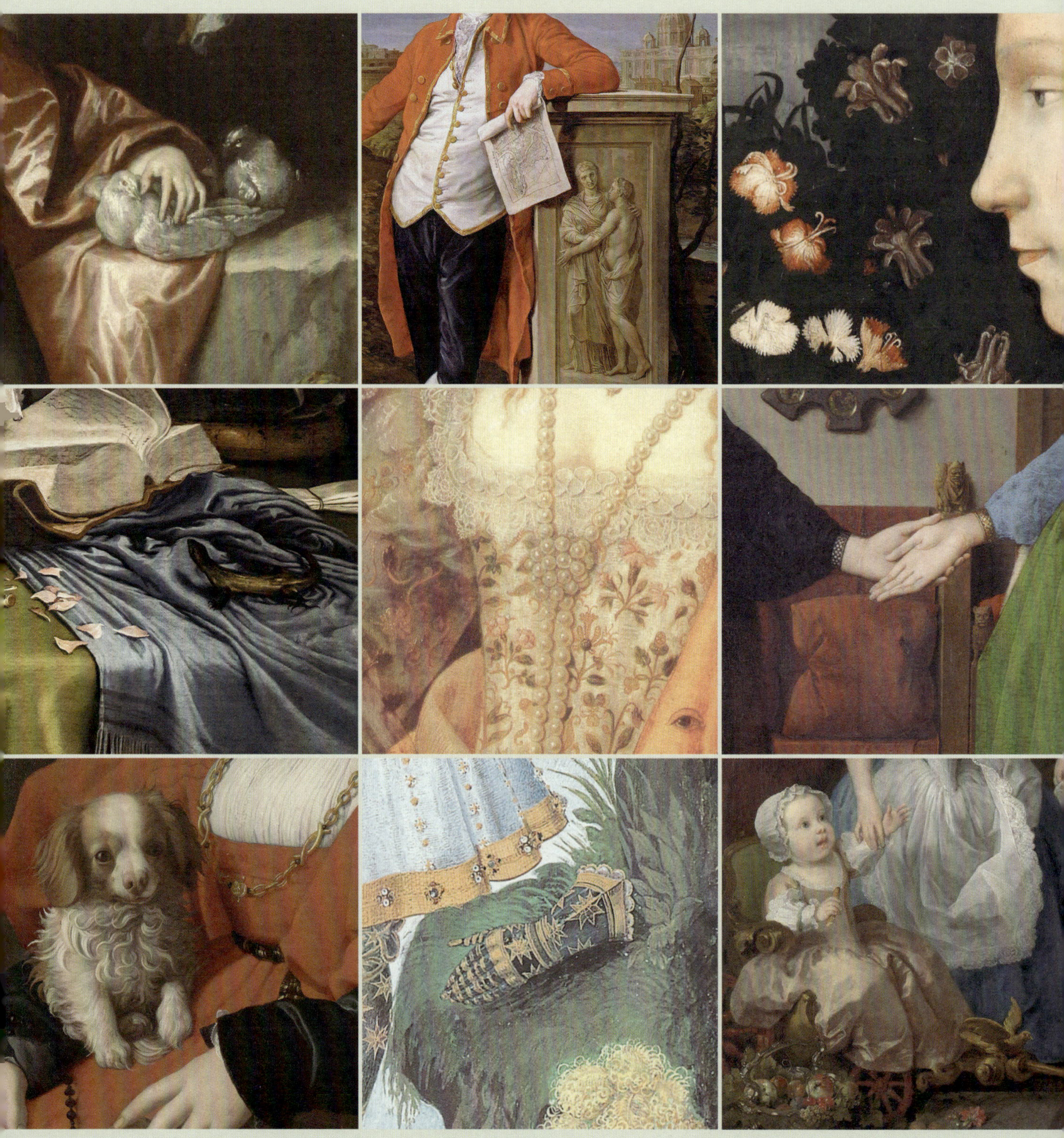

CHAPTER TWO

PORTRAITS

ANTONIO PISANELLO

A Princess of the House of Este

1433

Her hair is remorselessly drawn back and her eyebrows and hairline plucked to create the high, round forehead considered fashionable at that date. No girl of a marriageable age could appear in public with her hair unbound.

There is some doubt as to the identity of Pisanello's sitter. Embroidered on her sleeve is the symbol of the Este family, a two-handled amphora. There is a suggestion that she is Margherita Gonzaga, wife of Lionello d'Este, but there are clues in the girl's clothing that indicate she is Ginevra d'Este: Ginevra means 'juniper' in English, and the Princess is shown against a juniper bush and wearing a sprig of juniper. Her pale and spotless complexion signifies a life of decorative idleness. Her bosom is forced flat by a rigid bodice. She looks a trifle smug, but she had very little to be smug about. She was both the niece and then wife of Sigismondo Malatesta, a daring military leader, a poet and patron of the arts. He was also a rapist, adulterer, murderer and torturer who violated anything that took his fancy, from nuns to both his daughters and his sons-in-law. He married Ginevra in 1434 and had her poisoned six years later, when she was only twenty-two.

The Red Admiral butterfly in the top left corner symbolises the resurrected human soul. In the background the juniper bush contains several symbols. The carnations often symbolise betrothal, but its Greek name, *dianthus*, means 'the flower of God'. But symbols can be slippery: carnations sometimes contain a message of loss and regret, and both the columbines and the sprig of juniper can also symbolise death. Maybe Pisanello added these symbols later, after Ginevra had been murdered?

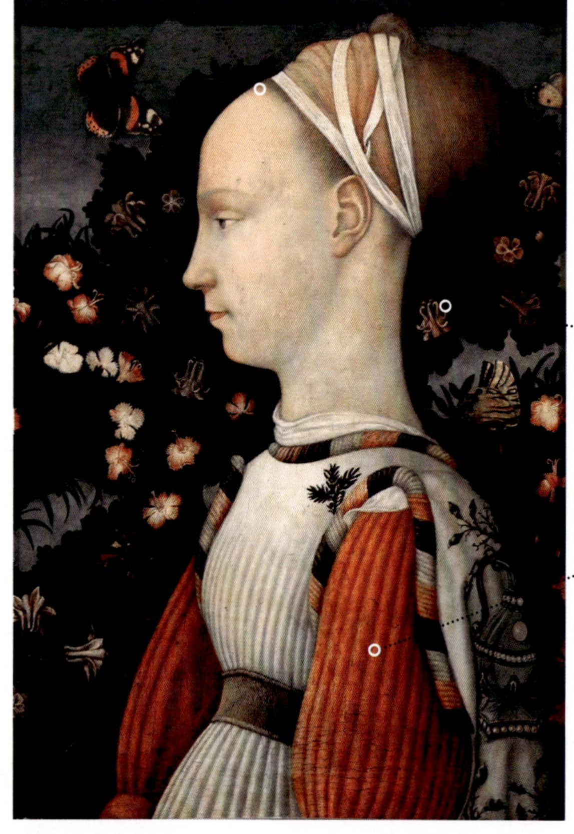

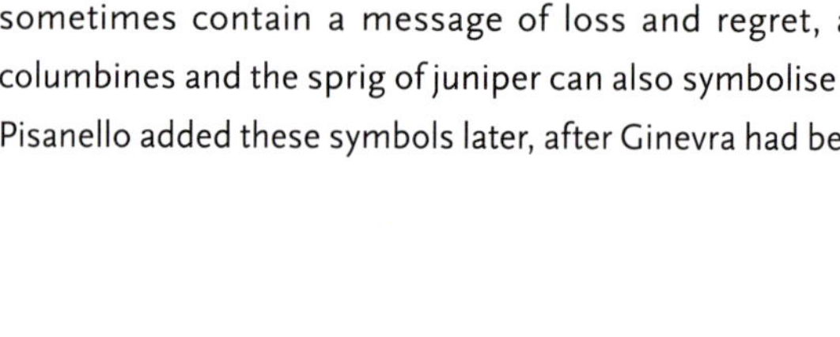

The columbine, which literally means 'like a dove', was so named because the shape of the flower was thought to resemble doves in flight. Hence the flower is a symbol of the Holy Ghost.

These sleeves are probably detachable, enabling her to transform an outfit simply by changing them. The number of sleeves a woman possessed was limited by sumptuary laws that prevented the use of dress to advertise a person's wealth and status.

JAN VAN EYCK

The Arnolfini Portrait

1434

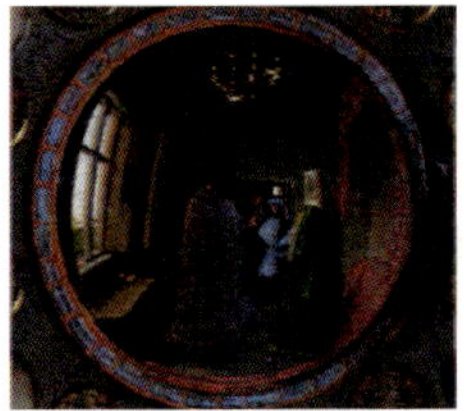

The mirror shows the back view of the couple, a self-portrait of Van Eyck and another man whose identity is unknown.

It has long been thought that this famous painting showed a marriage ceremony between the Italian merchant, Giovanni Arnolfini, and Giovanna Cenami. However, recent research shows that they did not marry until thirteen years after the picture was painted. Another theory is that the couple are Arnolfini's cousin and his wife. But the fact that she died in childbirth a year prior to the portrait's signature has encouraged speculation that it is a memoriam portrait.

Everything about this couple demonstrates their affluence: his velvet cloak lined with sable, her fine wool dress trimmed with ermine, their jewellery, the elaborate brass chandelier, oriental carpet, glazed windows and the luxurious bed covered with expensive red cloth. The glass mirror is another sign of wealth; the middle classes usually had to make do with polished metal. Even the oranges on the window sill are a sign of prosperity, as they were imported to the Netherlands from Spain or Portugal.

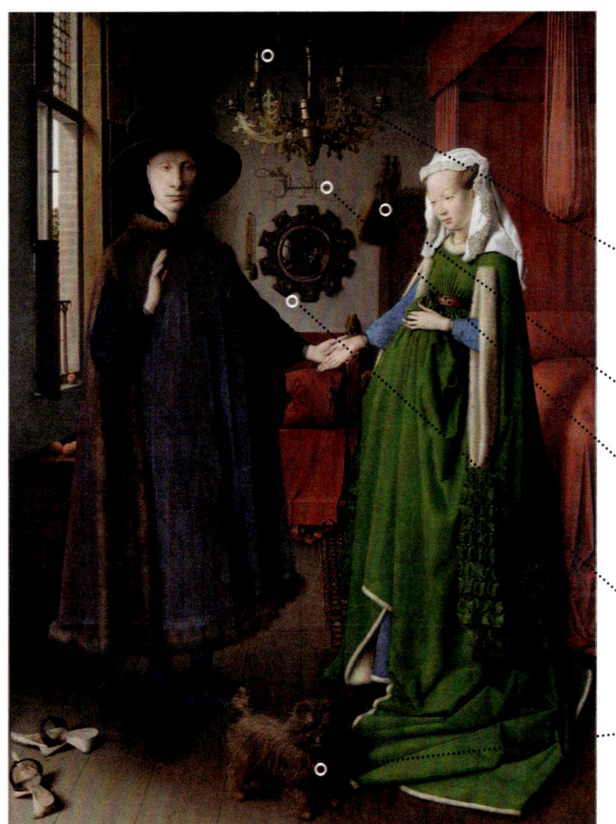

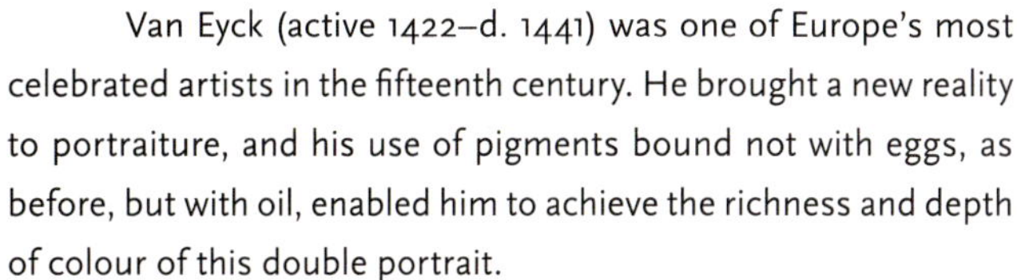

Van Eyck (active 1422–d. 1441) was one of Europe's most celebrated artists in the fifteenth century. He brought a new reality to portraiture, and his use of pigments bound not with eggs, as before, but with oil, enabled him to achieve the richness and depth of colour of this double portrait.

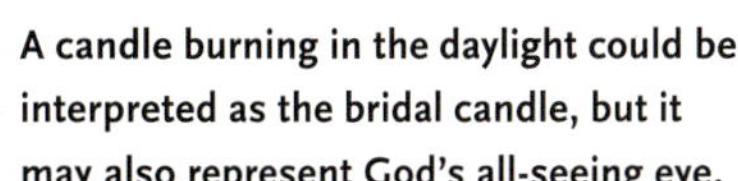

A candle burning in the daylight could be interpreted as the bridal candle, but it may also represent God's all-seeing eye.

This wooden figure represents St Margaret, the patroness of pregnant women.

The Latin inscription reads: 'Johannes van Eyck was here. 1434.'

The frame of the convex mirror is inset with tiny medallions depicting scenes from the life of Christ.

The little dog, a symbol of devotion since time immemorial, stands for conjugal fidelity. The clogs may signify the wooden floor as 'holy ground'.

LORENZO LOTTO

Portrait of a Gentleman in his Study

1528–30

Idiosyncratic and highly accomplished, Lotto (*c.* 1480–1556/57) could be considered the true inventor of the Renaissance psychological portrait. In this refined and contemplative image, he is not just aiming at a likeness but probing beneath the surface to reveal the young man's inner thoughts.

Art historians have 'read' the portrait in different ways. One theory is that the youth is mourning the end of a relationship, symbolised by the blue silk shawl, withered rose petals, open letter, ring, gold chain and the lizard. Alternatively, the young man has reached the age and stage when he must abandon youthful pastimes, such as hunting and music playing, and henceforth must shoulder family responsibilities. As to his identity, most scholars agree that he is a member of the Rovero family of Treviso, either Cristoforo or Alvise. Various events in the life of Cristoforo, such as the recent death of his mother, would fit the theory that life had suddenly become dauntingly serious. Documentary evidence of Alvise's melancholic temperament would fit either theory.

Although Lotto was born in Venice, he spent much of his life moving restlessly from town to town. When he died, he left eloquent written testimonies to his own anxious, isolated and often depressive cast of mind. Towards the end of his life, he entered a monastery and became a lay brother.

With his straight nose, downy upper lip and pale complexion, this is a handsome and sensitive face.

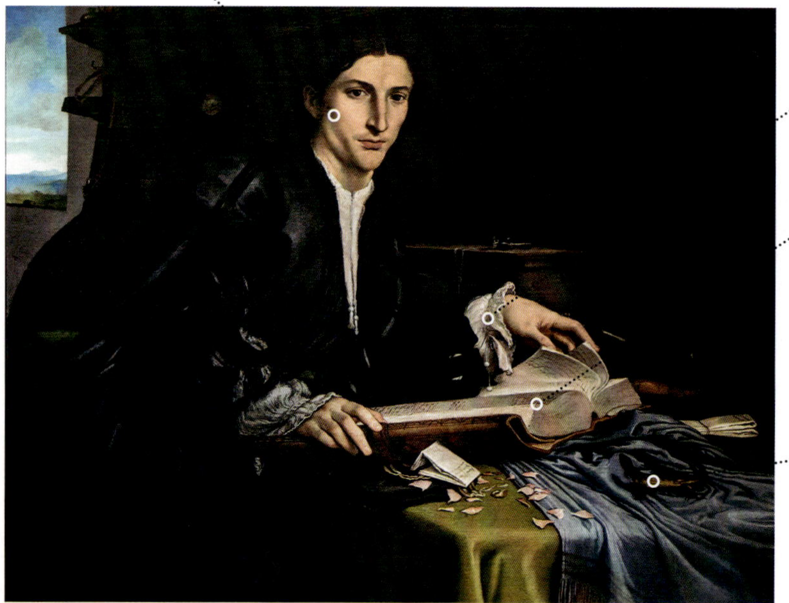

He is dressed elegantly in a velvet tailored suit with flouncy white cuffs made of the purest lawn.

One theory is that the leather-bound double-entry account book alludes to the young man's new role as manager of his family's affairs. Another theory is that the pages of the book represent the years he has lived and those that remain to him.

The lizard sitting on the blue shawl is a symbol of jealousy and deception. But it can also allude to death and rebirth.

AGNOLO BRONZINO

Portrait of a Lady in Red

c. 1533

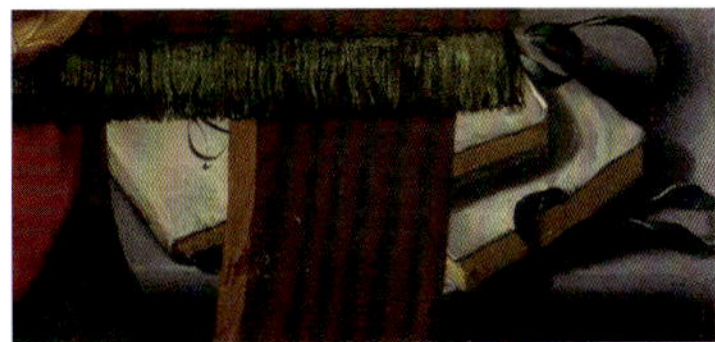

The books resting on the* pietra serena *bench allude to the lady's love of letters.

Bronzino (1503–72) was the pupil and adopted son of fellow Florentine, Jacopo Pontormo, to whom this painting was initially attributed. But Pontormo was not known for lingering on such details as the crisp folds of the white shirt, the curls on the chest of the little dog or the intricacies of the sitter's jewellery. In his *Lives of the Artists*, Giorgio Vasari recounts that Bronzino's portraits were 'extremely natural and done with incredible diligence ...'

Rather than revealing the character of his sitters, Bronzino aimed to convey their status, elegance and self-restraint by the attributes he included in their portraits. Here, it is the lady's sumptuous garments, rather than her haughty demeanour and distant gaze, that place her among the highest echelons of Florentine society. Only the wealthy could clothe themselves in fabric dyed with vermilion, the pigment that was as costly and precious as gold, while her pure and untarnished complexion embody the feminine ideal.

Bronzino became the favourite portraitist of the Medici after Cosimo I became Grand Duke of Tuscany in 1537 and secured his family's absolute hereditary rule until the eighteenth century. Bronzino's numerous portraits were copied at Cosimo's request and used as diplomatic gifts.

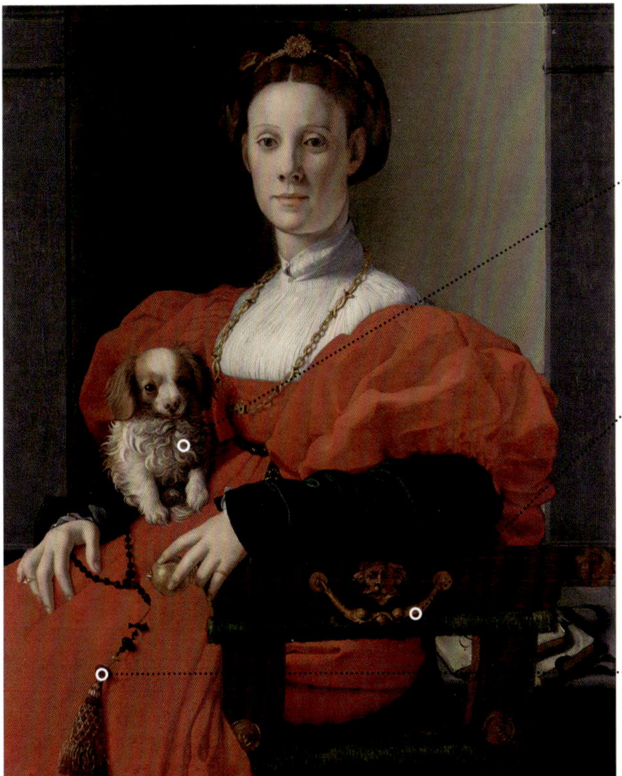

This small spaniel was a particularly fashionable breed at this date. Little dogs often appear in portraits as a symbol of marital fidelity.

This handle, which takes the form of two dolphins clutching a ball between their mouths, was an emblem of the Medici family. Above the handle, Bronzino employs the ancient Roman tradition of fantastical decorations known as grotesques.

The rosary, with its beautifully painted tassel, refers to the lady's piety.

NICHOLAS HILLIARD

George Clifford, 3rd Earl Cumberland

c. 1590

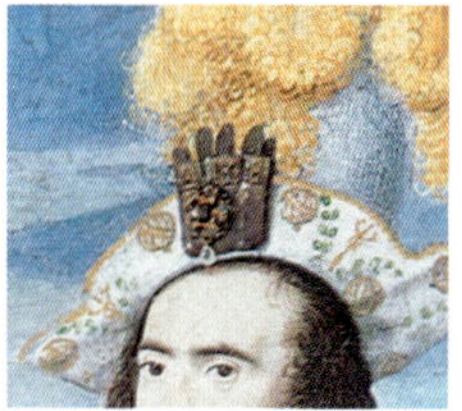

As a mark of the Queen's favour, her glove is pinned to Clifford's bonnet by a rose jewel with a pendant pearl.

This is not just an image of a tall man in a short skirt, but Queen Elizabeth I's champion as he appeared in the tiltyard on her Accession Day, 17 November 1590. The series of tournaments held annually, when the Queen's knights tilted (jousted) in her honour, were the most important festivals of the Elizabethan age and the major public spectacle of the year.

The Tudors lived in a world that was full of symbolism, and everything they wore or carried conveyed messages about belief, allegiance, heredity and loyalty. The art of portraiture faithfully reflects this. Nicholas Hilliard (1547–1619) specialised in painting miniature portraits. The English art of limning, as it was called, was unparalleled anywhere else in Europe, and Hilliard was one of its finest exponents.

Clifford wears his star-studded armour, over which he wears a surcoat, its sleeves banded with gold braid and adorned with jewels. The surcoat's lining is embroidered with a pattern of Tudor roses and armillary spheres – symbols for heavenly wisdom. With his right hand he supports a tilting lance.

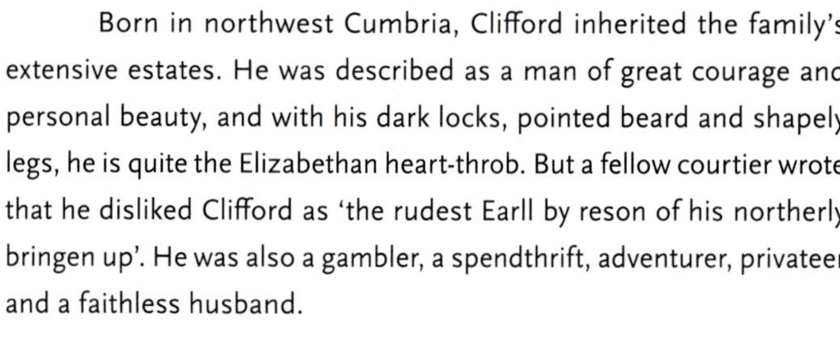

Born in northwest Cumbria, Clifford inherited the family's extensive estates. He was described as a man of great courage and personal beauty, and with his dark locks, pointed beard and shapely legs, he is quite the Elizabethan heart-throb. But a fellow courtier wrote that he disliked Clifford as 'the rudest Earll by reson of his northerly bringen up'. He was also a gambler, a spendthrift, adventurer, privateer and a faithless husband.

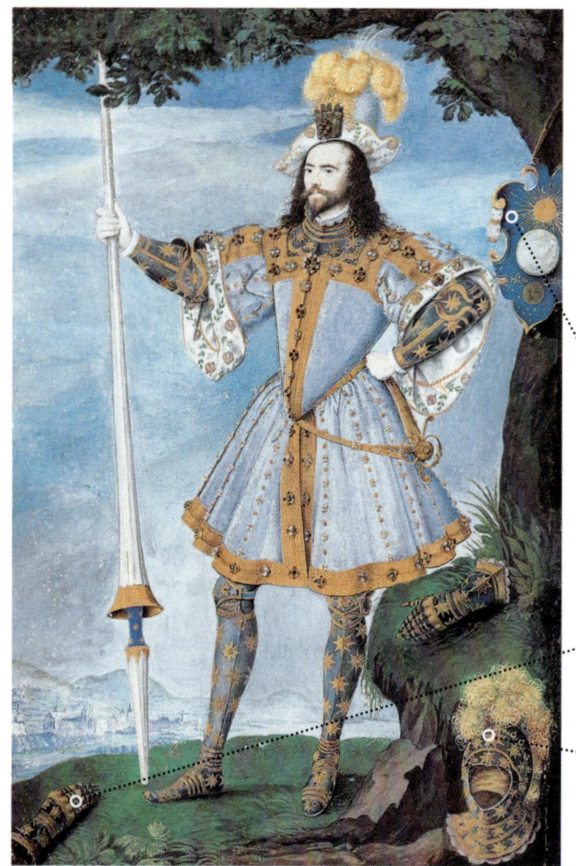

High in the tree hangs Clifford's emblematic parade shield for display at the tilts. It bears an *impresa* (device) that proclaims that he will be the Queen's challenger until earth, sun and moon pass into eclipse.

Clifford's right gauntlet is thrown down in front of him, as if in challenge.

His ostrich-plumed helmet, together with the left gauntlet, lie at the base of the oak tree.

ISAAC OLIVER

The Rainbow Portrait

c. 1600

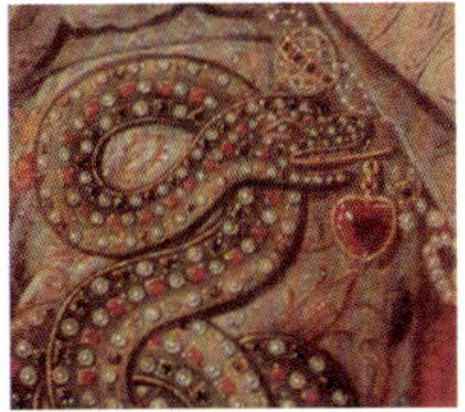

The bejewelled, coiled serpent with a heart-shaped ruby in its mouth represents the Queen's cunning and wisdom.

Although nearly seventy when this portrait was painted, Queen Elizabeth I – who never married or had children – carefully controlled her image as the Virgin Queen throughout her reign. Artists such as Oliver presented her in regal splendour, arrayed in fantastic garments and dripping with jewels, the bald patches on her scalp and the facial scars caused by smallpox concealed by a striking array of wigs and thick layers of white lead make-up. She was famed for her love of fashion – an inventory compiled in 1587 stated she owned 628 pieces of jewellery and, at her death, over 2,000 gowns were recorded in the royal wardrobe. It took her two hours to squeeze into one of these magnificent outfits.

Elizabethan art and architecture was filled with ciphers and hidden meanings, and this portrait is layered with symbolism, all of it alluding to the queen's majesty. The pearls, for instance, scattered about her person, are symbols of hope, power and virginity.

Oliver (*c.* 1565–1617) was born in France and came to England as a Huguenot refugee. A pupil of Nicholas Hilliard (see facing page), he became famous as a miniature painter and was one of the artists, together with musicians and authors – among them Shakespeare and Edmund Spenser – whose portraits contributed to the 'Cult of Gloriana'.

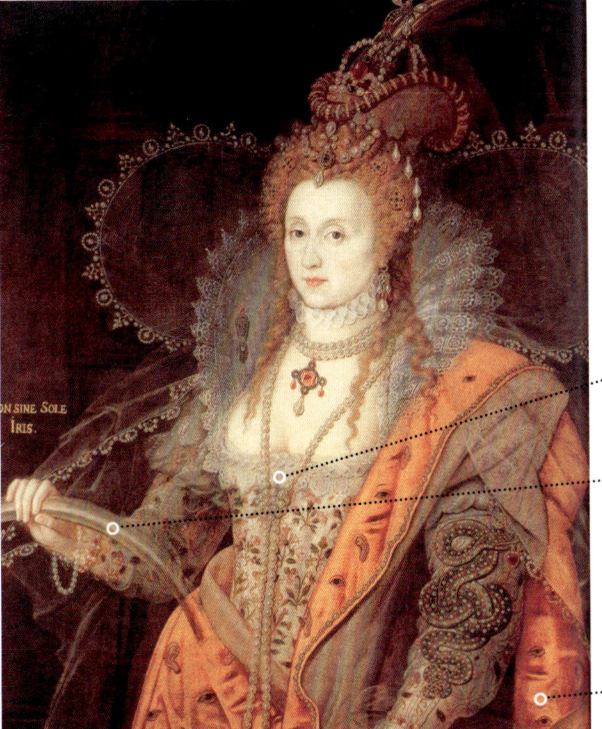

The knot in the rope of pearls suggests virginity.

This curious object in her right hand is a rainbow, a symbol of peace. The Latin motto above it reads *non sine sole Iris*, meaning 'no rainbow without a sun', the sun being Elizabeth.

The lining of her cloak is decorated with human eyes and ears, suggesting Elizabeth was all-seeing and all-hearing. She had a formidable spy network that she relied upon to warn of challenges to her reign.

ANTHONY VAN DYCK

Venetia, Lady Digby

c. 1633–34

Having been a star pupil in Peter Paul Rubens's workshop in Antwerp, Van Dyck (1599–1641) pursued an independent career around Europe before establishing himself in London where he was appointed court painter to Charles I. The diplomat and intellectual, Sir Kenelm Digby, was a member of the Stuart court who became a close friend. In 1625 Digby married Venetia Stanley, celebrated for her beauty and intelligence but also said to have enjoyed a colourful past. Perhaps to quell rumours of her promiscuity, Digby commissioned Van Dyck to paint an allegorical portrait of her that casts her in the role of Prudence trampling on Profane Love. Since Van Dyck was no allegorist, he asked Digby who was 'alwayes his most generous friend and protector' to suggest the allegorical references. The aim of Digby's design is clear: if a diagonal line is drawn from the top left corner to the bottom right, everything that is good is to the right of the line and all to the left is bad. Van Dyck possibly painted this portrait as a posthumous tribute to Lady Digby, who died unexpectedly, aged thirty-three, the year it was painted.

Lady Digby's left hand rests gently on one of two turtle doves, symbols of married love. The doves and the snake allude to St Matthew, Chapter 10: 'Be ye therefore wise as serpents and harmless as doves.' Winsome little angels crown her with a laurel wreath as a symbol of her victory over the vices.

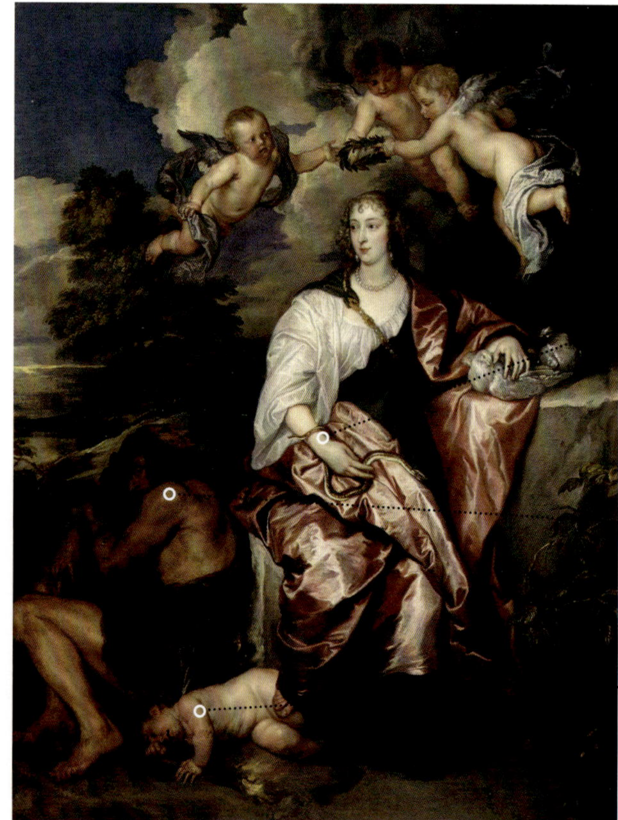

Coiled in Lady Digby's lap and around her arm is a serpent that is – rather surprisingly, given its reputation in the Garden of Eden – associated with wisdom.

Rough and swarthy, his hands bound, a defeated two-faced Deceit cowers beside her.

Cupid, the symbol of lust – and love – lies subdued beneath her feet, his torch of flaming desire about to go out.

WILLIAM HOGARTH

The Graham Children

1742

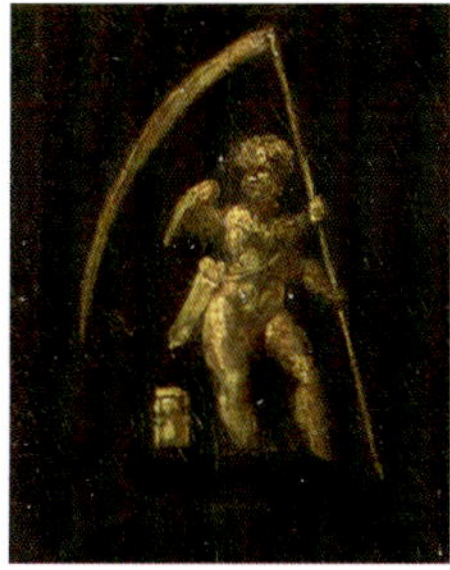

On top of the clock Cupid holds an hour glass and scythe, symbols of death.

Hogarth (1697–1764) was the most English of artists. He was opinionated, pugnacious, moralistic, philanthropic and tireless in his defence of the poor. Although Hogarth's marriage was childless, he loved to paint children. When commissioned to portray the family of the prosperous royal apothecary Daniel Graham, he produced one of his largest and most spectacular portraits, in which the figures are life size. From the flowered headdresses worn by the girls to the silver basket of fruit to the bristling whiskers of the predatory cat, Hogarth has painted every detail with infinite care. The viewer's first impression is of four bright, beautifully dressed and carefree children. Yet, beneath the surface the painting contains tiny threats, allusions to the passage of time and to mortality.

Seated in his gilded carriage, two-year-old Thomas is clutching a rusk and reaching out for the cherries that his sister Henrietta is holding. With the gentlest touch, she restrains him. Beside her, seven-year-old Anna Maria proudly displays her flower-strewn dress. By turning the handle of the 'bird-organ' Richard, oblivious of what is going on behind him, hopes to encourage the goldfinch to sing. But the bird, its wings outstretched, is cheeping with terror because it knows what is on the cat's mind. A goldfinch was a favourite childhood pet, but its presence in paintings often has a hidden meaning.

Cherries were symbolic of the 'Fruit of Paradise' and given to the virtuous.

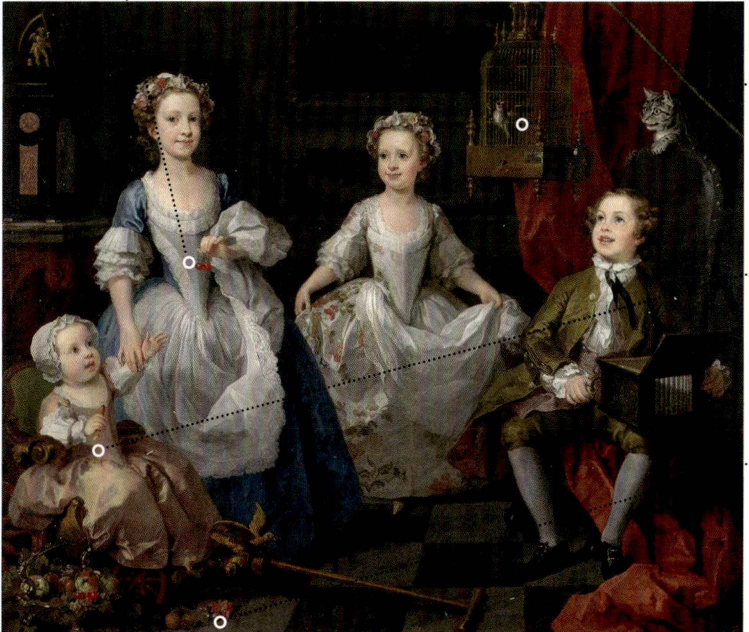

According to legend, the goldfinch acquired its red spot when it plucked a thorn from Christ's brow on the road to Calvary. Thus, it symbolises Christ's Passion.

Before Hogarth completed the portrait, the baby Thomas died, yet another victim of the spectre that haunted every family in the eighteenth century: infant mortality.

The pink carnation by the baby is not as random as it looks. The flower has several meanings: one is that it represents the tears of the Virgin Mary, hence motherhood. In this context, it is signalling a mother's sacrifice.

POMPEO BATONI

Francis Basset

1778

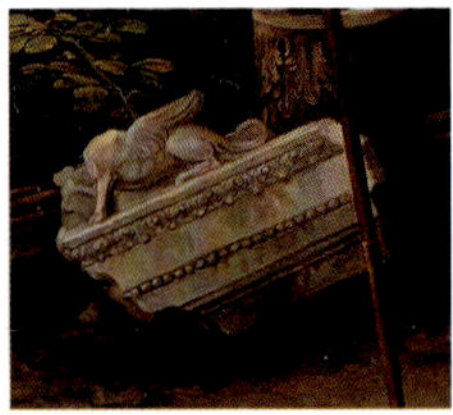

This fragment of an ancient marble frieze, surmounted by a sculpted griffin, frequently appears in paintings by Batoni.

By the eighteenth century, portraits increasingly contained attributes rather then symbols – objects which indicated the sitter's interests or attainments. Against a background of the Roman *campagna*, elegantly clad in scarlet with his tricorn hat and walking stick in his right hand, the twenty-year-old Francis Basset leans nonchalantly against a marble pedestal. He has reached the southernmost point of his leisurely journey through the cultural centres of Europe. Known as the Grand Tour, these travels – which could last up to four years – acted as a rite of passage for rich and titled young men who had left school and university but were faced with an awkward gap before they were obliged to come to grips with Real Life. Some used these years wisely, expanding their horizons and learning foreign languages, but others frittered them away and might just as well have stayed at home.

Batoni (1708–87), who had a splendid studio in the centre of Rome, derived a great deal of his income from wealthy visitors, especially those from Britain. This portrait, however, was never destined to end up on the walls of Basset's home. Despatched to England on board a British frigate, the *Westmorland*, the ship was seized by the French and its cargo, including this portrait, sold to the Spanish – which explains why the painting is now on the walls of the Prado in Madrid.

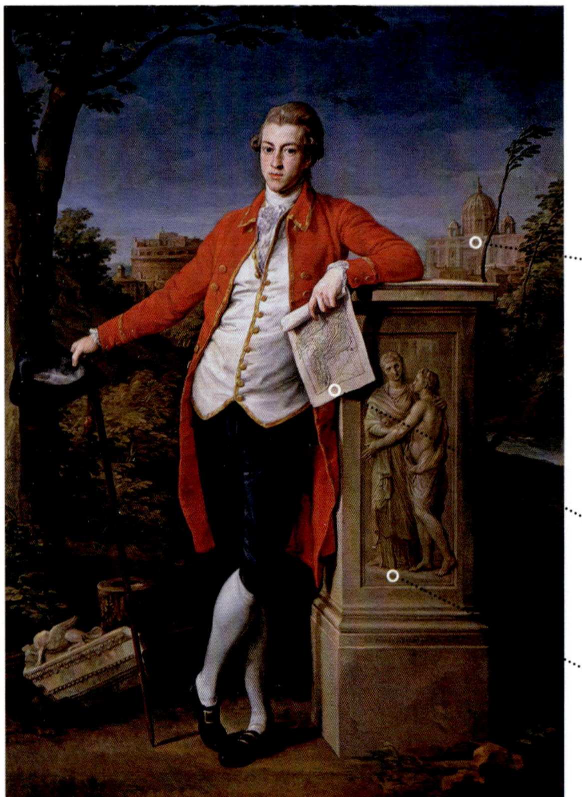

The backgrounds of Batoni's portraits often include glimpses of famous buildings. This is the distinctive Baroque dome of St Peter's Basilica in Rome. Over Basset's right shoulder is the Castel Sant'Angelo.

Basset holds a partly unrolled map of the city of Rome.

Batoni has invented this pedestal, but the relief carving is based on a well-known ancient sculpture.

FRANÇOIS BOUCHER

Madame de Pompadour

1756

The letters, the quill pen and ink demonstrate that she has cultivated the art of correspondence.

When Madame de Pompadour became the official mistress of Louis XV, she occupied a second-floor apartment at Versailles. Whenever Louis could decently escape his royal duties, he would ascend her private staircase to be with her. But by 1756, when this portrait was painted, their relationship had evolved from a sexual one to one of intimate friendship (a relief to Madame de Pompadour as she had endangered her already frail health by her attempts to boost her flagging libido with a diet of truffles, celery and vanilla). To mark her new status, she moved into a large apartment on the palace's ground floor. She now had more space for the countless *objets d'art* with which she liked to surround herself, which included numerous pets, both furred and feathered.

Boucher (1703–70) was Mme de Pompadour's favourite artist, and together they epitomised the elegance, wit and refinement of the Rococo period. In this portrait he has caught her beauty, poise and grace. Her supreme asset was her exquisite taste, and the Pompadour style would be her most lasting memorial. She had managed to survive the slings and arrows of a spiteful court, divert the king – whose besetting sin was boredom – but it had exhausted her. To his profound distress, she died at the age of forty-two. They had been inseparable for nearly twenty years.

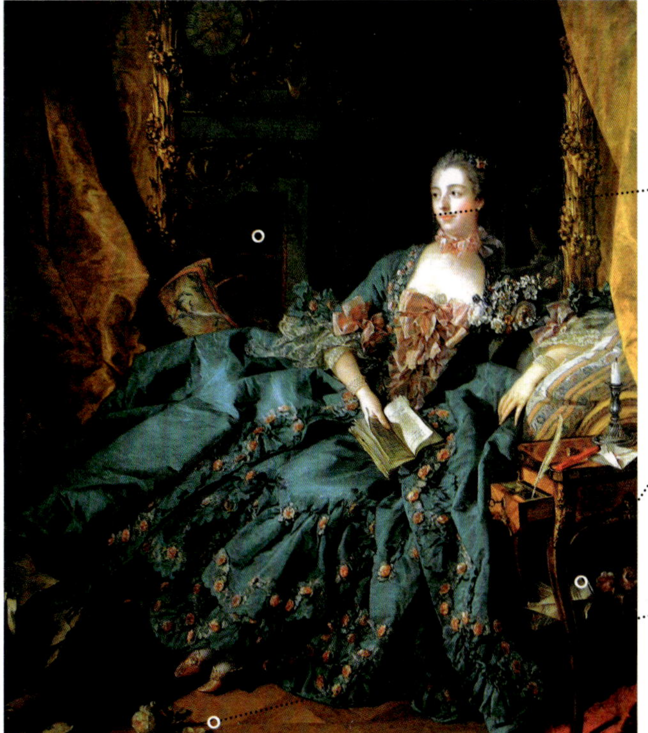

Mme de Pompadour was a passionate reader. The bookcase reflected in the mirror behind her contains volumes of the most advanced writers and thinkers of her age. It was said that her personal library contained 3,525 books.

The sheet music bulging from the folder indicates her musicality. She was taught music and singing and was an influential patron of the arts.

The roses at her feet indicate that her apartments were always filled with flowers.

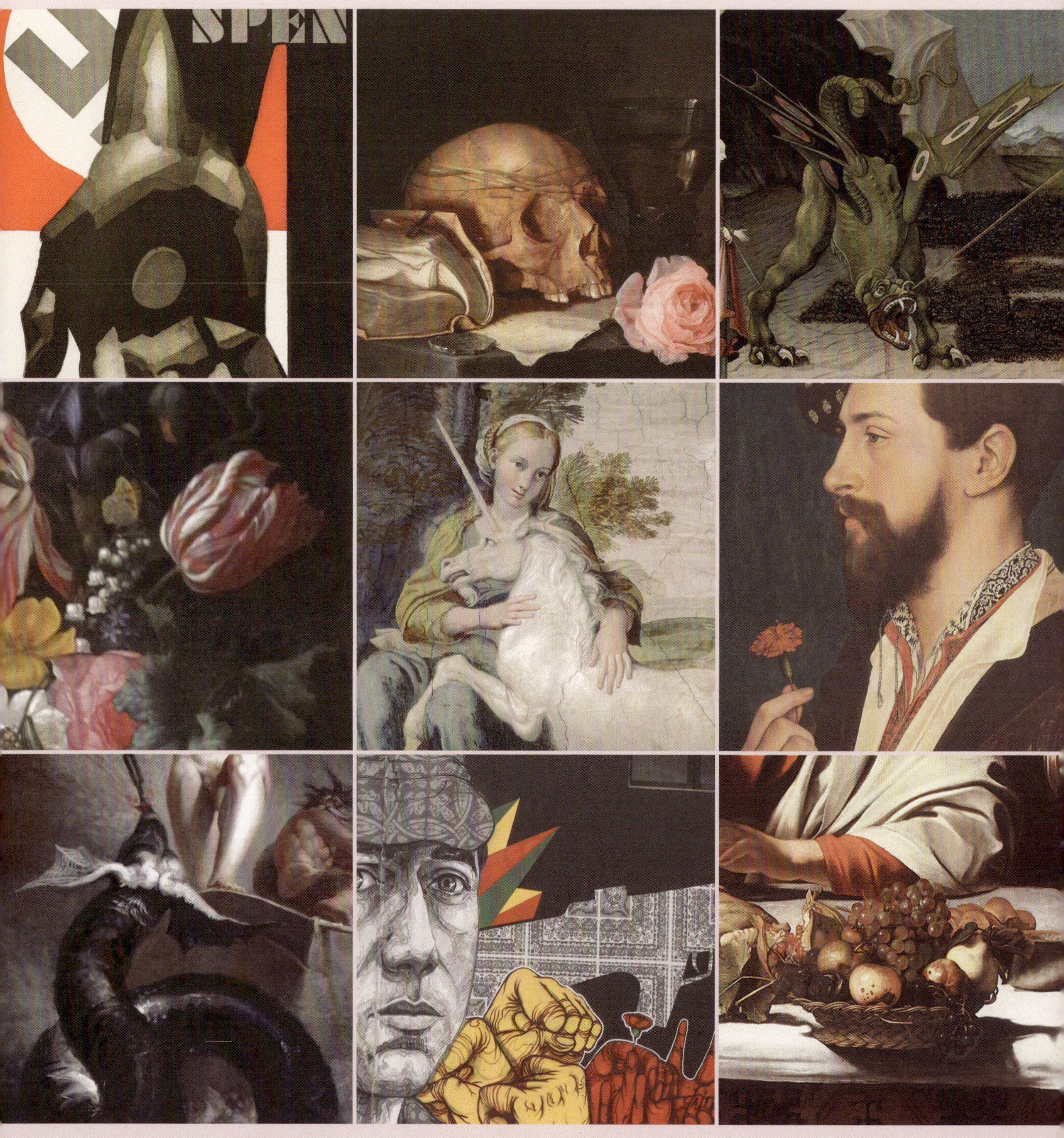
SPEN

CHAPTER THREE

THE ENDURING POWER OF SYMBOLS

Art is replete with symbols and many of them do not fit neatly into subject classifications. In some cases, single objects – a flower, a Sanskrit sign for good luck, a mythical beast – have become freighted with significance, their meaning evolving over the centuries.

Still lifes are particularly rich in symbols, many of them religious or philosophical. There is no better memento mori *than a decaying flower or an overripe fig. Contemporary viewers would have immediately interpreted the allusions emobodied in, for example, pomegranates, wheat and butterflies. The process of symbols evolving is on-going: doves, carnations and swastikas have all changed their meaning over the last century to convey political and propaganda messages that are very far from their original connotations.*

STILL LIFE

The English term 'still life' comes from the Dutch word *stilleven*, an indication of just how much this type of painting is associated with Dutch artists. The Dutch were obsessive picture buyers – more so than any other European country. In 1641, the English diarist John Evelyn was astonished to see paintings for sale outdoors at the Rotterdam fair.

Still-life subjects took several forms. The *vanitas* paintings were to remind the viewer of the transience of life, the worthlessness of worldly pleasures and the futility of earthly possessions. Some still lifes contained exotic objects – a Ming vase, a rare nautilus shell or a Persian rug – that people had never seen before. Women artists in particular excelled at complex flower pieces. The different blooms, skilfully woven together into a riot of fiery colour, reflect the fact that the Dutch were the leading horticulturists in Europe.

In Spain, too, still life was a popular genre, bought principally by highly educated collectors. In spite of their apparently mundane subject matter, the paintings were often invested with religious meaning, conveyed by symbols that were readily understood by the contemporary viewer.

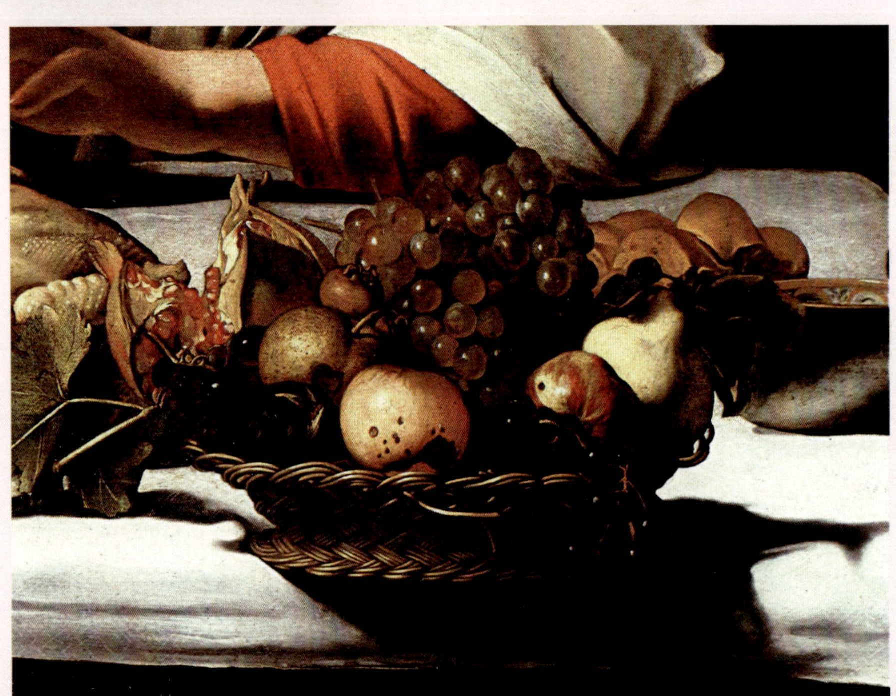

Caravaggio, *Supper at Emmaus*, *c.* 1601
(Top) The artist was famed for the reality and drama he brought to religious subjects. Here he depicts the miraculous appearance of Jesus to two of his apostles within days of his Crucifixion. Neither of them recognises him until his blessing of the bread recalls the Last Supper. (Left) The basket of fruit teetering on the edge of the table is an exquisite still life in its own right. The overripe apples and figs stand for original sin while the pomegranate and grapes symbolise Christ's Resurrection. The shadow on the basket's right is shaped like the tail of a fish, the ancient sign for Jesus Christ.

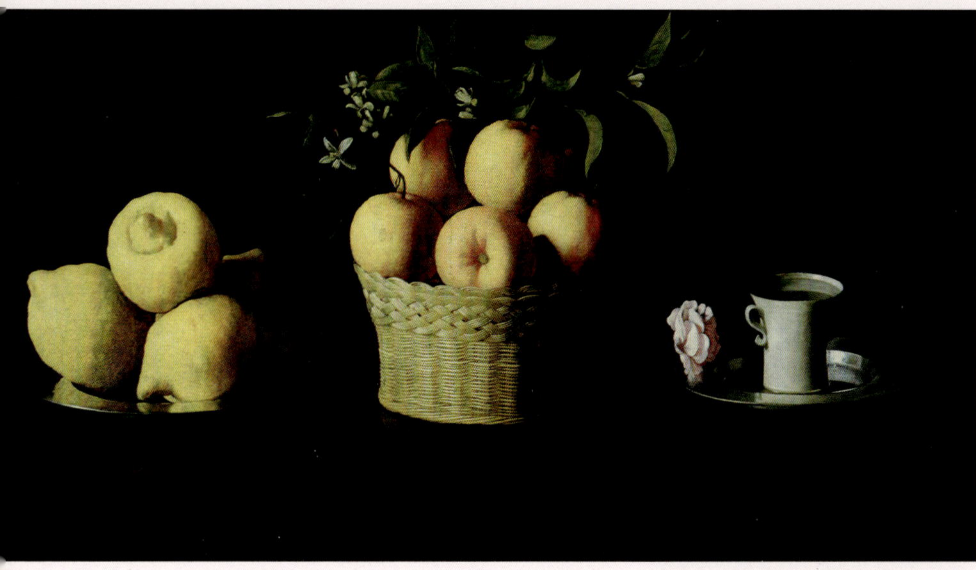

Francisco de Zurbarán, *Still Life with Lemons, Oranges and a Rose*, 1633
The measured placement of the three groups is an allusion to the Holy Trinity. The fruit symbolises the sweetness of heaven; the cup of water and the rose allude to the Virgin's chastity and purity. The spotless, mirror-like surface reflects God's love. This is the only signed and dated still life that Zurbarán is known to have painted.

Jan Davidsz. de Heem, *A Vanitas Still Life with a Skull, a Book and Roses*, *c.* 1630
The skull evokes human mortality, while the wheat stalks woven around it symbolise the changing seasons. The document and the book are emblems of human knowledge. The roses are doomed to wither and die.

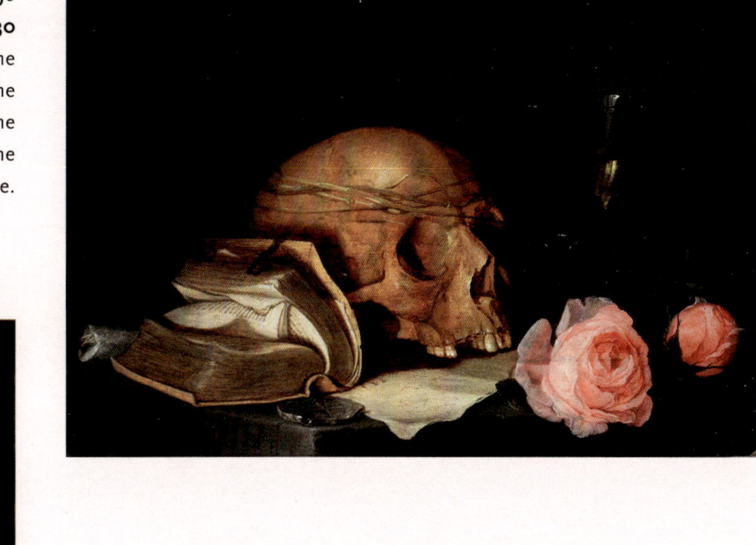

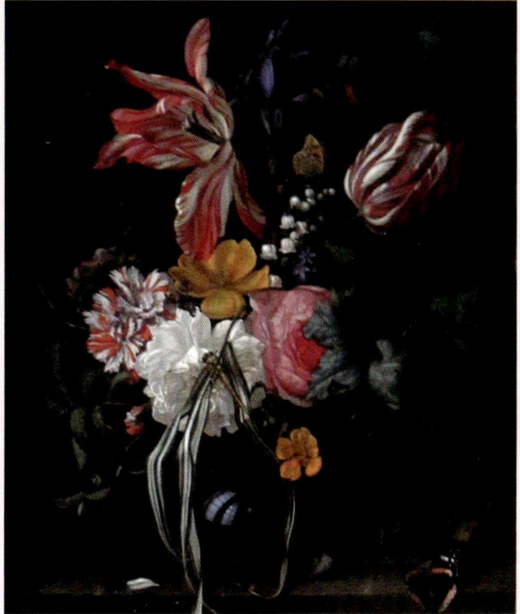

Maria van Oosterwijck, *Vase of Tulips, Rose, and Other Flowers with Insects*, 1669
Oosterwijck was one of the most successful woman flower painters of the Netherlands. Her pictures often contain butterflies, like the Red Admiral on the table's edge, which symbolises both the brevity of life and the resurrected human soul.

MYTHICAL BEASTS

A mythical beast is one that never existed in reality. Some of them were based on actual encounters or on garbled accounts by travellers. The unicorn came about when a wild ox was wrongly translated as a unicorn in the Bible. A few combine the human with the animal, hence the centaur. In different cultures mythical creatures have different meanings: in the ancient East a dragon was a beneficent deity, but in Christian culture it was seen as representing the Devil and all his works.

Providing heroes – such as St George and the Archangel Michael – with fitting opponents in their fight against evil was one of the most important functions of the more ferocious beasts. In the *Odyssey*, Odysseus vanquishes various monstrous creatures including the Cyclops, Scylla and Charybdis. Other tales relate how Medusa was defeated by Perseus, the Minotaur by Theseus. Some, like the griffin, which had the body of a lion and the wings and head of an eagle, made excellent guardians of treasure. Throughout history, certain artists have set out to create shocking or dramatic scenes, and the stories surrounding these mythical beasts have provided them with boundless inspiration.

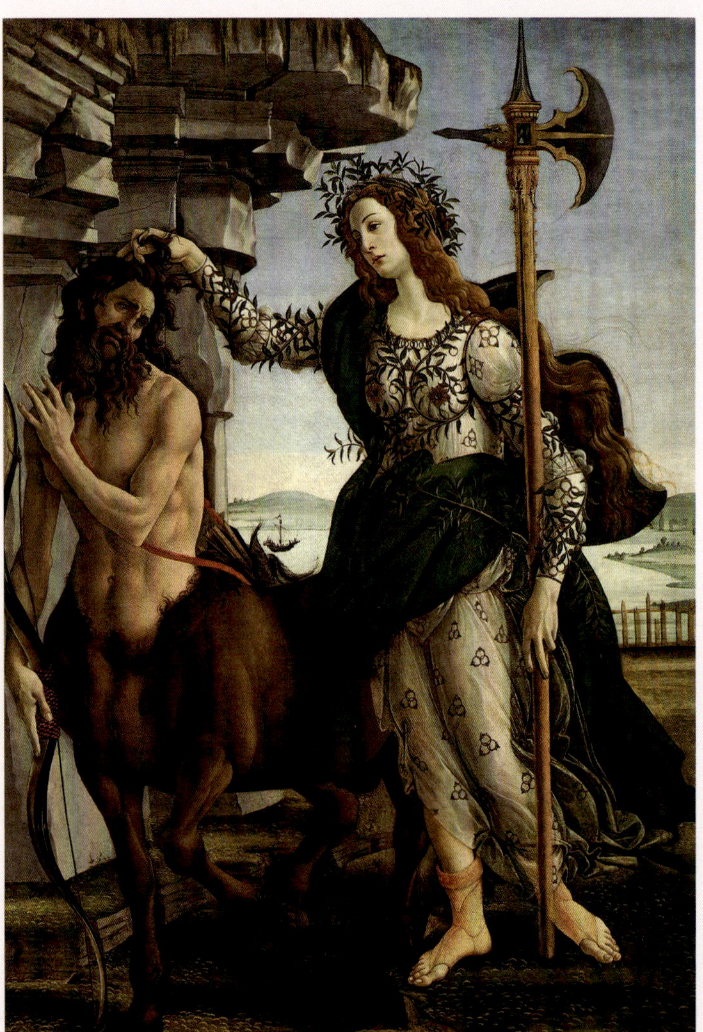

Sandro Botticelli, *Minerva and the Centaur*, c. 1482
In Greek mythology, centaurs have the reputation of being brutal, drunken and lecherous. Representing the lower instincts, here the centaur is equipped with quiver and bow, symbols of earthly love. Minerva, holding the halberd that is her attribute as the goddess of war, is subjecting the distinctly discomfited beast to her superior power and wisdom. She is credited with creating the olive tree, and her clothes and hair are decorated with sprigs of olive. The interlocking rings embroidered on her dress are an emblem of the Medici family.

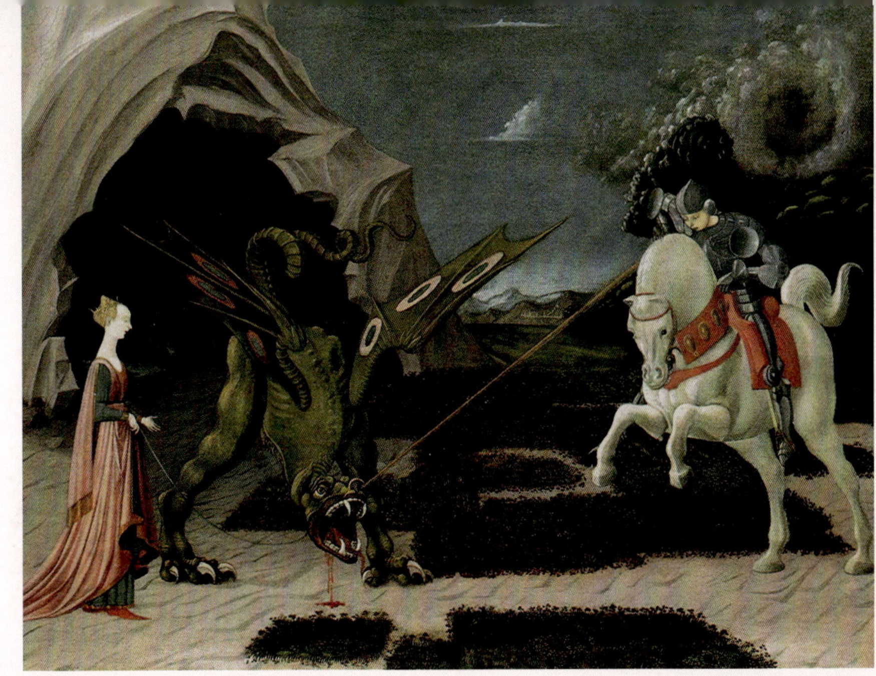

Paolo Uccello,
***Saint George and the Dragon*, 1470**
Originating in Georgia, but popularised in western Europe by *The Golden Legend*, the myth relates the story of a dragon that was terrorising a city called Cyrene in Libya. It had eaten all the sheep, then began on the children. A princess was next on the menu, and she was delivered to the dragon's cave. But St George arrived on his white steed and helped her catch the dragon, then tie her belt to it and lead it to the city. There he promised the citizens he would kill it if they all converted to Christianity. They hastily agreed, and George struck off the dragon's head.

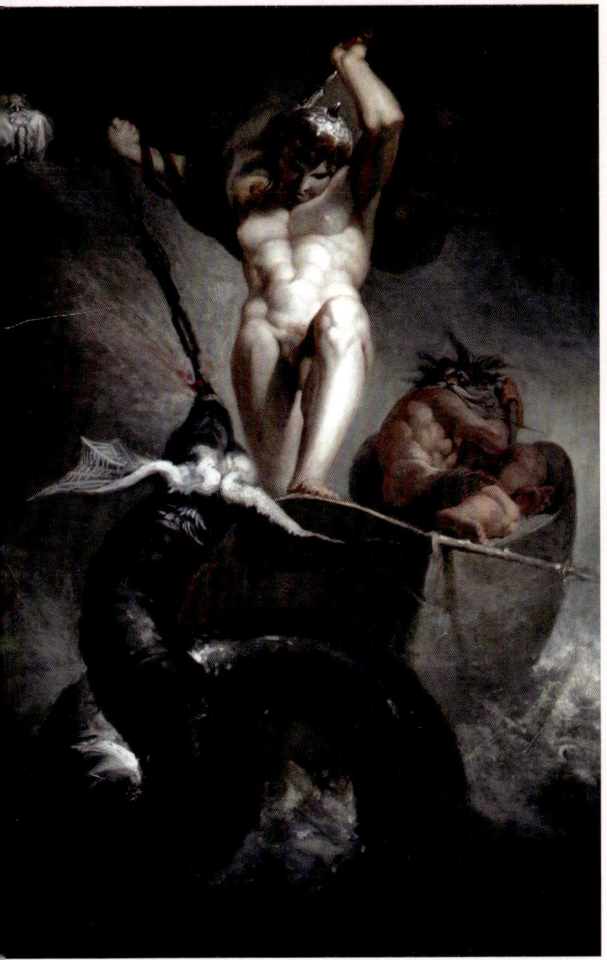

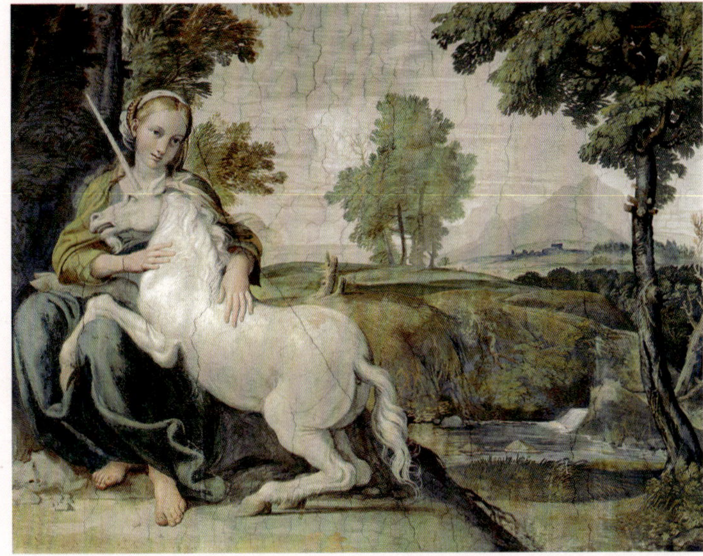

Henry Fuseli, *Thor Battering the Midgard Serpent*, 1790
In this dramatic scene, taken from Norse mythology, a muscular Thor looms above the serpent's thrashing coils, while the giant Hymir cowers in the stern of the boat. Thor's battle was said to reflect Fuseli's support for the French Revolution, the serpent representing the *ancien régime*.

Domenichino, *Virgin and the Unicorn*, c. 1602
The unicorn was proud, noble and fiercely courageous, but also gentle and serene. Seen both as a symbol of Christ and of worldly love, he was said to be so swift, he could only be captured by a virgin.

EVOLVING SYMBOLS

Some symbols have evolved from their original meaning – or meanings – to represent something completely different. Often their route to their new derivation can be unexpected, even serendipitous. The swastika has been especially active: for thousands of years it had been a symbol of good fortune for almost every world culture, but in the twentieth century it became, and remains, synonymous with fascism.

The poppy, too, has travelled far. Having been a symbol of sleep, degeneracy and death, today it is familiar in Britain and the Commonwealth as a symbol of Remembrance for those who died in the First World War and in every conflict since. Its evolution was inspired by a poem written in 1915 by a Canadian who had just witnessed the death of a friend. It begins: 'In Flanders' fields the poppies blow/Between the crosses, row on row ...' A poppy's seeds lie dormant in the ground, but the churning up of the soil on the battlefields exposed them to light and they flourished in their millions.

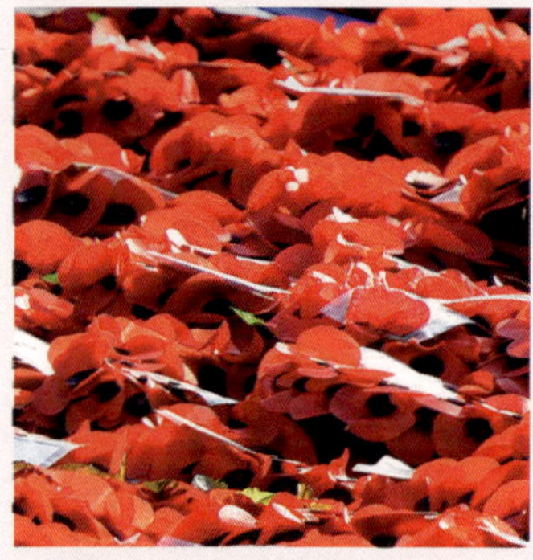

Part of the great sea of poppies around the Cenotaph in Whitehall on Remembrance Day.

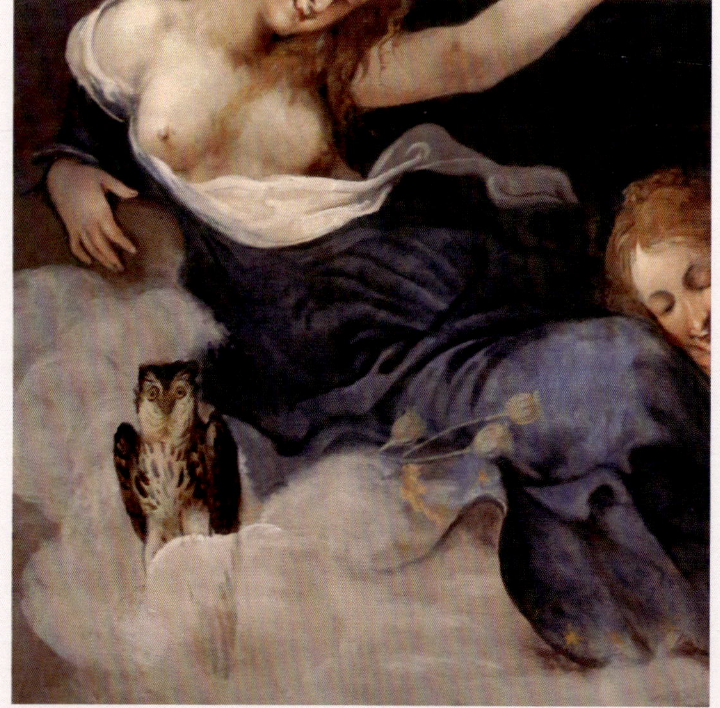

Giovanni da San Giovanni, *The Night with Aurora and Cupid*, c. 1635 (detail)
The image shows Night covering the sleeping Dawn (Aurora) with her cape while the owl, sacred to Night, stares unblinkingly out of the painting. To the right of the owl are some poppy heads. These are not randomly placed but are a reference to the poppy's sleep-inducing qualities. Sap extracted from the head of *Papaver somniferum* is used to make opium and is the key source for many narcotics. Opium is one of the ingredients in laudanum, popular in the nineteenth century as a painkiller and tranquiliser. Ancient cultures, such as the Egyptians and Greeks, clearly used the poppy in its various forms. Poppies seldom appear in Christian art, apart from occasions where they represent the blood of Christ. Despite its tainted history, the poppy has become one of the most famous floral symbols of the modern age.

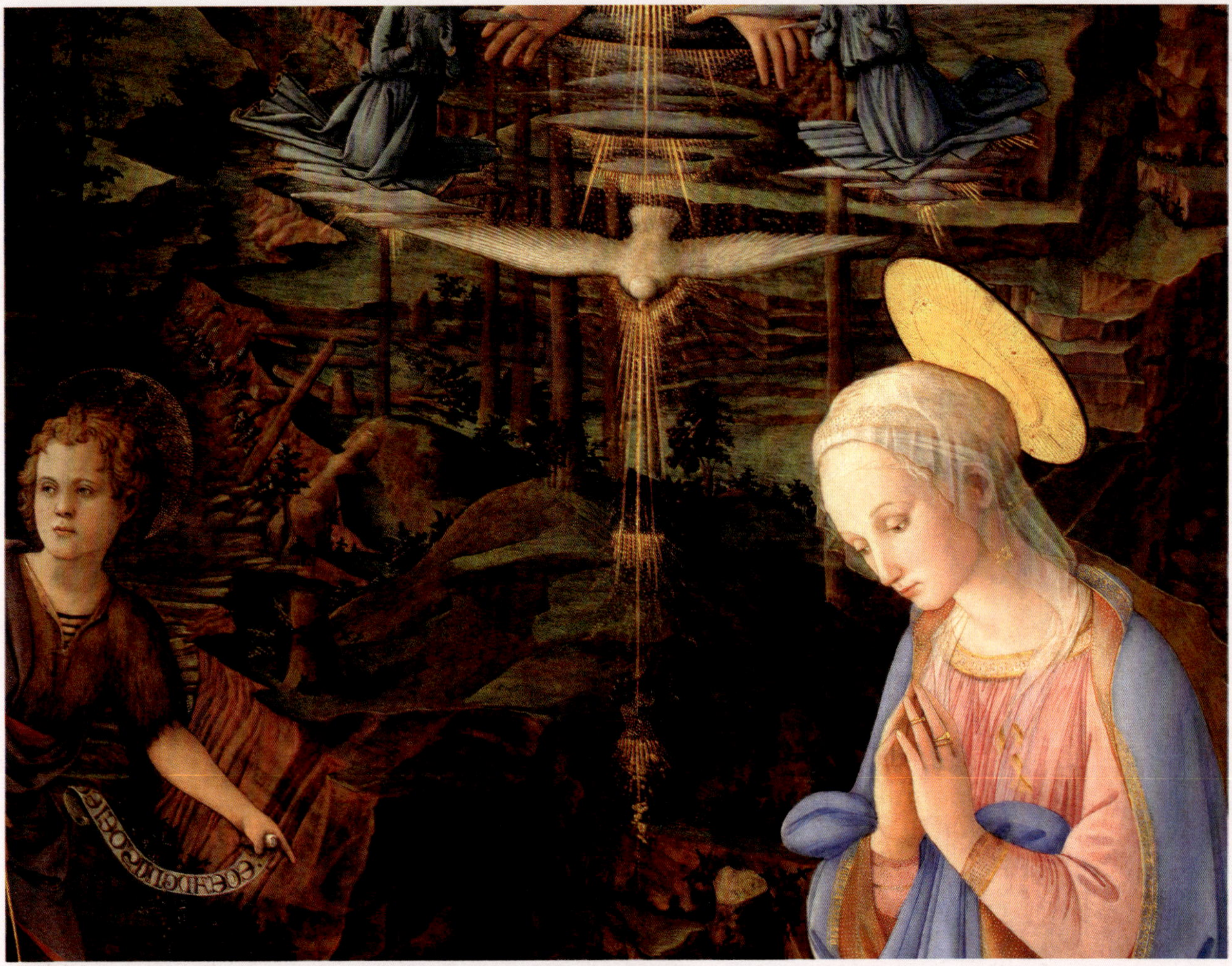

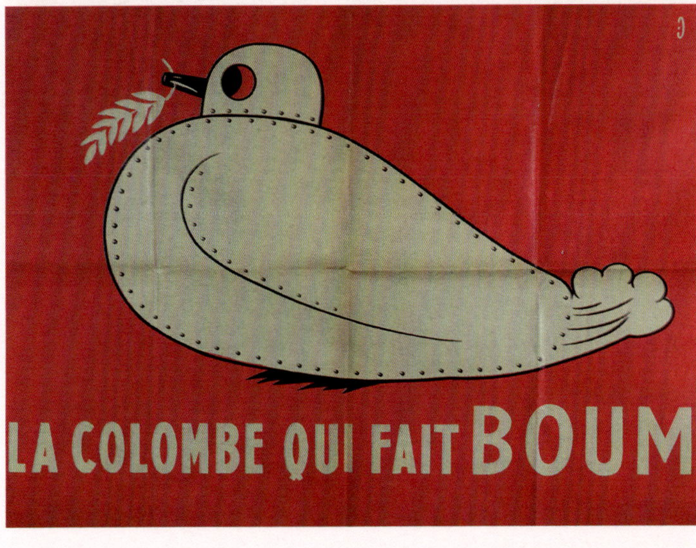

Fra Filippo Lippi, *Adoration of the Child with St Bernard*, 1463 (detail)

The dove is one of Christianity's oldest symbols, associated with purity, peace and the human soul. As a symbol of the Holy Ghost, it is the third part of the Holy Trinity. Here, it hovers between God, Mary and the Christ Child who is lying on the ground.

'The Dove that Goes Boom!', anti-communist poster, 1952–53

The Paix et Liberté movement, founded in 1950 to attack the Soviet Union and communist ideology, distributed thousands of posters throughout France. This one, in which the dove changes into a Soviet tank, was a parody on Pablo Picasso's Dove of Peace, chosen to symbolise the World Peace Congress in 1949.

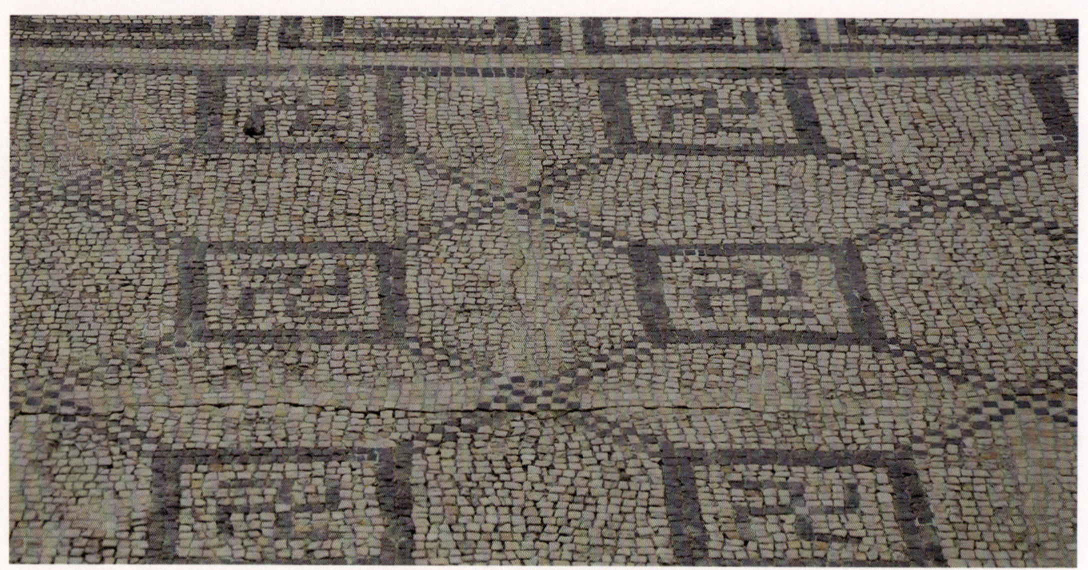

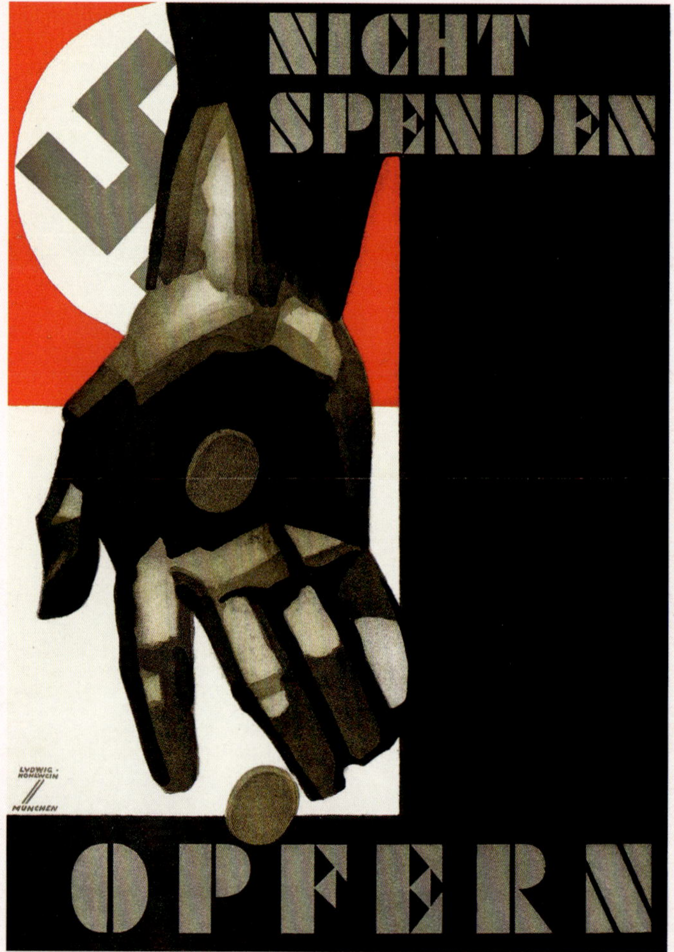

Roman mosaic, Conímbriga, Portugal, third century AD
No symbol has changed its meaning more radically or sunk lower in the public mind than the swastika. For millennia it remained true to its Sanskrit meaning of 'well-being' or 'good fortune' in almost every culture in the world. To the Romans it was a symbol of good luck, hence its appearance in a wealthy citizen's villa, the House of the Swastika, in the ancient city of Conímbriga.

Nazi propaganda poster, *c.* 1933
The swastika's downfall came in 1920 when Adolf Hitler designed the Nazi flag. He flipped it and combined it with the three colours of the German Imperial flag: red, black and white. In the 1930s the Nazis, believing it to be a symbol of an 'Aryan' master race, adopted it and corrupted it for ever. This poster, instigated by Germany's insolvency following the First World War, urged the people to donate their money to charity, not to spend it. The artist, Ludwig Holwein, worked closely with Joseph Goebbels and the Ministry of Propaganda and Enlightenment.

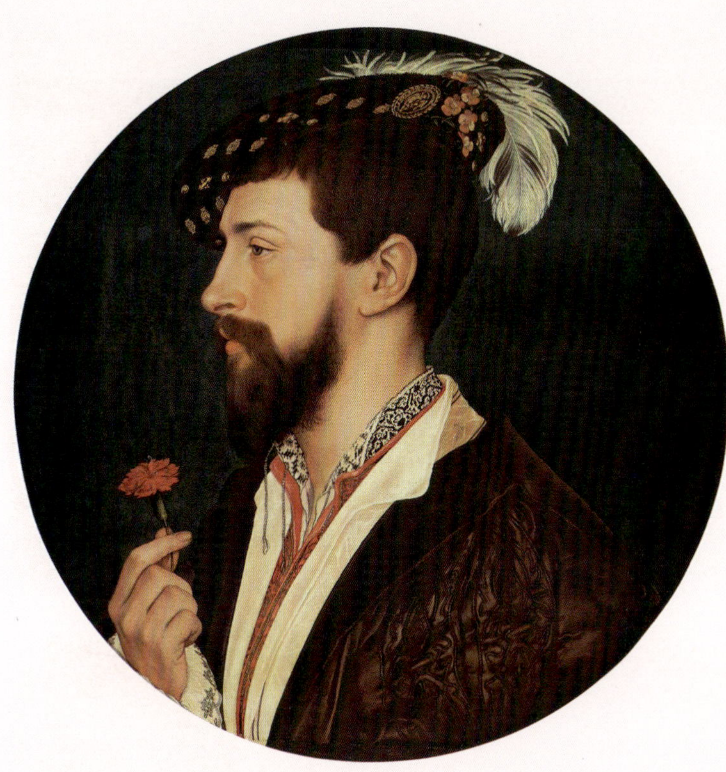

Hans Holbein the Younger, *Portrait of Simon George of Cornwall*, *c.* 1535–40
The sitter's red carnation is a symbol of his betrothal. It also symbolises Christ, since its Greek name, *dianthus*, means 'the flower of god'. Carnations can represent maternal or compassionate love, as they were said to grow on the ground where the tears of the Virgin Mary fell at the Crucifixion.

Graffiti of the leader of the Carnation Revolution, Lisbon, Portugal, 1974
The image shows Fernando Maia, the leader of the military coup that overthrew the authoritarian government that led to Portugal's transition to democracy. No shots were fired during the coup; instead, the people offered carnations to the soldiers and placed them in the muzzles of their guns hoping that the flowers would pacify them

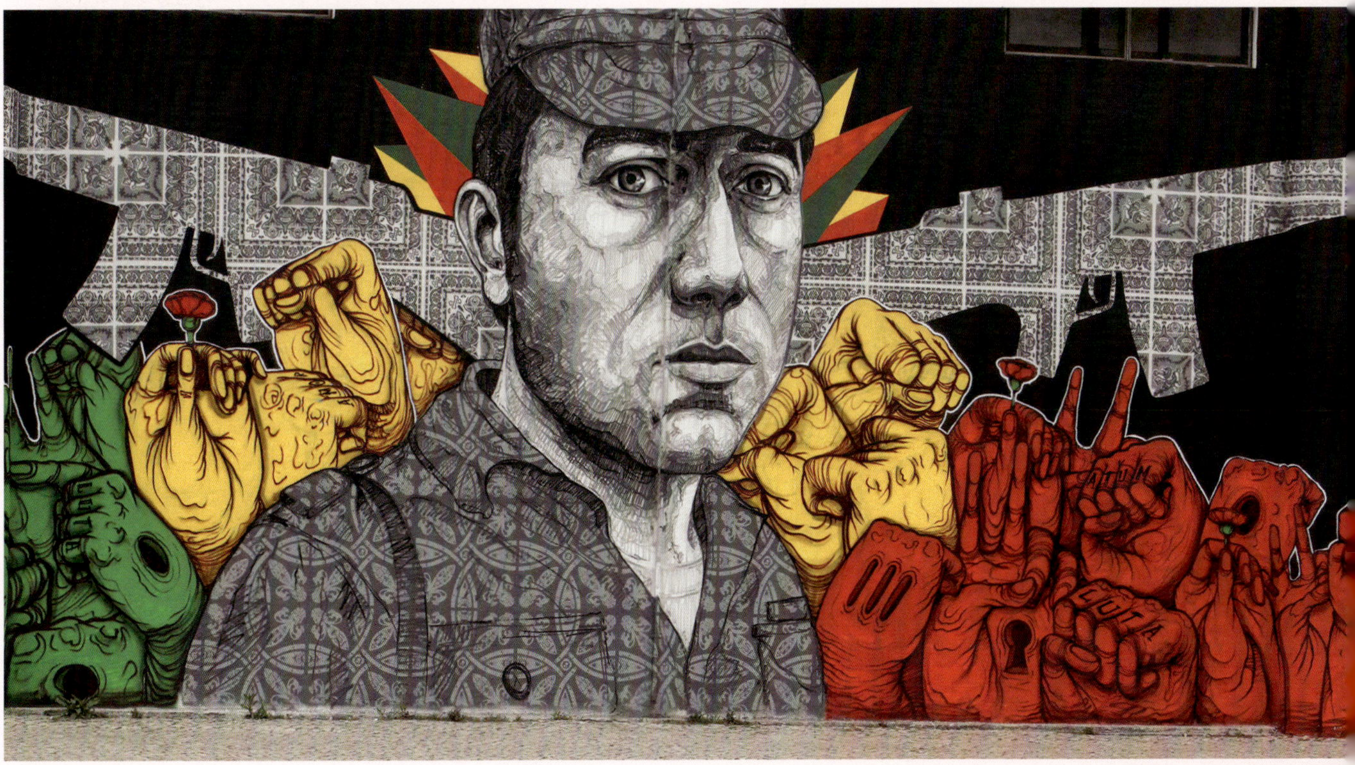

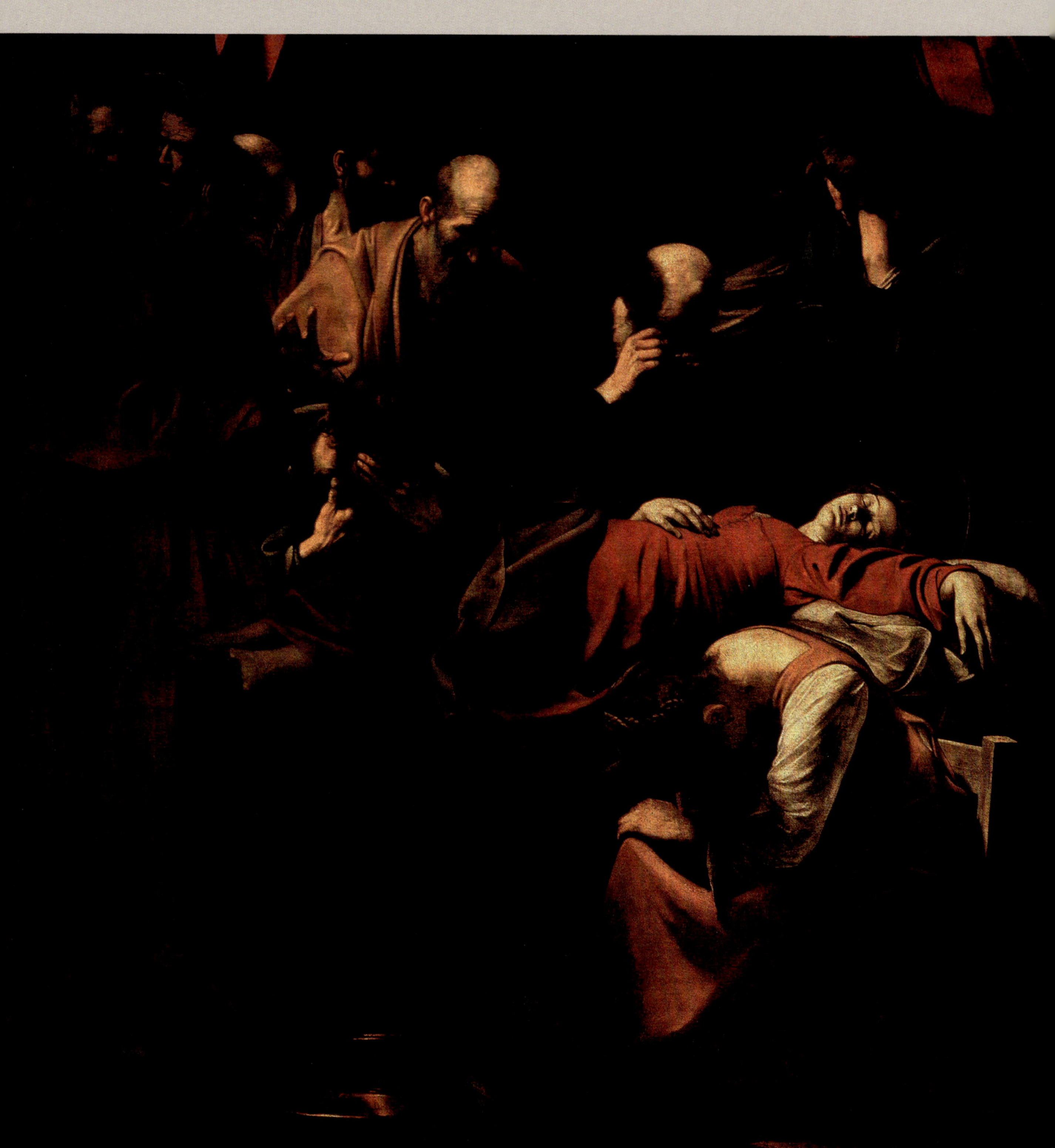

CARAVAGGIO, *Death of the Virgin*, 1606 (detail)

Part Two

WHAT'S GOING ON?

Contemporaries of the artists featured in these pages would have had no problem interpreting their paintings. They were steeped in stories from the Bible, the classical world and in mythical and religious iconography, and would have instantly recognised the characters and scenarios they depict. Today's viewer not only has to decode the 'lost' language of symbols, but also has to unravel the meanings of these paintings, some of which are purely narrative but nonetheless draw on a world view that can feel alien and impenetrable. Faced with a seething crowd of biblical characters, a vision of the Holy Land that owes a puzzling debt to Renaissance Europe, a vast array of myths and legends from classical antiquity, a pantheon of pagan gods and bizarre and surreal juxtapositions of both time and location, it is hardly surprising that many modern viewers ask the question 'What's going on?'.

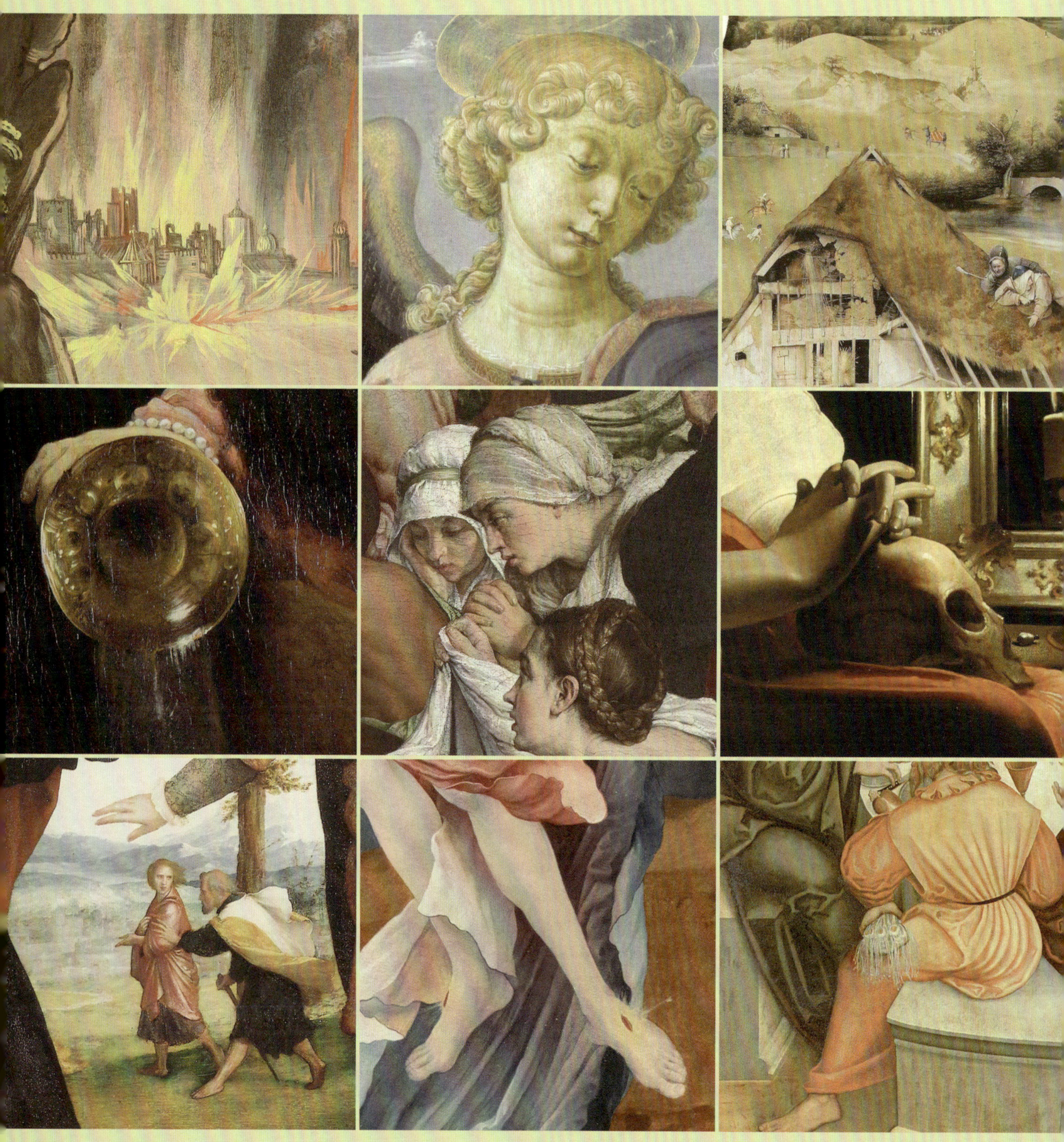

CHAPTER FOUR

BIBLICAL SCENES

FILIPPO LIPPI

Madonna and Child with Scenes from the Life of the Virgin

1452

Seated on a throne at the centre of this *tondo*, with the Christ Child on her lap, the Madonna regards the viewer with a gently enquiring gaze. The Child, his toes endearingly splayed, has picked out a seed from the pomegranate she holds for him. The background shows a well-appointed interior of a fifteenth-century Florentine palace in which women of the wealthy classes and their servants attend what appears to be a birth. But why is the woman in bed wearing a halo? Rather confusingly, Lippi has portrayed two episodes in the life of St Anne, the Virgin Mary's mother, simultaneously: St Anne's reconciliation with her husband, Joachim, and giving birth to their daughter. According to *The Golden Legend*, Mary's parents had been childless for twenty years. Humiliated and ashamed of his sterility, Joachim retreated to the wilderness, but in a vision was instructed to be reunited with Anne. Mary was conceived when the couple embraced and kissed – hence Mary's conception was immaculate, as it was untainted by original sin.

Lippi (*c.* 1406–69) painted this scene on a birth tray. Orphaned as a child, he was brought up by the Carmine monks in Florence. He became both a painter and a monk, but eloped with a nun and had children with her. One of his most distinguished pupils was Sandro Botticelli.

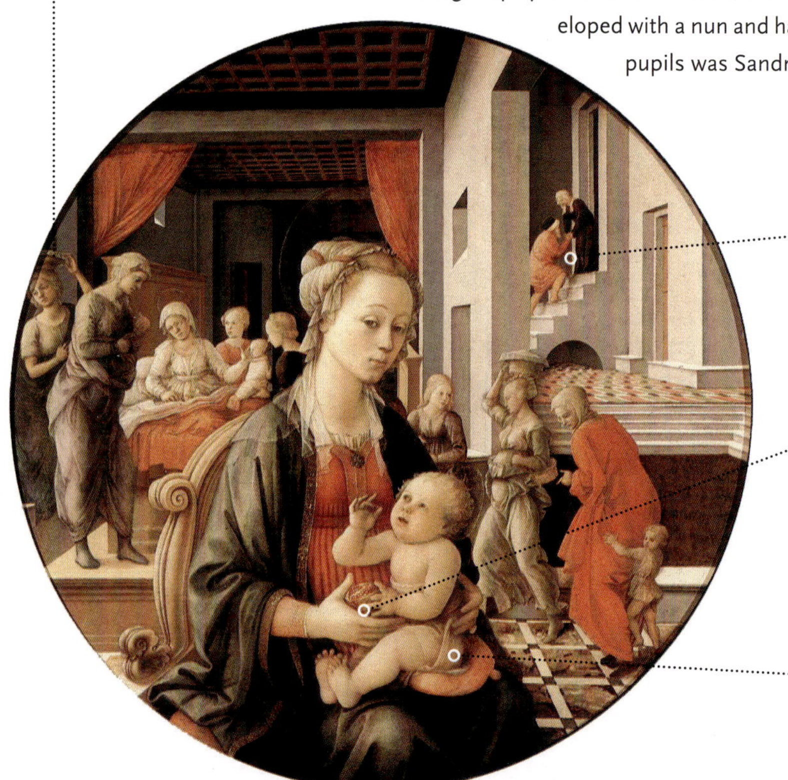

It was the custom to present a woman who had just given birth with sweetmeats on a birth tray. Here, a servant approaches Anne with a tray balanced on her head.

Anne meets her husband after Joachim's return from the wilderness. The staircase leads to the Golden Gate, one of the entrances to Jerusalem.

Because of its countless seeds and tough skin, the pomegranate is a symbol of fertility, chastity and of the Church, which contains many souls. When held by the Christ Child, it is a premonition of the Passion.

Indicative of his high status, the Christ Child sits on a red cushion. But could this piece of cloth be a Renaissance nappy?

ANDREA MANTEGNA

The Death of the Virgin

c. 1462

According to the Apocryphal Gospels, after the Archangel Michael announced to the Virgin her earthly end (or 'Dormition', that is, the 'falling asleep'), she summoned the apostles to come to her. All but St Thomas, who was preaching in India, gathered at her bedside. In the centre St Peter, dressed in bishop's robes and holding a prayerbook, conducts the service. Others hold candles. To the left of St Peter an apostle holds holy water in one hand and blesses the Virgin with the other. The upper part of this work was mutilated at some point in its early life. The missing section represented Christ receiving the soul of the Virgin. Mantegna's mastery of perspective, his ability to give each apostle an individual character and the dreamy landscape beyond the window, combine to make this work a masterpiece.

This painting has an interesting past. It was once owned by Charles I of England who, during his reign, assembled one of history's greatest art collections. Following the king's execution in 1649, the collection, numbering around 1,500 pictures and 500 sculptures, was sold under the Commonwealth. Despite the best efforts of his son Charles II to recover the collection following the Restoration of the monarchy in 1660, many of the most valuable works were already in foreign hands, including this Mantegna, which is now one of the Prado Museum's most treasured possessions.

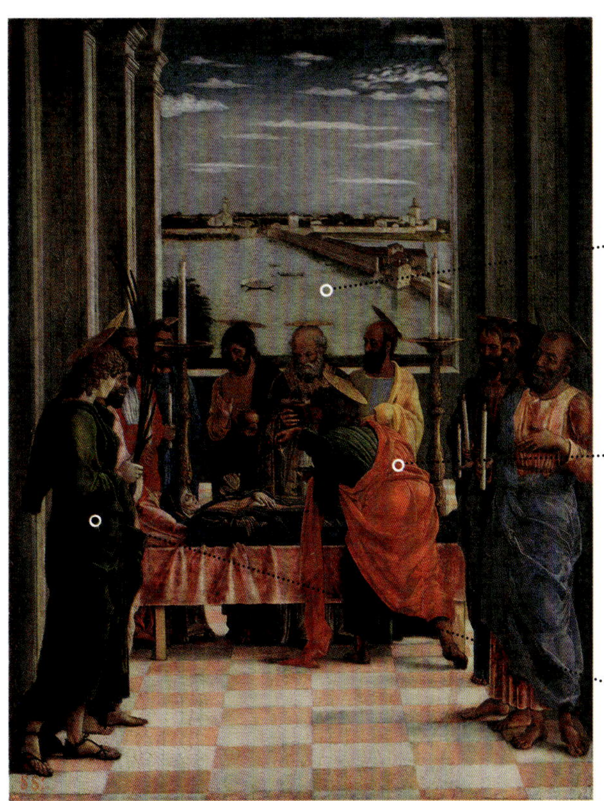

The lake scene is a detailed reproduction of the bridge and the Castello di San Giorgio in Mantua. Mantegna's painting was originally part of the decoration of the Castello's chapel.

This apostle is swinging a censer of incense over the Virgin's recumbent form. Because the smell of burning incense was so powerful, it was often used at funerary ceremonies as it helped to smother the scent of decay.

St John holds a palm branch, handed to him by the Virgin on her death bed, a symbol of her victory over death.

WORKSHOP OF ANDREA DEL VERROCCHIO

Tobias and the Angel

c. 1470–75

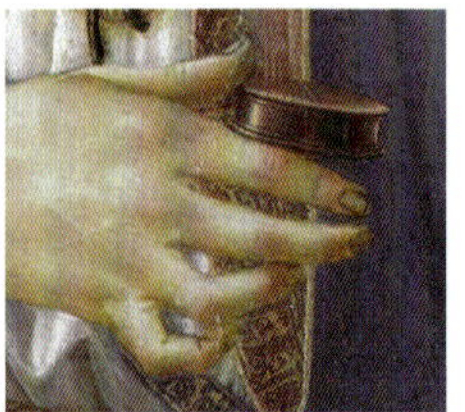

Raphael is carrying a little box that contains the vital organs of the fish that Tobias made into a special ointment.

This is a puzzling image: an angel and a youth, arm in arm, striding along at such speed that their garments are billowing out behind them. And why is the boy carrying a fish on a string? The answer lies in the biblical Book of Tobit – regarded as of doubtful authenticity by Jews and Protestants – that tells the story of Tobit, an old, blind Jewish merchant who dispatched his son Tobias to the country of Media, near Assyria, to collect a debt.

God sent the Archangel Raphael (disguised as a relative of Tobias) to accompany Tobias and his dog on their journey. When they stopped for a rest by a river, Tobias was attacked by a 'monstrous' fish, which he overcame. Raphael told him to gut it but to preserve its vital organs. While on their journey they visited Tobias's cousin, Sarah, who was possessed of a demon and had lost seven husbands. Undeterred, Tobias decided to marry her. He used the ointment he had made from the fish's organs to drive out Sarah's demon and to cure his father's blindness.

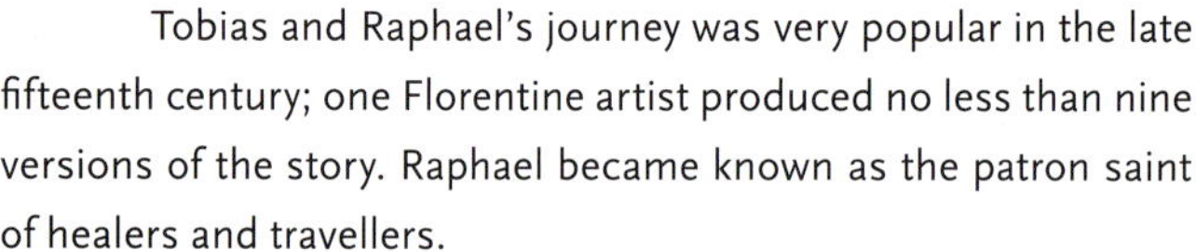

Tobias and Raphael's journey was very popular in the late fifteenth century; one Florentine artist produced no less than nine versions of the story. Raphael became known as the patron saint of healers and travellers.

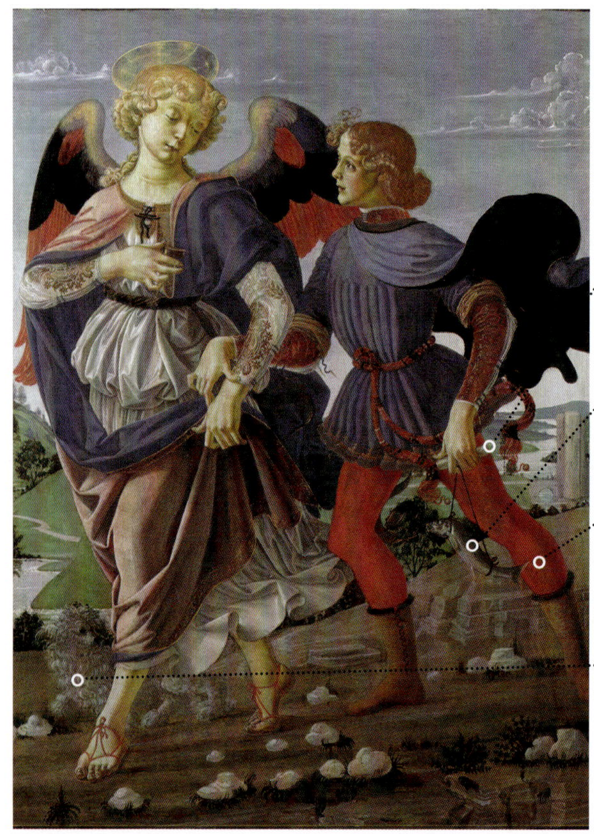

This rolled up parchment labelled 'Ricordo' is the record of the debt that is owed to Tobit.

In the story, Tobias is attacked by a 'monstrous' fish, so this small specimen is clearly a symbolic fish.

Any Florentine would know that Tobias was the son of a successful businessman by his red tights, which were the most desirable fashion item for men in the late fifteenth century.

Scholars have suggested that both the dog and the fish, which were clearly added later as the background is visible through them (and possibly Tobias's curls) were painted by Verrocchio's most famous pupil, Leonardo da Vinci.

MARTIN SCHONGAUER

Temptation of St Anthony

1470–74

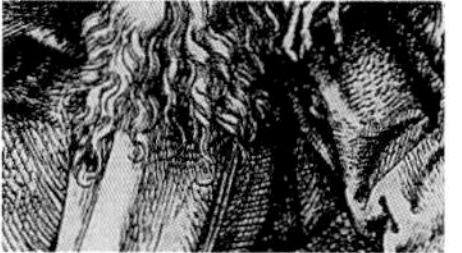

Fine cross-hatching can be seen in St Anthony's drapery. It was an excellent way to give volume to an image made out of black lines.

According to the fourth-century theologian, Athanasius of Alexandria, St Anthony Abbot had a vision during his years in the wilderness (see page 19) in which he had levitated into the air and was attacked by demons and tormented by erotic visions. Schongauer (*c.* 1448–91), one of the earliest exponents of the art of engraving, has used his fertile imagination to produce some truly horrific devils. Apart from the lugubrious fellow with the spikes (top left), they all seem to be thoroughly enjoying their tempting and tormenting. St Anthony, on the other hand, is the picture of patience and stoicism. He epitomises the Christian's struggle to resist evil temptations. He appears not to mind that the owner of the dangling, claw-like foot is hauling on his scarf, that sundry fiends are belabouring him with sticks or that a disgusting apparition is combing his hair with its fingernails. Yet, as a result of Schongauer's direct observation of nature, the softness of fur, the complexity of scales and the membranes of the wings of these imagined creatures are remarkably convincing.

According to Vasari, Michelangelo – then aged about thirteen – was so impressed by this engraving by Schongauer that he made a 'perfect pen-and-ink copy'. But he went further: he produced a painting of it. Such was his attention to veracity that he reputedly studied fish in Florence's fish market.

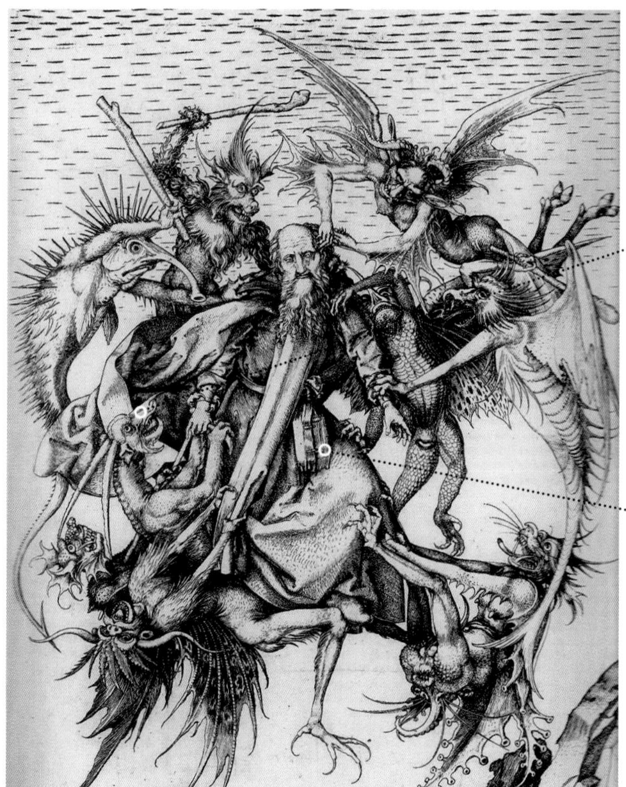

St Anthony appears to be disputing possession of his crutch-shaped staff – known as a *tau* – with a hideous demon with long horns. There is no sign of the saint's other attributes, his pig and his bell.

These small portable books, known as girdle books, were worn by medieval European monks. The book hung upside down and backwards so that when it was swung upwards it was ready for reading.

HIERONYMUS BOSCH

Adoration of the Magi Triptych

c. 1494

This is the central panel of a triptych, painted by perhaps the greatest master of fantasy who ever lived. This image, however, appears to lack the grotesques and freaks that usually haunt Bosch's work. That is, until various elements are examined more closely. The three kings are as they should be, their gifts all present and correct. Mary sits stolidly outside the crumbling stable with a rather scrawny Christ Child on her lap. But who is the disturbing figure posing in an off-the-shoulder scarlet gown with his pallid skin, tanned face and bizarre headgear? More unsettling still is the gang of villains lurking behind him. He is the Antichrist, who is announced in the Bible as one 'who denies the Father and the Son'.

In the background, to the right and left, are two armies of men on horseback which appear to be riding towards each other. On the basis of their Oriental headdresses, they have been identified as Herod's soldiers searching for the Christ Child to kill him. In the far distance, across an arid and lumpy landscape, are the weird and wonderful spires and towers of a city. Jerusalem or Bethlehem?

Very little is known about Bosch (*c.* 1450–1516). He was born in the Dutch town of 's-Hertogenbosch and became famous for his terrifying representations of the powers of evil and for his incredible powers of invention.

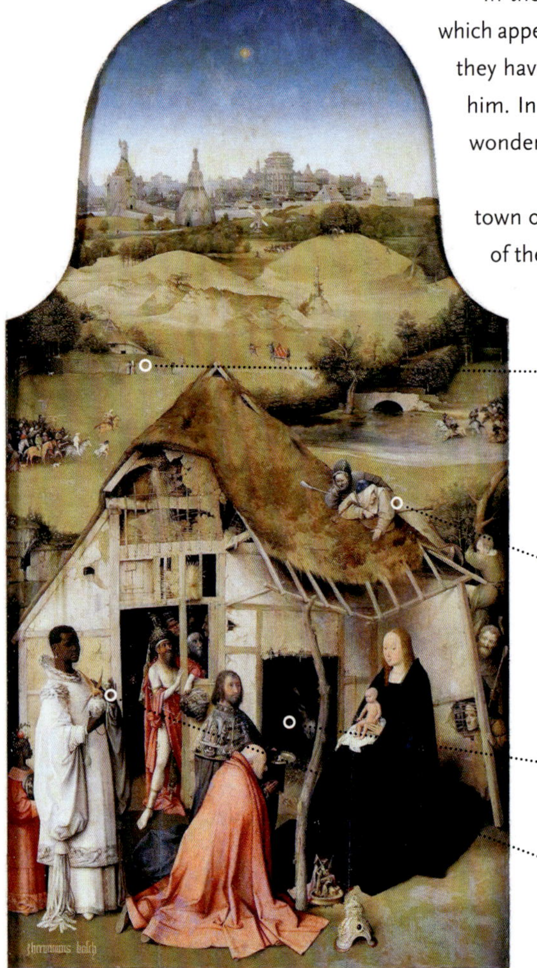

Although very difficult to see, this house is identified as a brothel by the swan on its flag. A man pulling a mule that is ridden by a monkey, an allusion to lust, is heading towards it.

According to the biblical description of the Nativity, the shepherds leave their flocks to gaze in adoration at the Christ Child, but these men clambering on to the roof seem more like voyeurs.

Here is the donkey, but where is the ox?

The phoenix perched on Balthasar's pot of myrrh, with a pomegranate seed in its beak, is a portent of the Resurrection.

ALBRECHT DÜRER

Lot and his Daughters

c. 1496–99

The Old Testament is full of dramatic and often troubling stories, but few are more shocking than the one about Lot. Based on the account in Genesis, Lot, his wife and two daughters were living in the city of Sodom, thought to be situated on a former peninsula in the central part of the Dead Sea in Israel. They were visited by two angels who urged them to flee, as both Sodom and the neighbouring city of Gomorrah were about to be destroyed by God as punishment for their citizens' wickedness. The family were to leave at once and were commanded not to look back.

Lot, his haste exhibited by his flying coat tails, guided his girls – but not his wife – to safety in the mountains where they took shelter in a cave. Convinced there were no men left alive to father their children, the daughters conspired to get their father drunk and then to lie with him in order to continue the family line. Thus an inebriated and befuddled Lot is seduced by his daughters. Both these incestuous couplings resulted in the birth of sons, Moab and Ben-Ammi, founders of the Moabites and Ammonites.

Painter, printmaker and writer, Dürer (1471–1528) is regarded as the greatest German artist of the Renaissance. His technical mastery transformed printmaking into an art form equal to that of painting and sculpture.

Lot's wife, failing to obey God's command that the family were not to look back during their flight from Sodom, has been turned into a pillar of salt.

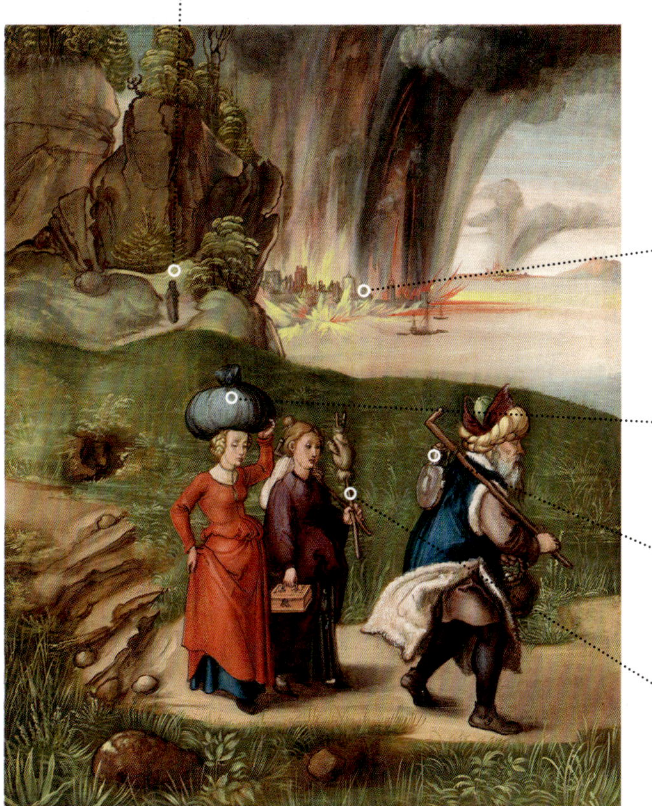

The cities of Sodom and Gomorrah in flames after God had rained down fire and brimstone on them for their godlessness and immorality.

The pumpkin-shaped bundle carried by the daughter in red probably contains the family's few remaining clothes.

Slung on Lot's stick is either a bottle containing water or the wine the daughters used to make their father drunk.

The purple-clad daughter is carrying a spindle, the house keys and her valuables in a little box.

GEERTGEN TOT SINT JANS

The Tree of Jesse

c. 1500

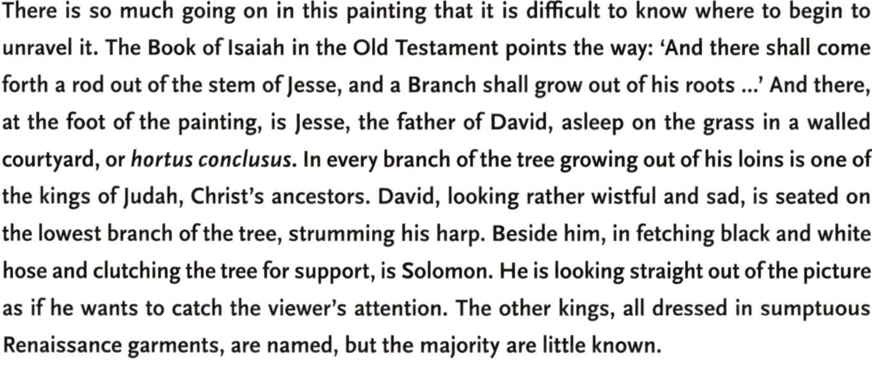

There is so much going on in this painting that it is difficult to know where to begin to unravel it. The Book of Isaiah in the Old Testament points the way: 'And there shall come forth a rod out of the stem of Jesse, and a Branch shall grow out of his roots ...' And there, at the foot of the painting, is Jesse, the father of David, asleep on the grass in a walled courtyard, or *hortus conclusus*. In every branch of the tree growing out of his loins is one of the kings of Judah, Christ's ancestors. David, looking rather wistful and sad, is seated on the lowest branch of the tree, strumming his harp. Beside him, in fetching black and white hose and clutching the tree for support, is Solomon. He is looking straight out of the picture as if he wants to catch the viewer's attention. The other kings, all dressed in sumptuous Renaissance garments, are named, but the majority are little known.

Geertgen, who died before he was thirty, has let his fertile imagination run riot in this painting. He is especially inventive when it comes to hats (see page 27). The Tree of Jesse often appears in stained-glass windows in medieval cathedrals. They were easy for the contemporary viewer, many of whom were illiterate, to understand and were normally 'read' from bottom to top.

Although difficult to pick out from this jigsaw of figures, the Virgin Mary and the Christ Child float above the assembled relations. They are flanked by two angels in blue satin.

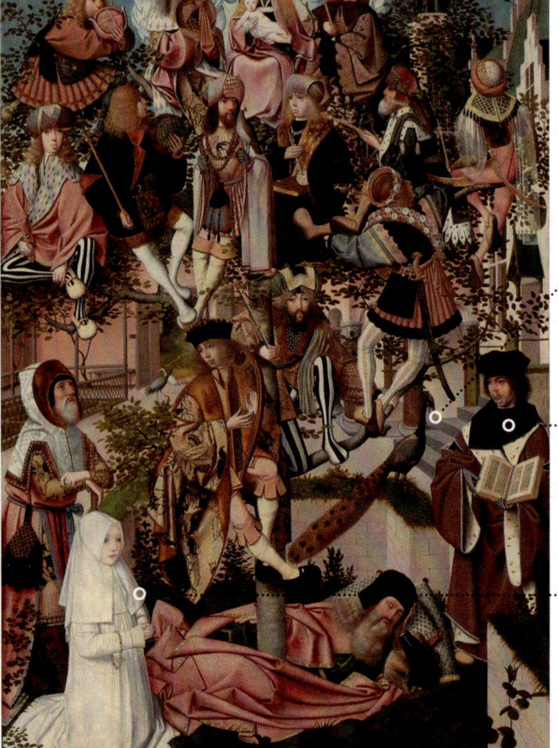

Peacocks, like the cranes on the left, were an ornamental feature of many gardens at the time. The peacock was a symbol of eternal life and of Christ's Resurrection.

This man with the open book, and the man opposite to him with a 'handbag' on his belt, are said to be the prophets Isaiah and Jeremiah.

The nun in a white habit, kneeling so demurely, her hands joined in prayer and a rosary on her arm, is the one who paid for the painting. It was not known that she was there until the picture was restored in 1932.

MATTHIAS GRÜNEWALD

Resurrection from the *Isenheim Altarpiece*

1512–16

This extraordinary image appears on one of the ten panels that depict scenes from the life of Christ, from the Annunciation to the Resurrection, which make up the Isenheim Altarpiece. It was painted by Grünewald for the Monastery of St Anthony in Isenheim. Almost nothing is known about the artist. Even his name is doubtful, and the dates when he was born and died (1470/80–1528) are extremely vague.

The Crucifixion scene is one of the most shattering ever painted: a twisted, tormented Christ, his flesh a sickly green and covered with sores, is lashed to the Cross that is set against a dark and lowering wasteland. It is a horrific record of suffering, created by an artist who does not flinch from taking the medieval preoccupation with sin and mortality to its furthest extreme. On a side panel of the altarpiece is this painting: no image could contrast more starkly with the Crucifixion than this joyous Christ as he rises from the tomb and soars upwards, his shroud leaving a trail of radiant light beneath him. He is transcendent, surrounded by the hot glow of the sun set in a night sky, his body now unblemished and an almost ethereal white. The Roman soldiers set to guard the tomb are shocked and bewildered by this sudden commotion, but oblivious of the miracle that has just taken place.

Christ demonstrates the wounds (stigmata) made in his hands and feet when he was nailed to the Cross.

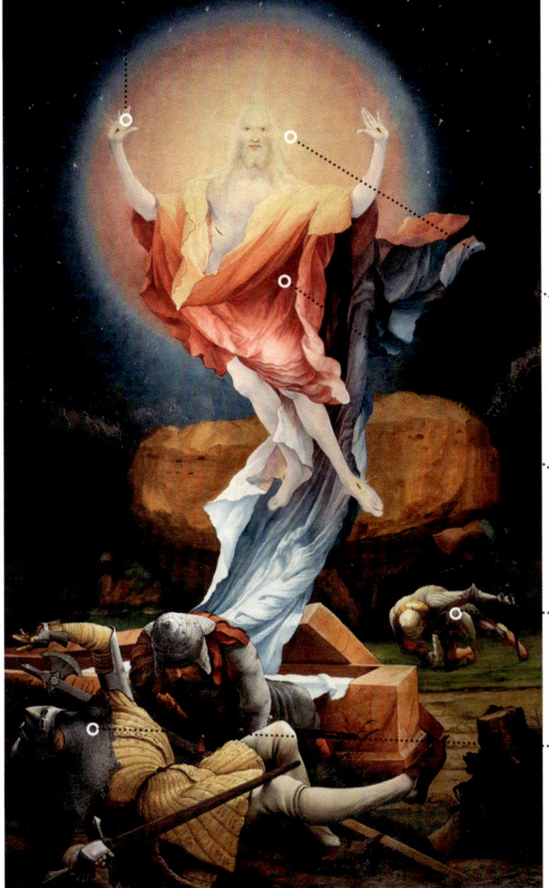

Christ's head and shoulders appear to be dissolving into the large circle of the sun, its brightness made all the more vivid by the deep blackness of the sky.

The scarlet robe alludes to Christ's suffering and incarnation.

Ungainly in his armour, this soldier has fallen forward like a stringless marionette.

This soldier, his visor over one eye, has flung his mailed fist above his head as if to ward off a blow.

JACOPO BASSANO

The Way to Calvary

1544–45

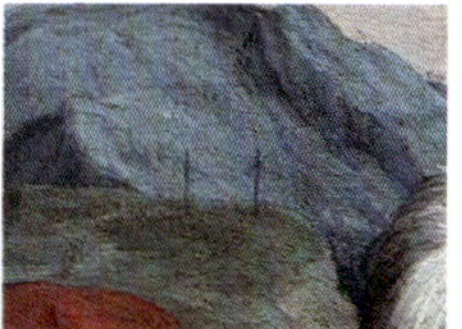

Barely visible in the distance, two crosses stand on the hill of Golgotha. They will soon be joined by a third.

Christ sinking under the burden of the heavy cross is clearly the focus of Bassano's painting, but among the confusing throng of figures accompanying him there is something else going on. The kneeling woman with the braided hair and dressed in red in the foreground is St Veronica. Her legend recounts that she offered Christ her white veil to wipe the sweat from his face and the image of his features was miraculously imprinted onto it. Her veil, the *Sudarium*, became a major relic, preserved in the Basilica of St Peter's in Rome, and venerated as a true picture of Christ.

The other figures can be divided into those who loved Jesus and those who were intent on his destruction. Mary wipes tears from her eyes with her blue cloak; St John the Baptist (just below the white horse) throws up his hands in anguish and despair; and the woman with her hands clasped in supplication is almost certainly Mary Magdalene. Their suffering is in marked contrast to the belligerence of the executioner who raises his fist to strike Christ, or the muscled torso of the Roman solider with his shield and helmet.

Jacopo Bassano (active about 1535–92) was the most famous of a family of Venetian painters. He was considered unique amongst his fellow Renaissance artists because of his ability to incorporate into his work the diverse influences of Dürer, Tintoretto and Raphael.

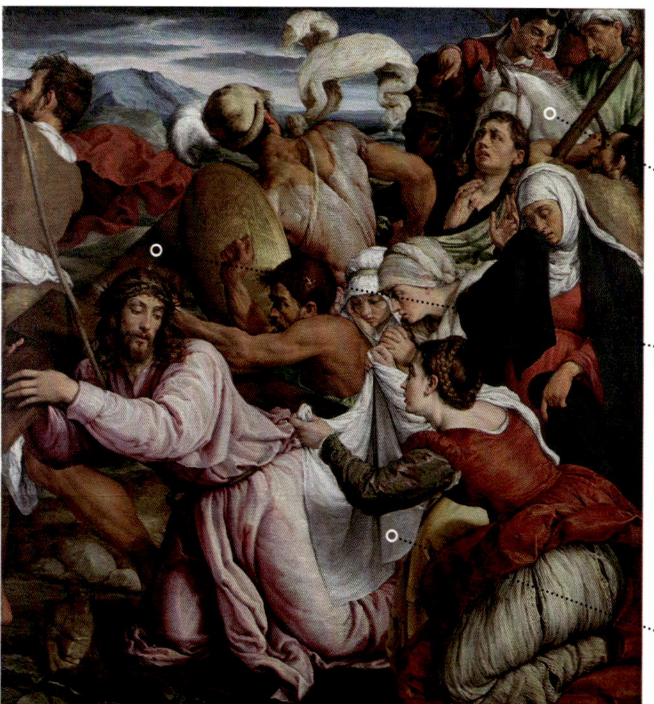

The men mounted on a horse and mule may represent the priests and Pharisees overseeing the event.

Christ bears the entire cross, although under the Romans a condemned man carried only the horizontal piece to the place of execution where the upright post was already fixed in the ground – an historical fact of which artists were clearly unaware.

St Veronica offers a white veil to the exhausted and fallen Jesus Christ.

HANS HOLBEIN THE YOUNGER

Noli me Tangere

1526–28

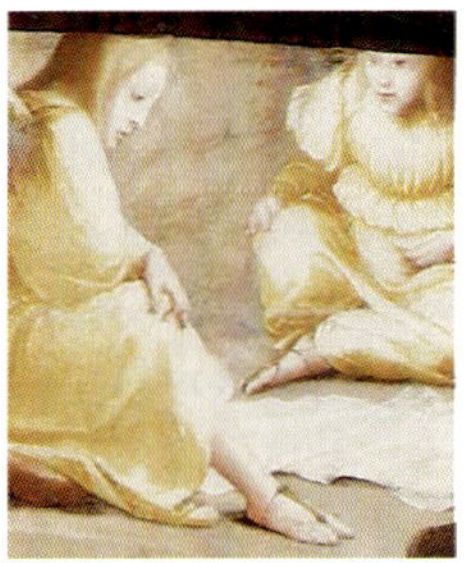

Of the two angels crouched in the sepulchre, one is looking directly out at the viewer of the painting.

In 1680, when the diarist John Evelyn saw this painting in Charles II's private Closet in Whitehall Palace, he recorded that he 'never saw so much reverence & kind of Heavenly astonishment, expressed in Picture'. This scene shows dawn breaking over a landscape in which two figures are caught in a moment of profound emotion. A weeping Mary Magdalene turns away from the brilliantly lit sepulchre, having found two angels in place of Christ's body, and encounters a man whom she mistakes for a gardener. When he utters her name, she recognises him. She reaches out to him, but Christ raises his hands as if to prevent her approach, and says: '*Noli me tangere*' (touch me not). The rich red and black of Christ's garments are mirrored by the garments of Mary, but in reverse. The flowers in the foreground have all been identified, as have the trees: on the left is an elm, in the centre a hawthorn and on the right a larch.

It is thought that this painting was commissioned from Holbein (1497/98–1543) by his friend Sir Thomas More, and may have found its way into the collection of Henry VIII when More was executed. Following the execution of Charles I, it passed to his widow, Henrietta Maria. When she died near Paris, it was returned to the Royal Collection.

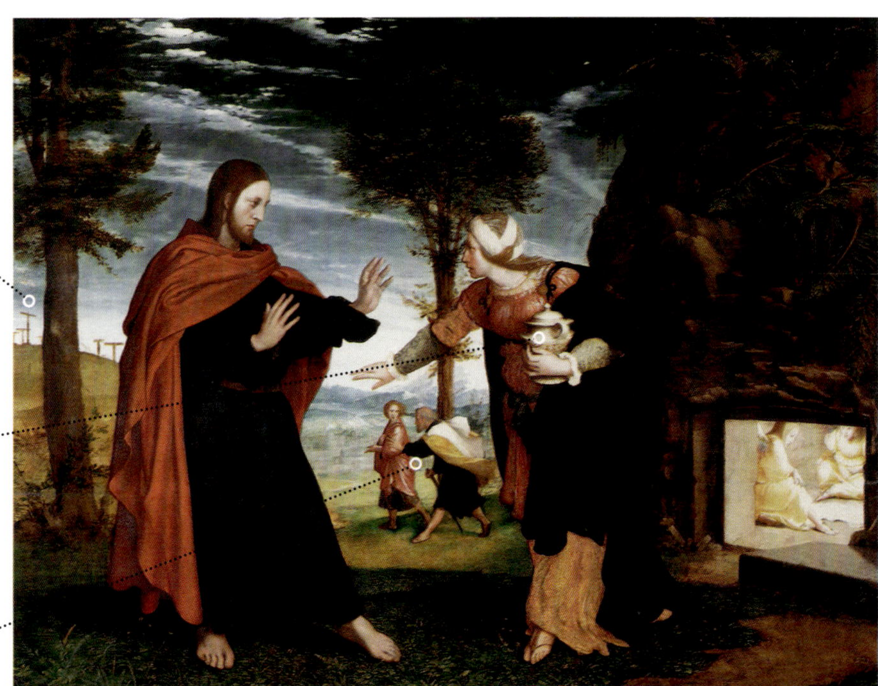

Silhouetted against the dawn sky stand crosses on the hill of Calvary. There are four of them, whereas the Bible only mentions three.

Mary Magdalene is always recognisable in paintings as she holds the casket of precious oils with which she anointed Christ's feet.

St Peter and St John are hurrying through the landscape towards a hazy city of Jerusalem in order to announce their discovery of the empty sepulchre.

PIETER BRUEGEL THE ELDER

Massacre of the Innocents

c. 1565–67

PIETER BRUEGEL THE YOUNGER, *Massacre of the Innocents*, n.d.

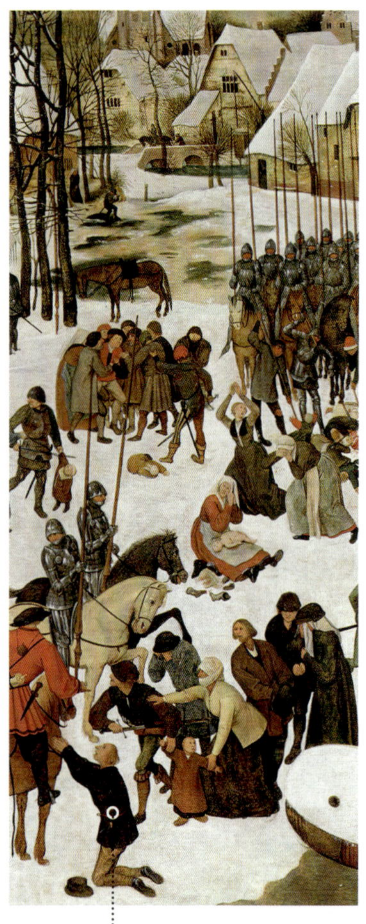

The kneeling man is pleading for the life of his child who is being threatened by a mercenary armed with a sword. In the altered original, the child has been changed to a calf.

According to St Matthew's Gospel, after hearing from the Magi of the birth of Jesus, King Herod ordered that all male children in Bethlehem under the age of two were to be slaughtered. Bruegel (*c.* 1525–69) followed the spirit of the biblical story precisely but set it in his own time so that the soldiers wear the distinctive clothing of the local officials who enforced public order. The artist also drew upon his experience of the exceptionally severe winter of 1564–65 to describe a village covered in snow, with icicles hanging from the rooftops and the pond in the foreground thickly frozen over.

This painting has a fascinating history: it was said to have been among the pictures carried off from the gallery of the Holy Roman Emperor, Rudolf II, by Swedish forces and to have been bought by Queen Christina of the Netherlands. In 1638 it was acquired by Charles II, King of England, and it remains to this day in the Royal Collection. But the painting that now belongs to Charles III is not as it was when it left the artist's easel. What Bruegel painted was a massacre of babies and infants, hence the title, and it was recorded as such in 1604. Seventeen years later it appeared in an inventory of 1621 as a 'village plundering'. What had happened to it in the interim?

When Bruegel created the work, the Netherlands was under the rule of Roman Catholic Spain. At a time of growing Protestantism, Rudolf did not want to own a painting that gave the impression that the spirit of Herod was alive and well, so the slaughtered babies were disguised as bundles, food, animals and even a large pitcher. On closer inspection of certain areas of the painting it is possible to see smudges, particularly in the snow, where smudges should not be.

The painting is full of anguish, desperation, supplication and barbarity, all of which make little sense if the viewer is ignorant of what has been hidden. A woman with her back to the viewer is apparently grieving over an array of hams and cheeses at her feet – her murdered child. To her right are a husband and wife who appear to be trading their daughter for a swan or goose held by the scruff of its neck by a soldier. This image is surreal until comprehension dawns: they are attempting to trade their daughter for their son. German mercenaries attempt to batter their way into the inn where more infants may be secreted: one wields an axe and one a battering ram, three climb in at the shutters, one kicks down a courtyard door.

In 1988 the painting underwent a complete restoration but it was decided to leave the more substantial (and historically significant) alterations to the figures. Besides, somewhere between 1686 and 1690 Bruegel's son, also Pieter, copied his father's original painting exactly, re-instating all the dead babies and infants (see left). This is incontrovertible proof of the cover-up.

The artist instructed to disguise the real story behind this painting has missed this scene in which a baby and a little boy are being brutally carried off.

Even in a scene of misery and bloodshed, Bruegel delights in showing the human side of life. Here a soldier urinates against a wall.

This mercenary in the striped hose is not killing a young boar, but a child. Protruding beneath a pile of livestock is the partially obliterated arm of a child – now a mere smear in the snow.

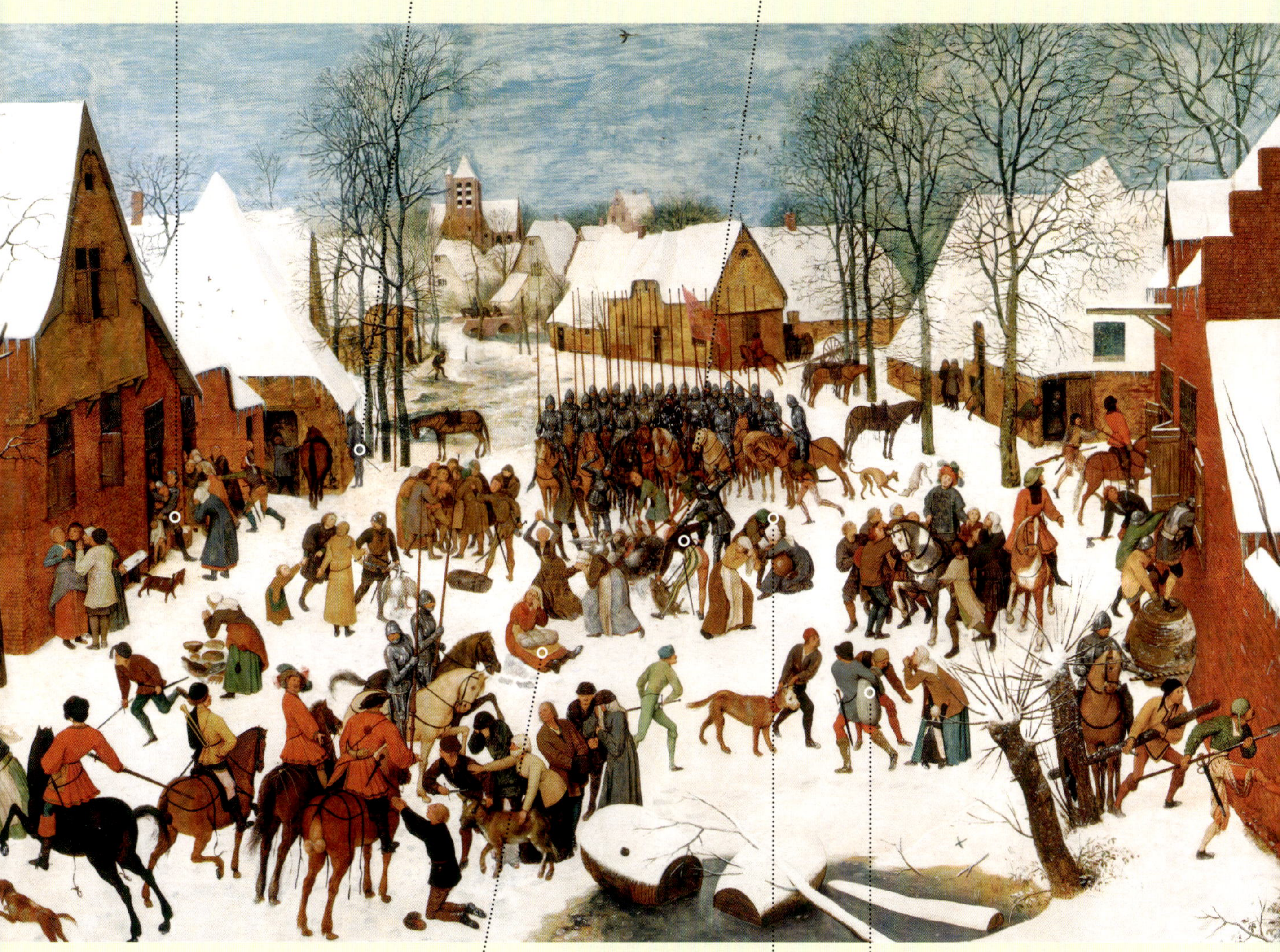

This woman sitting desolately in the snow is not mourning over the parcel in her lap but her dead child.

Here, a man stabs at this large red pitcher being cradled so desperately by the mother. It is her child.

This bundle is a child. To the right, the little girl lifting her arms to her mother has remained unaltered during the cover-up.

LUCAS CRANACH THE ELDER

Central panel of *The Wittenberg Altarpiece*

1547

The altarpiece was created for the Church of St Mary's in Wittenberg in Germany, the home town of Martin Luther and famous as the crucible of the Reformation. This panel of the altarpiece was painted by Cranach but other panels were painted by his son.

A round table for the Last Supper is very unusual. Also unusual is Cranach's use of portraits of several major Wittenberg personalities to represent Christ's apostles. Chief among these, the apostle turning to receive the chalice from the elegant cupbearer, clothed in red, has the features of Martin Luther. The grey stone walls, marble floor and windows would also have been recognised by the congregation as the very church in which they were worshipping. Martin Luther preached here, and this is where the practice of congregational singing and the taking of Communion first began. The apostles have taken their places on a stone bench, while Christ is seated on a separate square block. The image records the moment described in St John's Gospel when Christ announced at the supper: '... one of you shall betray me'.

Lucas Cranach (1472–1553) became one of the most versatile artists of the German Renaissance. He was a close friend of Martin Luther, and it is due to Cranach's portraits that Luther's appearance is known to posterity. Cranach was also the illustrator of Luther's translation of the Bible, his printed woodcuts acting as propaganda for the Reformation.

Christ's favourite apostle John rests his head on his chest.

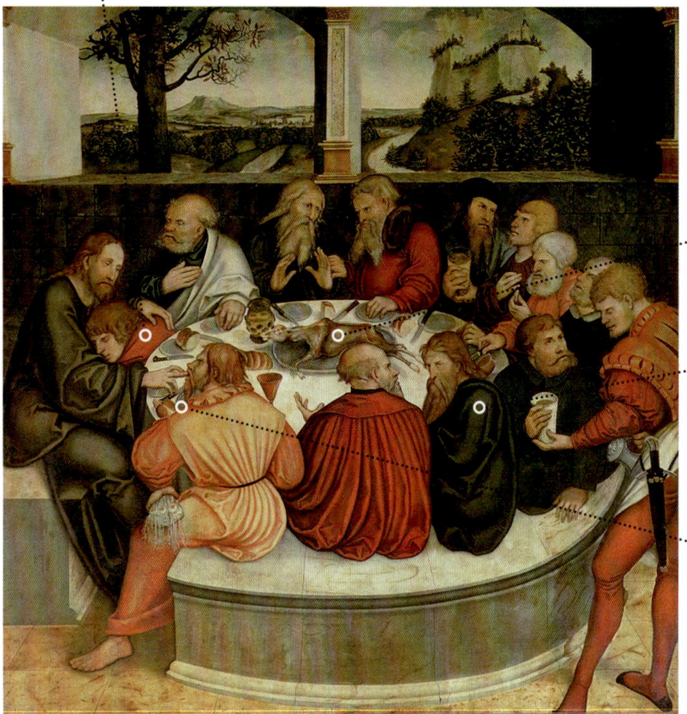

The unleavened bread and the Passover lamb – looking more like a tiny wizened cow – are ready on the table.

This is a portrait of Hans Lufft, the Wittenberg printer and publisher. He was commonly called 'the Bible Printer', because in 1534 he printed the first complete edition of Luther's Bible.

Having announced that one of the apostles would betray him, Christ offers a 'sop' to Judas Iscariot, the apostle seated on his right.

CARAVAGGIO

The Conversion of Saul

1600–01

Born in a little town near Milan, Caravaggio (1571–1610) arrived in Rome as an eager twenty-one-year old. Ambitious, arrogant and quarrelsome by nature, he was quickly absorbed into the violent, poverty-stricken underbelly of the city. He lived the latter part of his life as a fugitive, having killed a man in a duel. Yet throughout, he continued to transform legendary and biblical stories into mysterious, dark images, full of drama and suspense. For this picture, he keeps closely to the account in the Acts of the Apostles of Saul's (the future St Paul) miraculous conversion from a persecutor of Christians to a zealous evangelist that took place on the road to Damascus.

Eschewing conventional depictions of the story, Caravaggio plunges straight in with a huge skewbald horse and a fallen, swooning Saul. Blinded by a 'great light' and hearing a voice saying, 'Saul, Saul, why persecutest thou me?', he flings wide his arms in an ecstasy of acceptance that God is speaking to him. He is so close to the edge of the canvas that he seems to be entering the viewer's world. As the horse has no saddle, it has been suggested that the scene is taking place in a stable and the knobbly-toed old man is the groom. Caravaggio scorned 'ideal beauty' and the groom is typical of the urban and rustic models he preferred in his obsessive quest for depicting truth and reality.

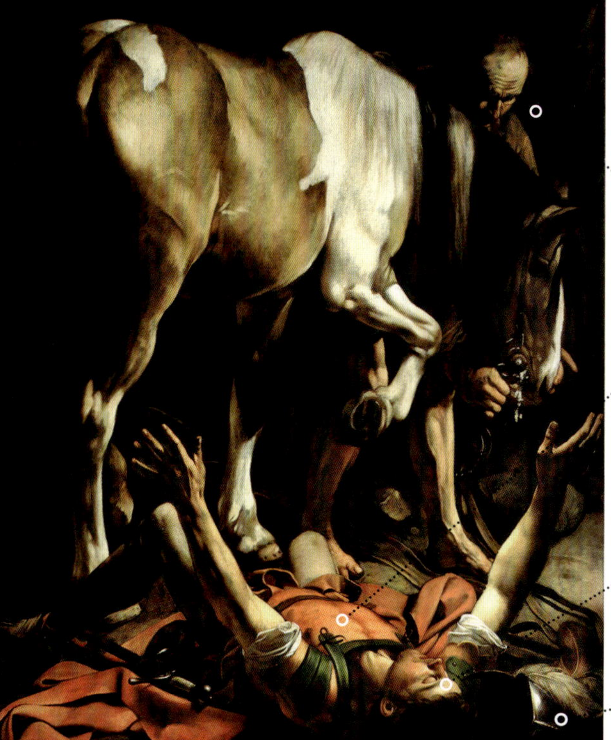

With furrowed brow, the groom stands quietly at the horse's head. He is aware of the light but is unable to hear Christ's voice.

Paul is dressed as a Roman soldier. His orange muscle cuirass is made of many layers of linen glued together to form a stiff shirt. His cape, adding a vivid splash of colour in the gloom, is beneath him. His sword lies by his side.

Paul's eyes are closed against the brilliance of the light. He was blind for three days before his sight was restored.

Paul's plumed helmet lies almost hidden in the shadows.

CARAVAGGIO

The Inspiration of St Matthew

1602

For sheer drama, Caravaggio has few equals. This swirling, whirling image in vivid red and orange is visible from every corner of the Chapel of San Luigi dei Francesi in Rome where it hangs over the altar. It is one of three paintings that the artist created for the French cardinal Matthieu Cointerel, who had decreed that the chapel be adorned with the life of his name-saint, Matthew the Evangelist, author of the first of the four Gospels.

This was Caravaggio's second attempt at this subject. The first, which depicted Matthew as a gnarled, humble old man, the angel leaning cosily over his shoulder, was rejected outright because the saint lacked dignity and his bare feet, which were large and thrust almost into the viewer's face, were offensive. By the second version, the saint has become a dignified, bearded sage who is startled by the sudden stratospheric arrival of the angel behind him. The angel's billowing white drapery is thrown into sharp relief by the velvety blackness of the background. Caravaggio developed a highly original form of chiaroscuro, called tenebrism, from Italian *tenebroso* (meaning dark or mysterious) which uses extreme contrasts of light and dark in the same image. The brightest colour he used in his paintings was a deep vermilion red. He appeared to dislike the colour blue, even clothing the Virgin Mary in red instead of the traditional costly ultramarine.

This line, which separates the dark brown area from the white drapery, is the edge of one of the angel's wings.

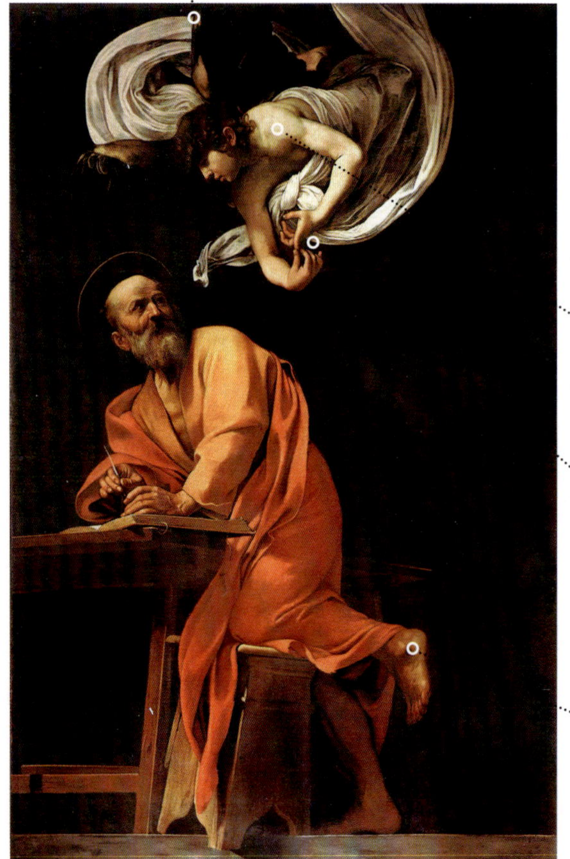

The angel resembles Caravaggio's workshop assistant and occasional model, who was also rumoured to be his catamite.

The angel is dictating the Gospel to St Matthew and counting off the verses on his fingers. He is the saint's inspiration. Matthew's role as a divine instrument is also implied by his name, which was believed to derive from the words *manus* (hand) and *theos* (god).

Caravaggio has taken care to paint the saint's feet in a more respectful manner than the first version of this subject, which was rejected.

GEORGES DE LA TOUR

The Penitent Magdalene

c. 1640

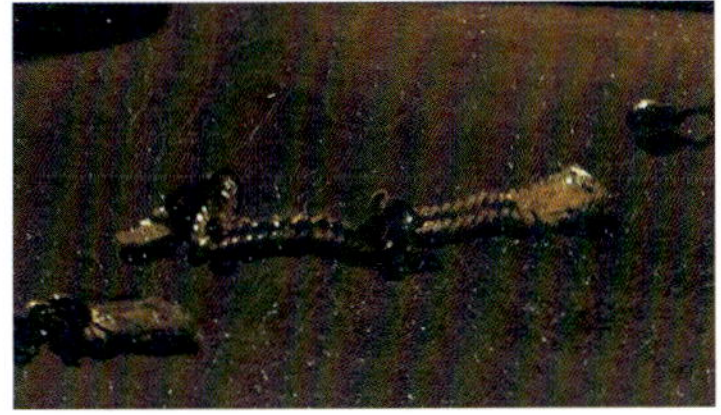

This jewellery has been discarded by Mary and lies on the floor at her feet.

At first glance this is a painting of a young woman regarding herself in a mirror. She appears to have just removed her pearl necklace, as it lies on the table before her. But on closer inspection the viewer becomes aware that she is not looking into the mirror but beyond it, and that her hands are resting on the top of a human skull. So what is going on? The answer is that this is a depiction of the well known biblical character, Mary Magdalene, who was said to have renounced the pleasures of the flesh for a life of penance and contemplation. La Tour has created an image that contains a stillness and tranquility, as if Mary has vanquished all past temptations and is at last at peace with herself.

Very little is known about La Tour (1593–1652). He was born and remained in Lunéville, a small town in France. He left no letters or drawings and only about thirty paintings, and these were not rediscovered until the early twentieth century, languishing in provincial museums or private collections. His style has been compared to that of Caravaggio because of its use of deep shadows and glowing highlights. But Caravaggio's light source tends to be outside the picture frame whereas La Tour's is nearly always *inside* the picture. La Tour painted at least four – all very similar – versions of this subject.

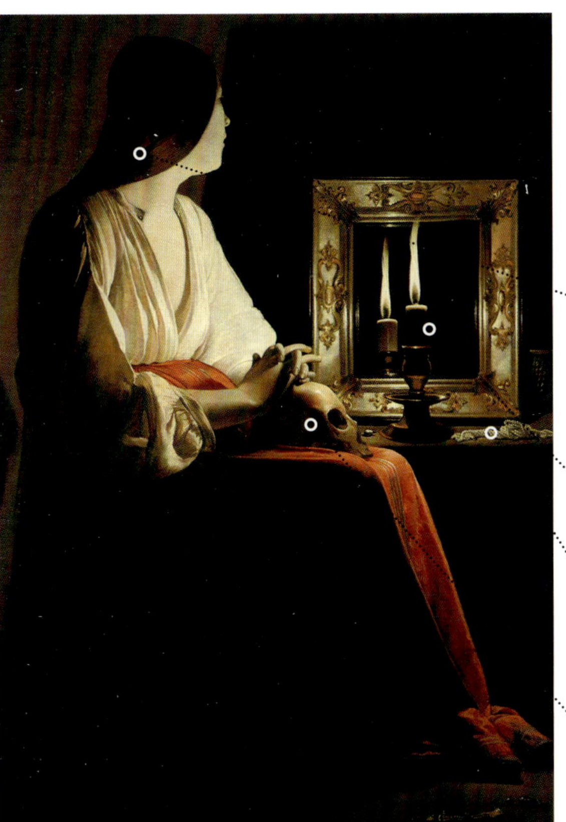

Typically, Mary's hair is untied, long and flowing. She was said to have wetted Christ's feet with her tears, wiped them dry with her hair and then anointed them with oil of myrrh.

The candle and its reflection are both references to life's transience.

The discarded pearls are symbols of the meaningless value of worldly possessions.

The skull beneath Mary's hands is to remind her of the brevity of life.

REMBRANDT VAN RIJN

Belshazzar's Feast

1636–38

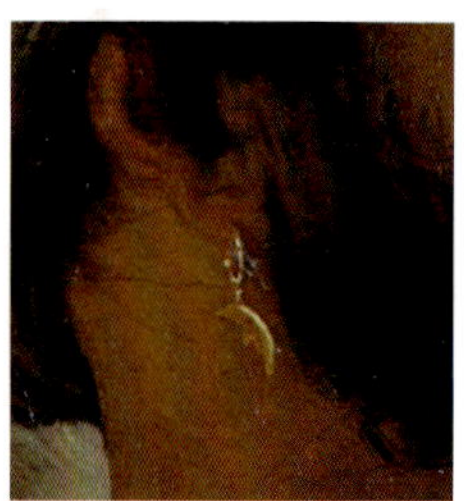

Easy to miss among the richness of the king's garments is this gold earring, shaped like a crescent moon.

Rembrandt van Rijn (1606–69) excelled at depicting moments of profound emotion or intense drama, often drawing on incidents in the Bible for inspiration. Biblical figures, particularly those from the Old Testament, were very popular in art at the time, especially in the Netherlands, since many Jews had fled there from Spain and Portugal to escape persecution.

Rembrandt has chosen to illustrate the account in the Book of Daniel of the feast given by Belshazzar, King of Babylon, for his nobles, wives and concubines. The account describes the king drinking before 'a thousand of his lords' and serving his guests wine in the sacred gold and silver vessels that had been looted from the Temple in Jerusalem. In the middle of the feast there came a sudden clap of thunder, and a ghostly hand appeared in a mysterious grey cloud. The hand wrote on the wall in Hebrew script: *Mene, mene tekel upharsin.* The king 'turned pale with fear. Such terror gripped him that his knees knocked together and his legs gave way beneath him.' Desperate to know the meaning of the sinister inscription, the king called for wise men to translate it, but none of them could decipher it. Belshazzar then summoned Daniel, a captive from Judaea, who told the king that the meaning was clear: 'Thou are weighted in the balances, and art found wanting.' Therefore God had brought Balshazzar's kingdom to an end and henceforth it would be divided and given to the Medes and Persians. That same night, the king was murdered.

The painting demonstrates Rembrandt's ability to conjure up a wealth of rich textures: sumptuous furs, lustrous gold plate, sparkling gems, the intricate embroidery of Belshazzar's cloak and waistcoat and the creamy folds of his turban, surmounted by a perky little jewelled crown. The effect of these separate elements is enhanced by the velvety shadows cast by the dazzling light emanating from the writing on the wall.

With their staring eyes and gaping mouths, Rembrandt has brilliantly conveyed the shock and horror of the guests. The woman on the right is so afraid that she shrinks away from the ominous writing and has spilt wine from one of the precious goblets onto the sleeve of her vermilion gown, while her left hand reaches out wildly for some support. The raised and clasped hands of the woman with the pearls register her fear at what is happening. The right hand of the terror-stricken king claws at one of the golden vessels while his left arm is flung out as if to protect himself from some hidden danger.

Rembrandt was born in Leyden, and trained in Leyden and Amsterdam. Although he never visited Italy, this painting shows the influence of Caravaggio. Like him, Rembrandt used real people as models instead of the classical beauties that peopled the canvases of the majority of Renaissance artists. He was about thirty years old when he executed this large-format canvas, but was already well known in Amsterdam as a superb portrait painter.

This woman looks like Rembrandt's wife Saskia, whom he married in 1634. He was a miller's son while she was the daughter of a wealthy mayor from Friesland, so it was an advantageous marriage for Rembrandt.

The tassel is attached to the turban with a large gem that Rembrandt has built up by using thick dabs of paint.

The Hebrew inscription reads from right to left, but the words are inscribed in vertical columns. The hand is positioned at bottom left for the logical reason that it has reached the final letter.

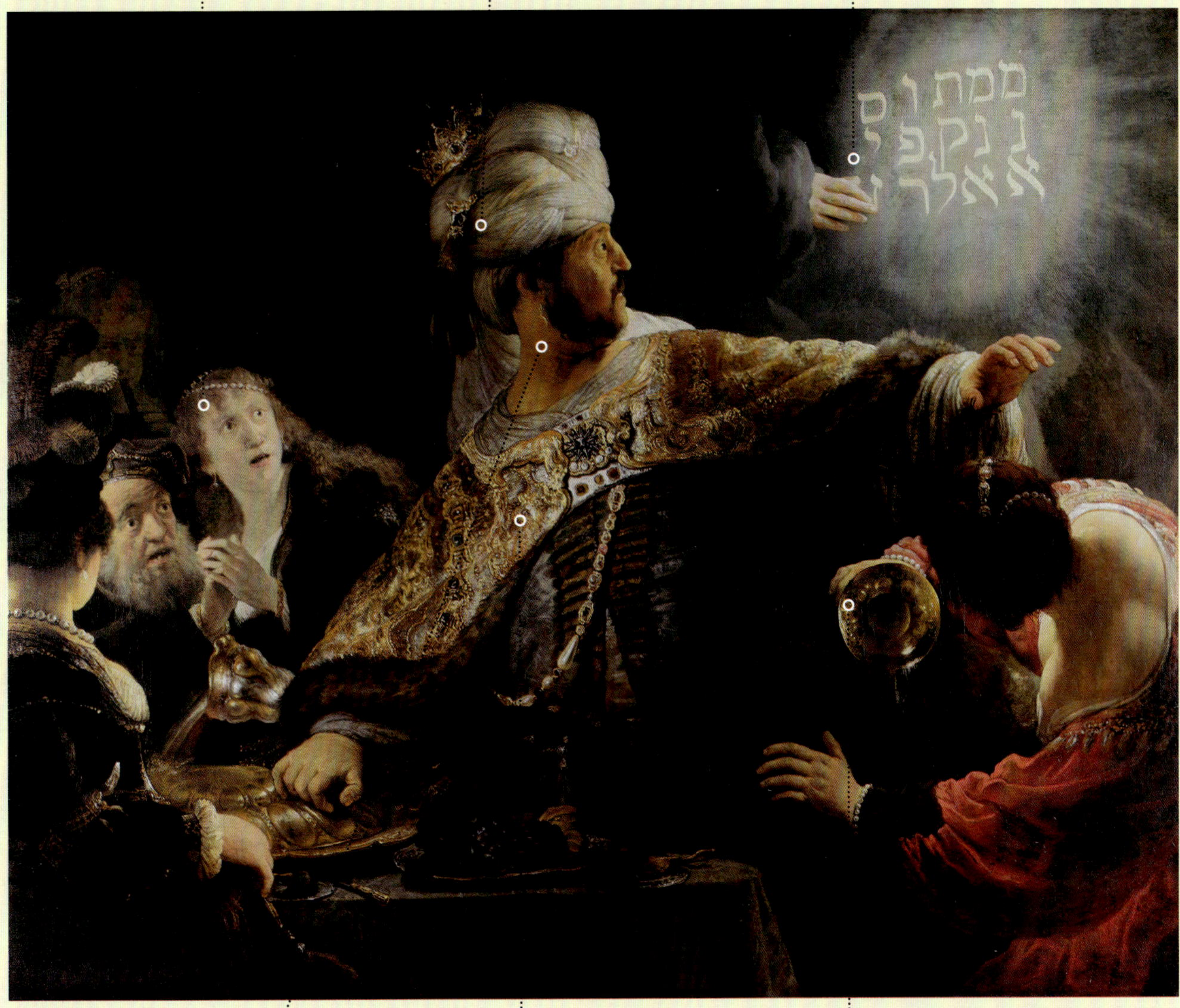

Rembrandt often used friends and family as models. The man posing as Belshazzar appears in several of his other paintings.

Rembrandt was a compulsive collector of art, antiquities, exotic costumes and weapons and used many of them in his paintings. Belshazzar's robe, turban, gold and silver cups may well have belonged to the artist.

Belshazzar's father, King Nebuchadnezzar, had looted the sacred gold and silver vessels from the Temple in Jerusalem. By drinking from them the guests were blaspheming the God of Israel.

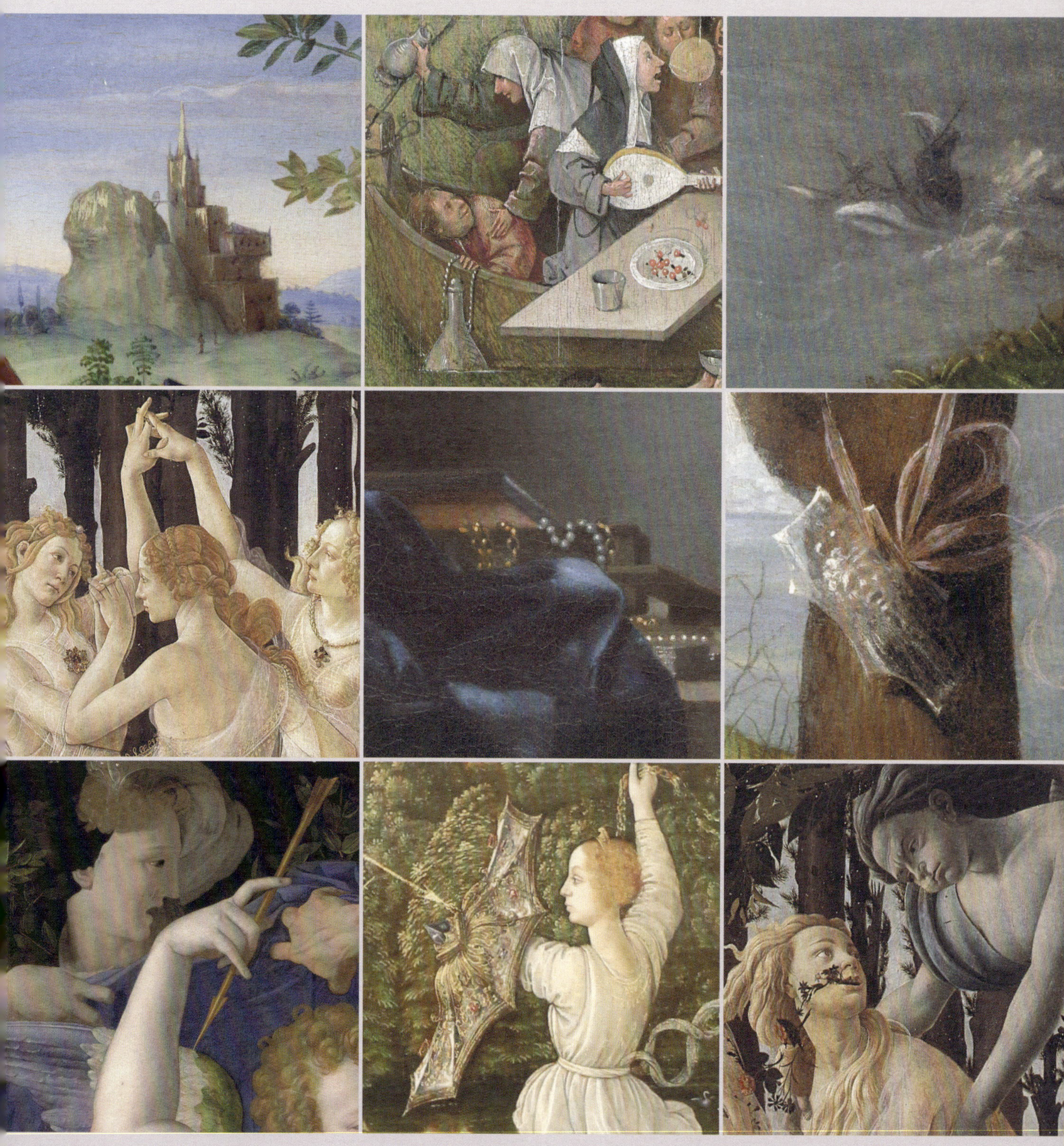

CHAPTER FIVE

ALLEGORY

SANDRO BOTTICELLI

Spring

c. 1480

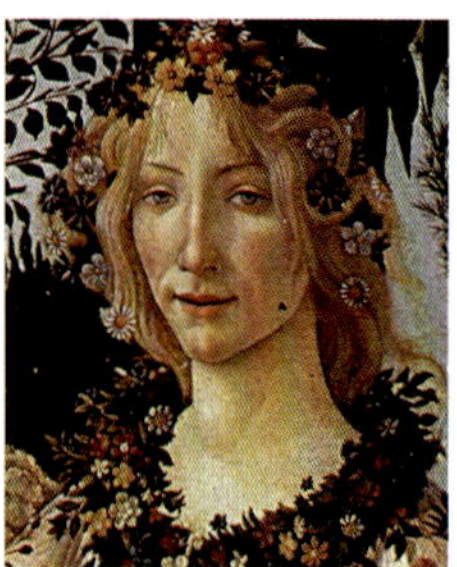

Flora's half smile is unusual. At this date few artists depicted a person smiling because of the parlous state of their teeth.

An allegory is a poem, play or painting in which the apparent meaning of the characters and events depicted is used to symbolise a more profound or spiritual meaning. Although scholars fail to agree on the interpretation of Botticelli's *Spring* (*Primavera*), one theory suggests that it is an allegory on the harmony of nature and humankind. Another theory maintains that it can be construed as a meditation on the nature of love and marriage. But, since the artist intended the painting to be read from right to left, it could be that it shows the progression of spring into early summer. Although the complex meaning of Sandro Botticelli's famous image remains a mystery, the painting is a celebration of love, peace and prosperity.

Botticelli created this painting for Lorenzo di Pierfrancesco, a member of Florence's most powerful family, the Medicis. In fifteenth-century Italy, most commissions were for devotional pictures destined to hang in churches. Commissioning large pictures on pagan themes was virtually unprecedented. Botticelli's inspiration came from a variety of classical and Renaissance literary sources, including the works of the Roman poet Ovid's description of the arrival of spring.

Turning a gentle, almost enquiring look on the viewer, the Roman goddess Venus, trailing a scarlet cloak, stands at the centre of an orange grove set in a paradisaical garden. Behind Venus is a myrtle tree, traditionally associated with the goddess of love. Her son Cupid hovers above her. Zephyr, the sickly blue figure on the right, is the west wind of spring. He is pursuing the virgin Chloris with evil intent. To Chloris's left, wearing an enigmatic smile and a flower-strewn dress, is Flora, the goddess of flowers, with a lap full of roses. On the left of the painting, Venus's companions, the Three Graces, join hands as they perform a stately dance. Two of them wear elaborate necklaces. Meanwhile Mercury, the messenger of the gods, is using his magic wand (*caduceus*) to chase away the spring clouds and usher in summer. He is always portrayed, as he is in this painting, as handsome, manly and athletic.

The figures that sway and droop so gracefully, are nearly life size. Botticelli, however, pays no heed to one of the major preoccupations of the early Renaissance: the accurate depiction of human anatomy. Instead, he distorts his figures in favour of elegant lines and the sinuous fall of drapery. The figures tread among the flowers on impossibly small feet and the pursued Chloris is about to overbalance and fall flat on her face. At least 138 species of different plants are all accurately depicted. The overall appearance, and size of the painting – almost 3 m across – is similar to that of the millefleurs (thousand flowers) Flemish tapestries that were prized more than paintings during the late Middle Ages and early Renaissance, as they were made with such expensive materials.

Venus's blindfolded son, Cupid, is poised to fire a flaming arrow at the Three Graces. The one who is hit will be destined to marry.

The oranges may be a punning allusion to the Medicis, as the family had golden balls on their coat of arms.

These are laurel trees, a punning reference to the name of the owner of the painting, Lorenzo di Pierfrancesco.

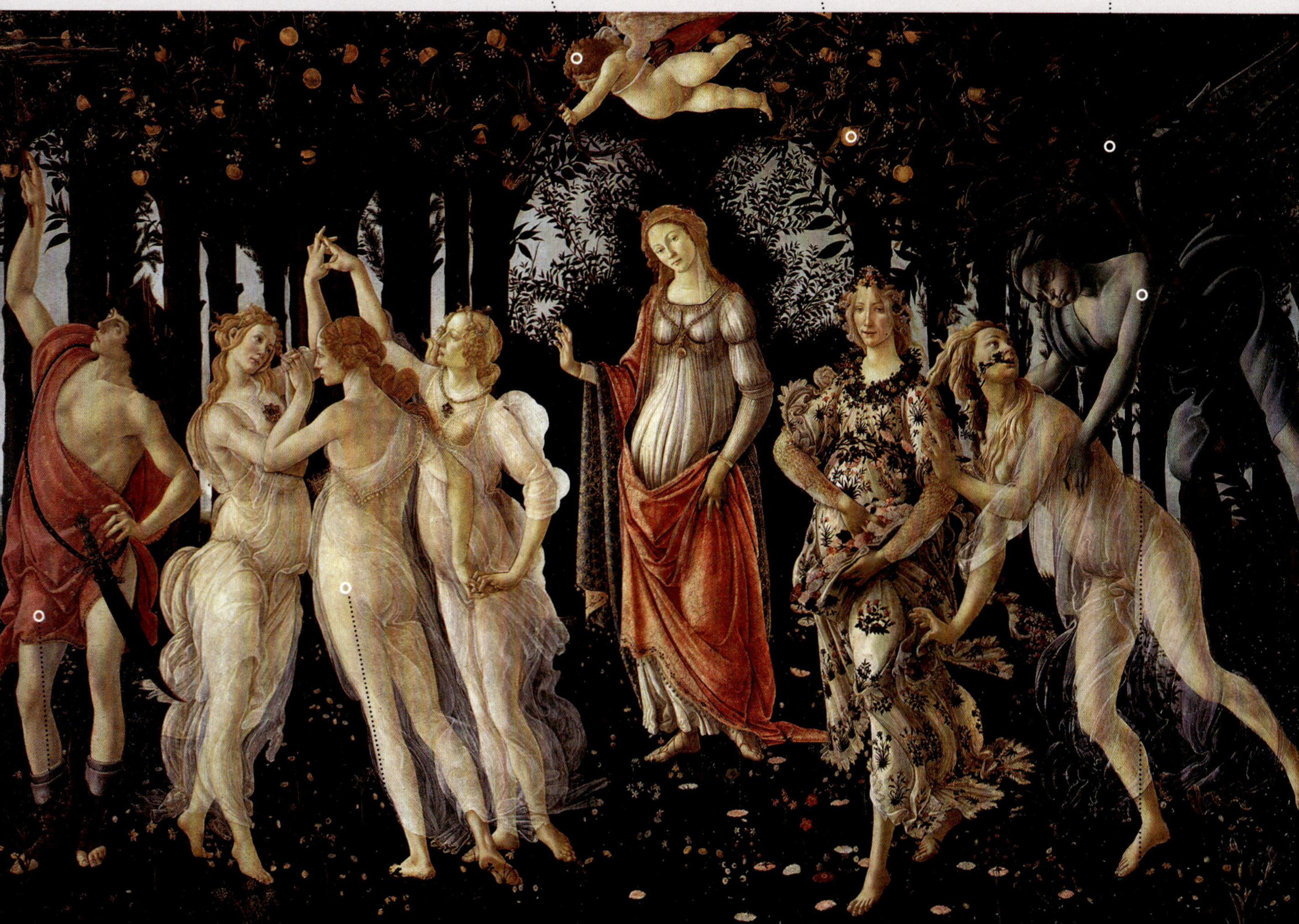

Mercury is chasing away the spring rain clouds. Although difficult to see, he is wearing his regular attributes of winged sandals and a helmet.

The Three Graces symbolise the three phases of love: beauty, desire and fulfilment. They are typically smiling maidens, either naked or transparently clothed.

Zephyr lunges at Chloris. When he catches and ravishes her, flowers spring from her mouth and she is transformed into Flora. Botticelli is using continuous narrative, thus Flora *is* Chloris.

GHERARDO DI GIOVANNI DEL FORA

The Combat of Love and Chastity

c. 1475–1500

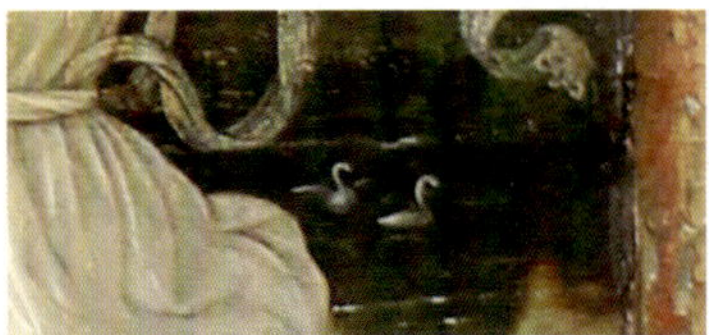

With wings outstretched, the male swan is battling it out with the female swan, a mirror of what is taking place in the foreground.

Gherardo (1445–97) was a Florentine painter and miniaturist who was inspired to illustrate a cycle of poems that were written in about 1370 by Francesco Petrarch, scholar and poet of the Italian Renaissance and one of the earliest humanists. The cycle, entitled 'The Triumphs', describes a series of mythological figures triumphing over each other in sequence: Love – as in physical love or lust – is defeated by Chastity, which in turn is defeated by Death, which is defeated by Fame, which is defeated by Time, which is defeated by Eternity. Gherardo painted all the episodes in the cycle as part of the same commission.

In this episode, the graceful female form of Chastity squares up to a naked, athletic Love, whose arrows bounce off her gold-embossed shield, leaving her unharmed. No wonder, as her shield is made of stout metal, ideally shaped for repelling arrows, and with a fearsome spike at its centre. The landscape behind this balletic combat is lush, dotted with neatly rounded clumps of trees, a lake on the right and the roofs of two houses on the left. Beneath the bare feet of the combatants the grassy sward is peppered with wild flowers, including clover, and Love's fallen arrows.

Renaissance society took the battle of Love and Chastity extremely seriously, as it represented the suppression of illicit passion in favour of fidelity in marriage. This was applied to women in particular.

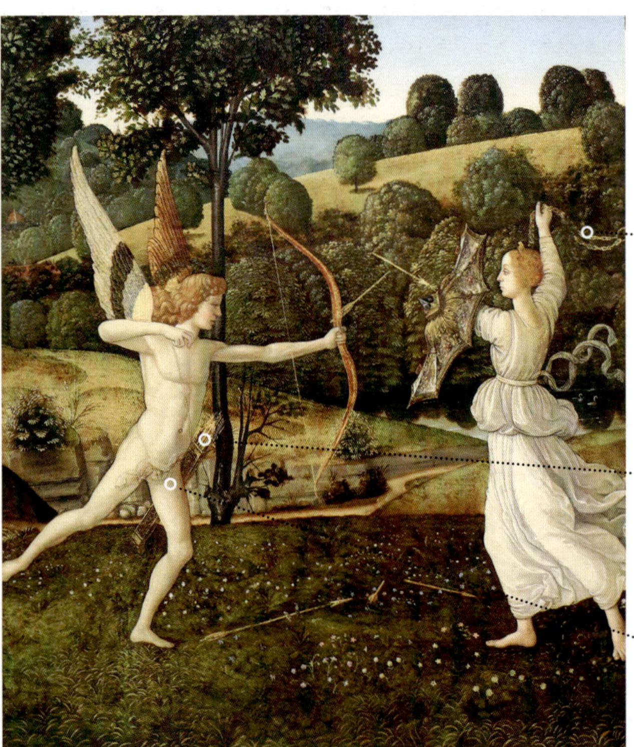

Chastity will use the chain that is swinging above her head to bind Love when he eventually capitulates. He will also have the feathers of his wings torn out and will be paraded as a captive in Chastity's chariot.

Love has enough arrows in his quiver for a prolonged but doomed onslaught against Chastity.

Love's loins are barely girded by a flimsy piece of gauze.

HIERONYMUS BOSCH

The Ship of Fools

c. 1494–1510

In the late Middle Ages, being designated a fool meant a person who had flaunted God's commandments, but it could also signify someone was a sinner. European society tended to deal with those deemed mad or bad by expelling them from towns and cities, thereby condemning them to vagabondage. Towards the end of the Middle Ages, so many of these criminals and unfortunates were on the move that they represented up to 30 per cent of the population. Bosch, who had a genius for highlighting humanity's faults and vices, has filled his fragile ship with a collection of fools and sinners and launched it onto a turbulent sea.

The bizarre passengers include a nun playing a lute who is consorting with a Franciscan monk. Both are singing lustily – and illicitly – together. Their attempts to eat the pancake dangling in front of them adds gluttony to their sins. The men with their mouths open are competing for the pancake. The barrel and the flask, which is half-submerged in the water, indicate drunkenness. The ship's mast could not bear a sail, the rudder made from a tree branch would not steer and the giant cooking ladle would not row. The ship is doomed.

The Church gets short shrift from Bosch. So does mankind. This painting is a powerful allegory that explores various aspects of human folly, vice and ignorance. No wonder Carl Jung declared that Bosch was 'The master of the monstrous ... the discoverer of the unconscious.'

The owl, representing wisdom, regards the shipload of fools cavorting below him with disdain.

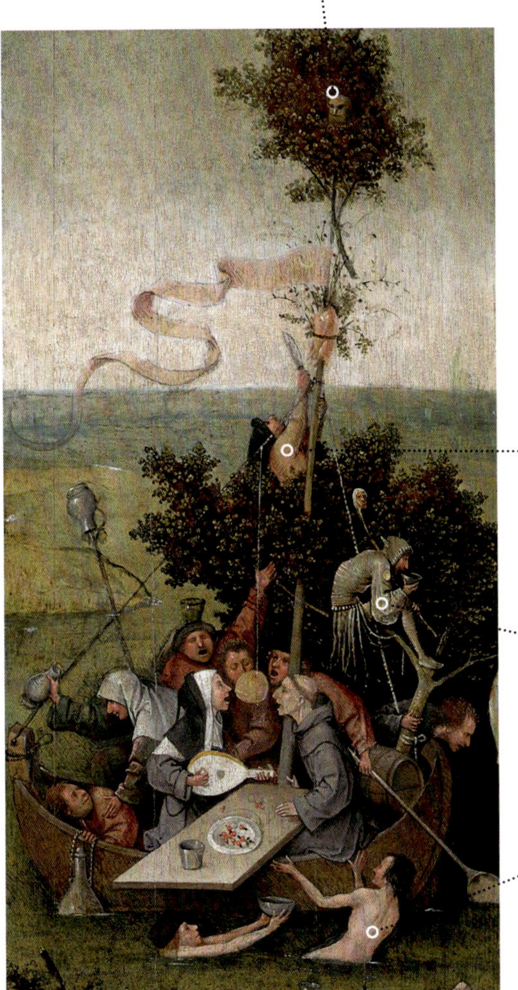

This man is trying to cut down a roast goose from the mast. His action recalls children competing to retrieve objects tied to the village maypole.

This figure in the fool's costume, sipping from a bowl, is turning his back on the other passengers. The asses' ears indicate stupidity – but perhaps he is the only sane one in the ship.

Naked figures in the water are almost always sinners in the metaphorical imagery of medieval times. Water was also associated with madness.

RAPHAEL

The Dream of a Knight

c. 1504

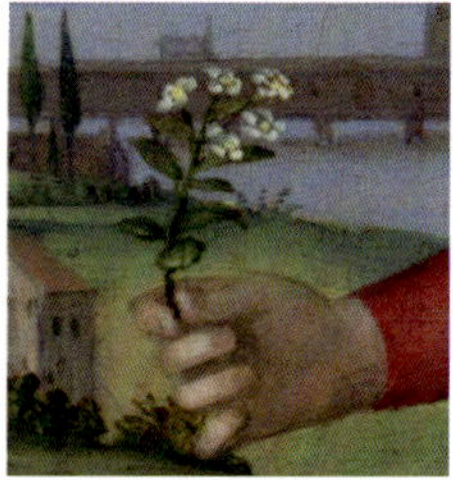

Myrtle is sacred to Venus. Since it was forever green, it symbolises everlasting love and conjugal fidelity.

This painting was inspired by a passage in the 'Punica', a first-century epic poem that recounts the story of the Second Punic War. Scipio, the young Roman hero, sleeps in the shade of a bay tree. The tree divides the picture in two. While asleep, he has a vision of Virtue and her adversary Pleasure. On the right, Pleasure holds out a sprig of myrtle to him. She is alluringly but chastely dressed and offers Scipio a life of charm and ease. (The drawing for this painting shows that Raphael originally drew Pleasure as a more seductive figure in a low-cut dress, but clearly thought better of it.) The woman on the left, her hair firmly restrained under a bonnet and wearing more sober garb, is Virtue. She shoulders a large sword and promises Scipio honour, fame and glory through victory in war. She also proffers him a book, representing intelligence and the contemplative life. Scipio, presented with a choice between virtue and pleasure, gallantly chooses Virtue.

In the background, an improbable church-like structure, its spire piercing the sky, is entered by a bridge suspended over an abyss. Beyond the church, roll endless blue hills. There is a lake, another bridge and another castle. This little picture is painted with minute attention to detail and a jewel-like finish. Sparing no expense, Raphael has used copious amounts of the two most expensive pigments, vermilion and ultramarine.

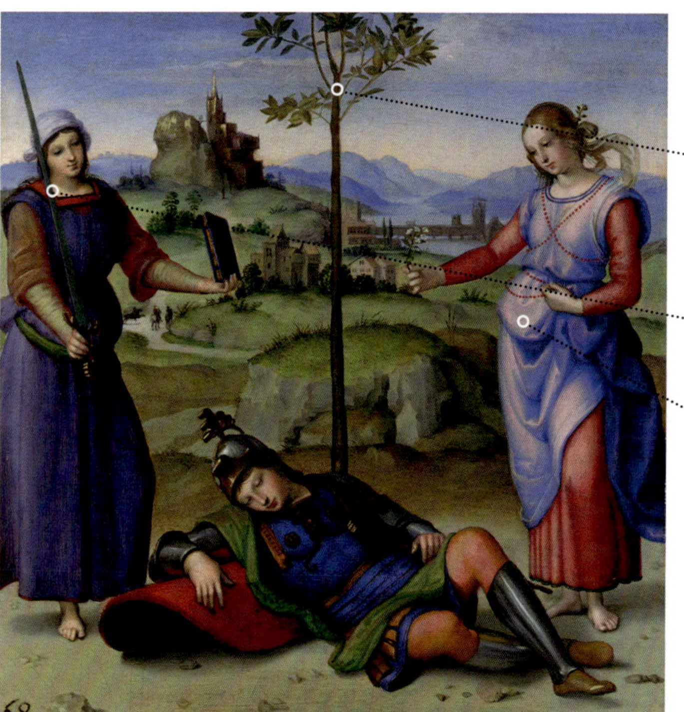

The evergreen leaves of the bay tree symbolise the honour a good knight could win through his military, scholarly and amorous activities.

The sword, a symbol of strength, is associated with heroic virtue and action.

The manner in which Pleasure's gown is gathered high under the breasts makes her look pregnant. Known as a *gamurra*, this was a fashionable style of dress in Raphael's day.

LORENZO LOTTO

Allegory of Virtue and Vice

1505

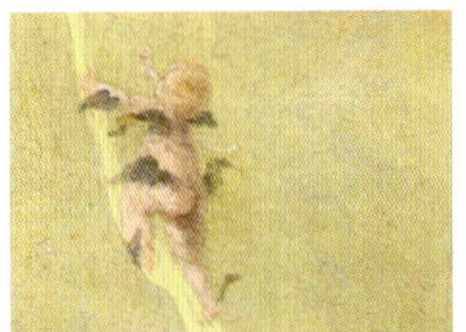

This nude infant has what appear to be little green wings sprouting from his shoulders, arms and ankles. But who is he, what does he represent and where is he going?

This is an exceedingly strange painting. The tree stump divides the image into light and dark, virtue and vice. On virtue's side, all is green, lush and sunlit. In the distance, a golden tree is silhouetted against the sky. Even the tree stump has vigorous new growth. A nude, fair-skinned child is crouched over a collection of objects lying on the ground. They are all symbols of the Liberal Arts: a flute represents music, a compass architecture, a protractor geometry and a scroll poetry. The two small red books are symbols of wisdom. Behind the child is a line of boulders and behind them again a small naked person is scurrying along a path that mounts the hill towards bright clouds.

On the right of the tree stump, all is disaster, dissipation and darkness. A swarthy satyr, with hairy goat's legs, embraces a jar of wine. He leers horribly and drunkenly into its depths. Other, presumably empty, vessels are strewn about. A large wooden ladle lies in the grass. Three trees loom like sentinels against a thunderous sky.

Lotto was commissioned to paint this picture by Bernardo de' Rossi, the bishop of Treviso, a city in the Veneto in northern Italy. The artist has paid homage to his patron by showing his coat of arms on a blue, painted shield propped against the foot of the tree.

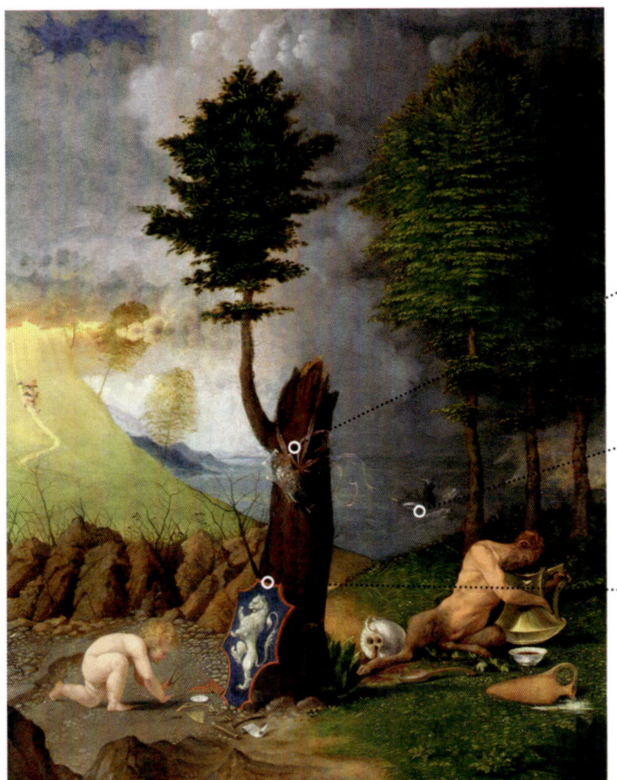

A translucent, shield-shaped object, decorated with a human face, is attached by a pink ribbon to the tree stump.

A huge commotion in the dark lake behind the trees shows where a sailing ship is sinking – a depiction of failure.

The Bishop of Treviso's shield on the left of the tree signifies that during his life he chose the narrow path of learning and virtue symbolised by the blonde child.

AGNOLO BRONZINO

An Allegory with Venus and Cupid

c. 1540–45

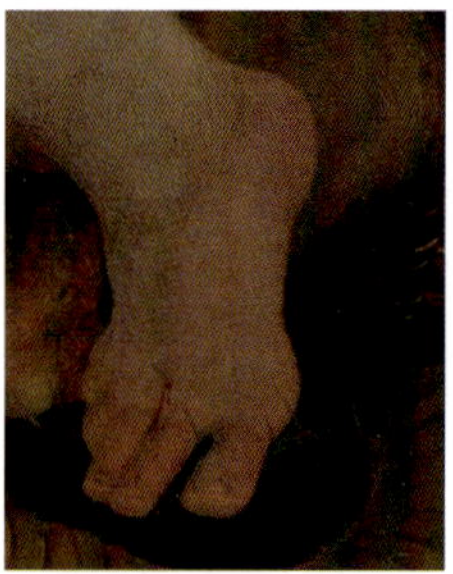

Pleasure seems oblivious to the thorn piercing his right foot. He symbolises the pain and pleasure of love.

This is a complex, enigmatic and erotic image. Bronzino painted it for Cosimo I de' Medici as a gift for Francis I of France. Its subject matter neatly catered to the French king's erudite but notoriously lecherous tastes. It shows a naked Venus, goddess of Love, being fondled by Cupid, her own son, while she attempts to disarm him by stealing an arrow from his quiver. Venus's milky white skin reflects the Renaissance ideal of beauty.

There are other strange things going on. The old man with staring eyes, wings and an hour glass on his shoulder is Father Time. He holds one end of a blue cloth, or curtain. The other end is held by someone with no back to their head, thus no brain and no memory. He is thought to be Oblivion. Is he, assisted by Father Time, trying to hide or reveal the actions of Venus and her son? The little smirking boy, about to shower Venus with rose petals, is foolish Pleasure. He wears an anklet of bells. Behind him, the girl with the beautiful face is Fraud: she has the body of a serpent, the paws of a lion, her hands are reversed and she holds a honeycomb. Perhaps her offer of sweetness has a sting in its tail? It has been suggested that this weird assembly forms an allegory that refers to the destructive power of love. But the overall meaning of the picture continues to baffle art historians to this day.

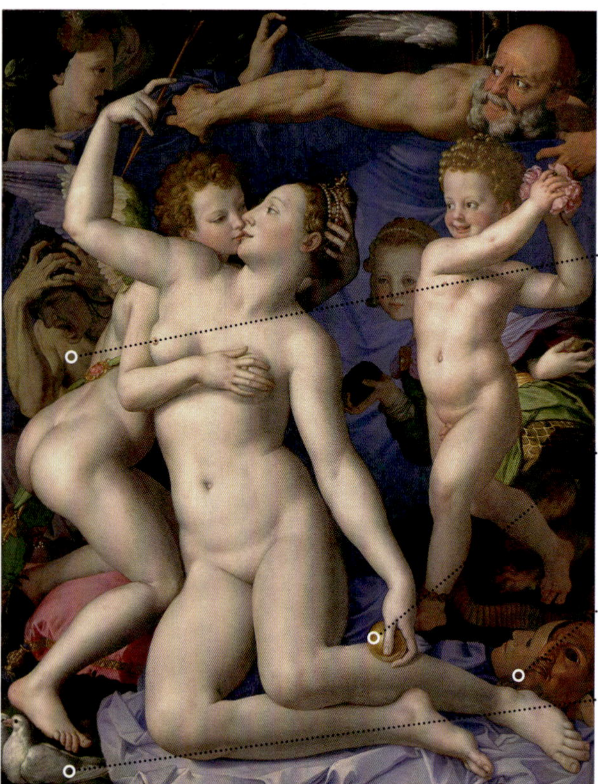

This screaming figure clutching its head has been variously identified as Suffering, Jealousy and even Syphilis.

Venus holds the golden apple which the Trojan Paris presented to her as the most beautiful of all goddesses.

Masks and disguises are often used as symbols of deceit and hypocrisy.

In his amorous approaches to his mother, Cupid is nearly crushing the dove – Venus's traditional attribute – beneath his foot.

JOHANNES VERMEER

Woman Holding a Balance

c. 1664

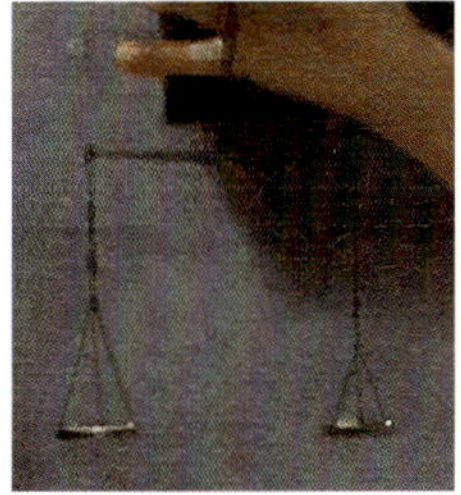

The painting's original title, Woman Weighing Gold, *assumed that she was weighing the gold coins on the table. But on examination by microscope it was found that the scales were empty.*

This painting is all about concentration – and silence. A wealthy merchant's wife, warmly dressed in a blue jacket trimmed with fur, stands before a sturdy table on which lie boxes overflowing with jewels, their glowing surfaces enhanced by the brilliant blue of the cloth beside them. Vermeer's consummate skill at lighting his subjects is demonstrated by the sliver of sunlight spilling into the room by the yellow curtain. It illuminates her face with its calm and thoughtful expression, but barely touches the scales which she holds so still, as if waiting for them to find equilibrium. Surely she is not about to weigh her necklaces, as they are too heavy for such a delicate receptacle. Besides, there are no calibrated weights on the table.

Art historians have long debated the hidden meaning of this painting, although they agree that it is allegorical. The clue – if it is one – may be the painting behind her. It shows the *Last Judgement*, the woman's head neatly dividing the blessed on the left from the damned. Could Vermeer (1632–75) be gently reminding the viewer to resist earthly possessions and instead lead an upright life in order to be numbered among the blessed on the Day of Judgement? Or is his message that riches and life itself are transient? Or the painting could just be a superb depiction of a calm and serene seventeenth-century Dutch interior.

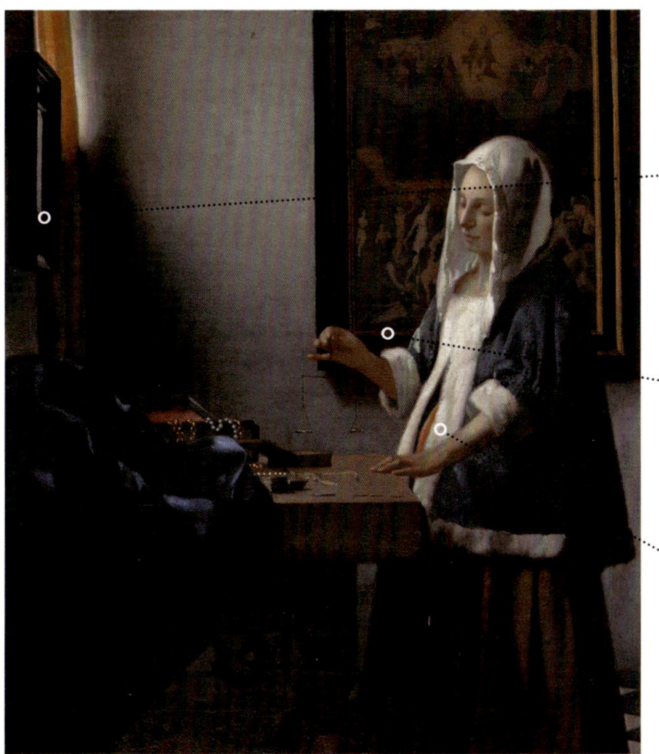

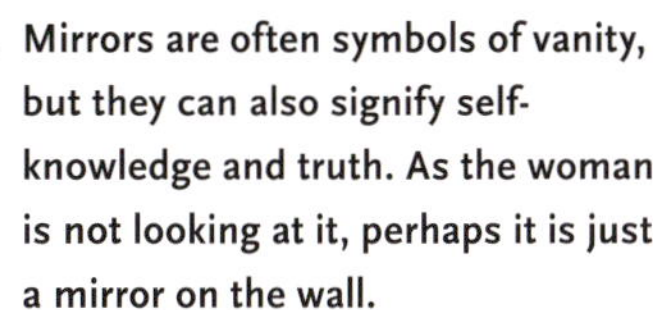

Mirrors are often symbols of vanity, but they can also signify self-knowledge and truth. As the woman is not looking at it, perhaps it is just a mirror on the wall.

The bottom of the frame of the Last Judgement is slightly higher here than it is behind her back, thus creating a neat space for the scales.

This bulge aroused speculation that the woman is pregnant – which she may be. But seventeenth-century Dutch fashion advocated a rounded shape.

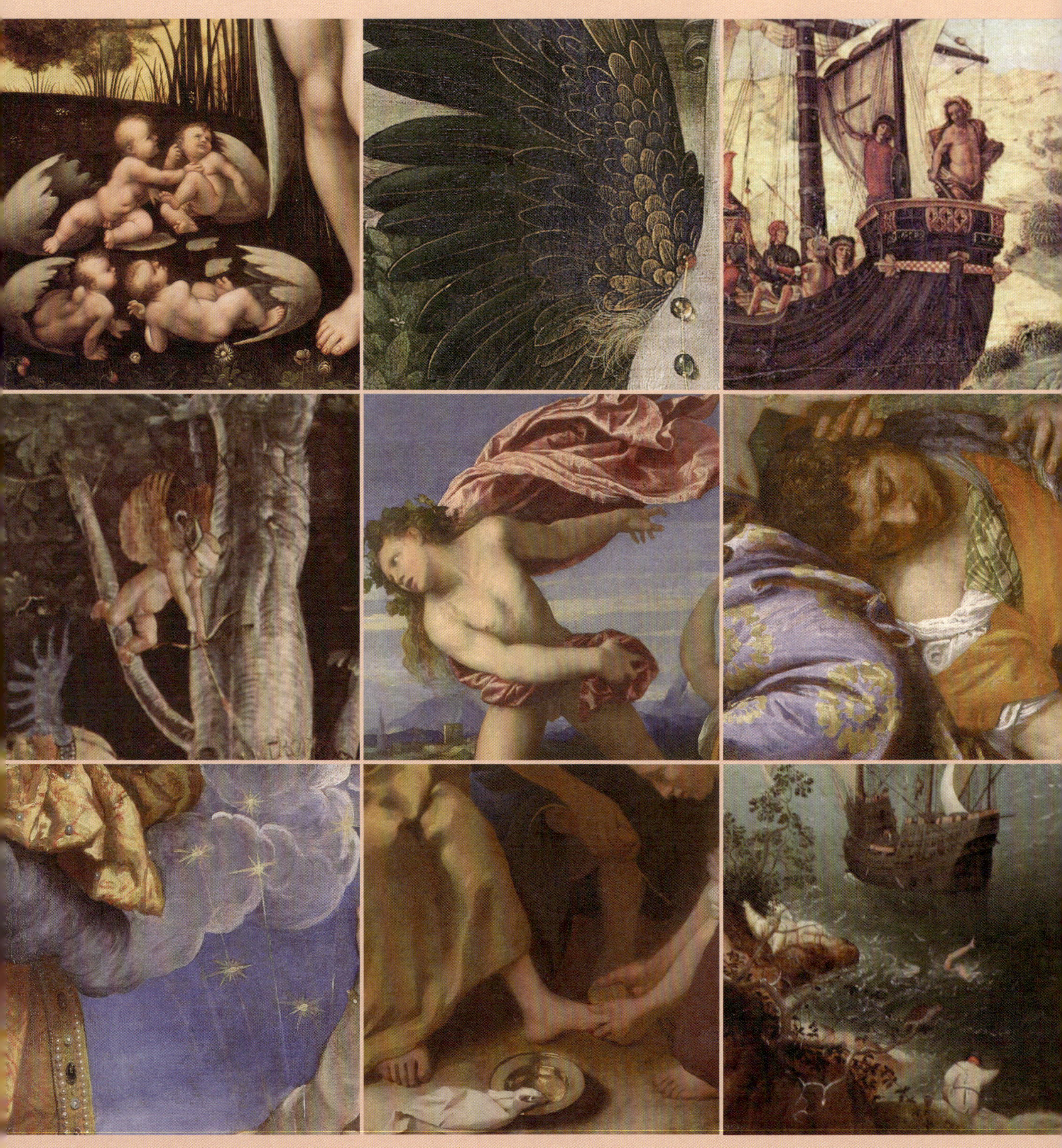

CHAPTER SIX

CLASSICAL MYTHOLOGY

88 LORENZO COSTA . *The Expedition of the Argonauts*, 1484–90

89 ANDREA MANTEGNA . *Parnassus*, 1497

90 FOLLOWER OF LEONARDO DA VINCI (CESARE DA SESTO?) . *Leda and the Swan*, 1505–10

91 NIKLAUS MANUEL . *The Judgement of Paris*, *c.* 1516–28

92 TITIAN . *Bacchus and Ariadne*, 1520–23

93 PIETER BRUEGEL THE ELDER . *Landscape with the Fall of Icarus*, 1558

94 JACOPO TINTORETTO . *The Origin of the Milky Way*, *c.* 1575

95 PAOLO VERONESE . *Venus and Adonis*, *c.* 1580

96 PETER PAUL RUBENS . *The Abduction of Ganymede*, 1611–12

97 JOHANNES VERMEER . *Diana and Her Companions*, 1655–56

LORENZO COSTA

The Expedition of the Argonauts

1484–90

Many mythological stories use the motif of a journey. In Homer's poem *The Odyssey*, the archetype of all travel narratives, he mentions Jason's quest for the Golden Fleece, and the wanderings of Odysseus may have been partly founded on Jason's story.

Jason, dressed in pink, figure-hugging body armour, is poised gracefully in the ship's bow. He was the rightful heir to the Kingdom of Iolcos in Thessaly until his uncle Pelias usurped the throne. Pelias, confident that he was sending Jason to his death, promised to return the throne in exchange for the Golden Fleece, a ram's fleece guarded by a ferocious dragon at Colchis on the Black Sea. For this risky expedition Jason built the largest ship ever seen, the *Argo*, assembled a band of heroes and set off on a journey that was to be fraught with numerous dangers. To illustrate this myth, Costa produced an almost surreal image: with billowing sails and floating on a milky-white sea, a vastly out-of-proportion ship approaches – or leaves – a rocky shore and a walled city. Could this be Colchis? With the aid of Medea, who lived in Colchis and was skilled at magical charms, Jason succeeded in seizing the fleece, returned with it to Iolcos and married Medea.

Costa (*c.* 1460–1535) was trained in Ferrara but worked in Bologna before succeeding Andrea Mantegna as the principal painter at the Gonzaga court at Mantua. Mythological scenes like this one often decorated wedding chests.

These Argonauts are four of the forty-nine heroes that accompanied Jason. They were said to have superhuman moral, intellectual and physical qualities.

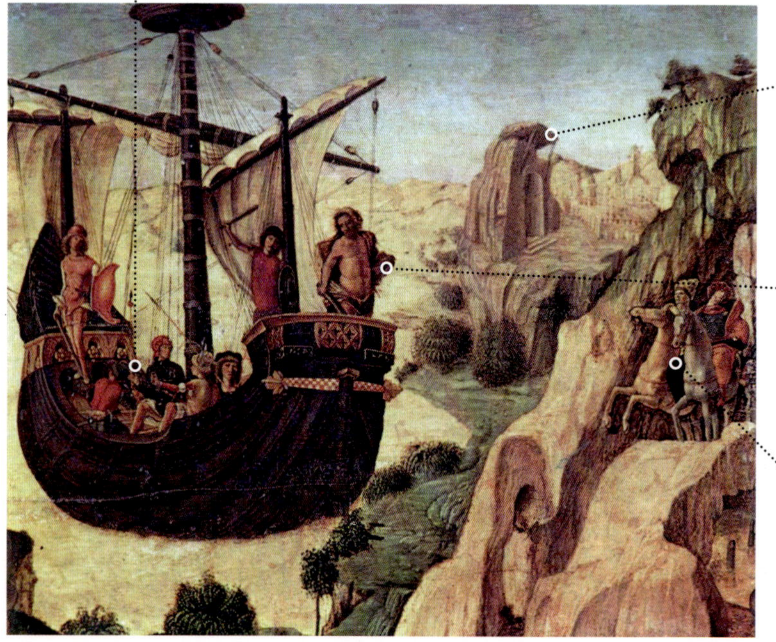

Depicting rocks appears to have been a problem for medieval and Renaissance artists who were apt to produce some very strange protuberances. Stranger still is this platform-like construction.

The lion skin and club identifies Hercules, a hero of Greek myth, who accompanied Jason on the first part of the voyage. Standing next to him is Hylas, his servant and lover.

As an earlier title for this painting was *Escape of the Argonauts from Colchis*, these horsemen may have been pursuing Jason and his men but have arrived too late.

ANDREA MANTEGNA

Parnassus

1497

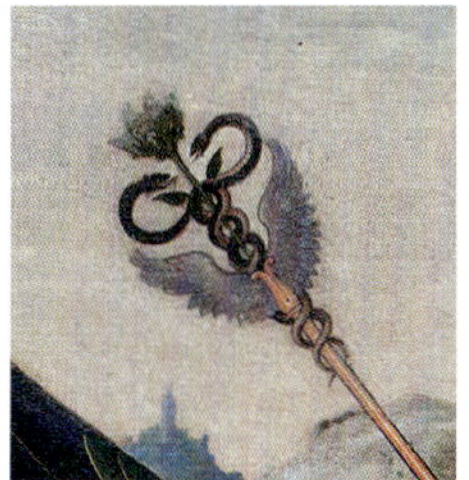

This is the head of Mercury's* caduceus, *set on an absurdly long staff. It was said that he once used it to kill two serpents, which are often shown wrapped around it.

Parnassus was sacred to the Muses and Apollo and thus the abode of poetry and music. Although the painting's theme is allegorical, namely the Victory of Virtue over Vice, all the characters represented are mythological. Mantegna created this painting for Isabella d'Este's *studiolo* – a small room set aside for intellectual pursuits – in the Ducal Palace at Mantua.

At the centre of the picture, standing on an arch of natural rock, are Venus, naked and beautiful, and Mars, god of war, suitably clad in plumed helmet and breastplate. Behind them is a large bed. To the left, Venus's son, Cupid, is causing mischief by aiming a dart at Venus's husband, Vulcan, to alert him to his wife's adultery. An enraged Vulcan, the god of fire (hence, volcano) erupts from his forge in the mountainside. In the foreground the nine Muses dance and sing to the music of Apollo's lyre. Traditionally, their song caused volcanic eruptions that could only be stopped by the winged horse Pegasus pawing the ground. Fortunately, the bejewelled, curly-haired horse is standing by. Another version of his story maintains that anywhere he stamped with his hoof a spring of water would burst forth, which may explain the stream in the foreground. Leaning against him is Mercury, messenger of the gods, recognisable by the winged hat and boots he wears to enable him to travel swiftly. He is the typical Greek youth, graceful and athletic.

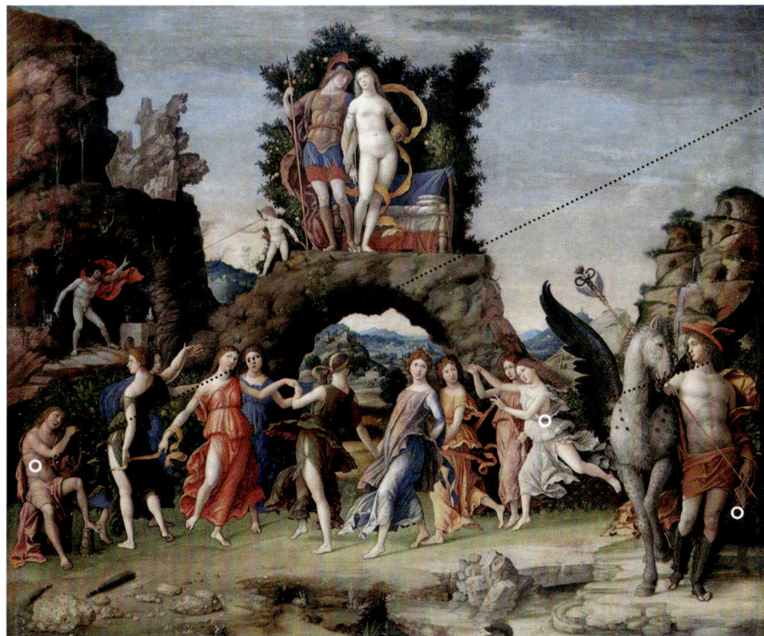

Apollo, the patron of poetry and music and leader of the Muses, sits abstractedly playing his lyre – said to be invented by Mercury. Behind him grows one of his attributes, a laurel bush.

This skipping, cavorting figure is probably Terpsichore, the Muse who represents dancing and song. She lends her name to the word 'terpsichorean', which means 'of or relating to dance'.

Mercury is holding a syrinx or pan pipes.

FOLLOWER OF LEONARDO DA VINCI (CESARE DA SESTO?)

Leda and the Swan

1505–10

Jupiter (Zeus) either fell in love with or impregnated – or both – a long list of women. It includes married women and even his own sisters. This myth relates that one day Jupiter comes upon Leda, the beautiful wife of the King of Sparta, bathing in a river. He falls in love with her, but disguises himself as a swan before appearing before her. They copulate, their union producing two eggs.

This story was an inspiration to several artists, some of them producing paintings which were little short of pornographic. It is known from preliminary sketches that Leonardo da Vinci painted this myth, but the picture has long since been lost. Several full-size copies were made of it by either his pupils or followers. Known as Leonardo's disciples or 'Leonardeschi', they were dubbed by Sir Kenneth Clark as 'the smile without the Cheshire Cat'. The Milanese artist Cesare da Sesto (1477–1523), who painted this copy, was one of the disciples. Leonardo also made two drawings of a kneeling Leda, with both the swan and the babies in attendance, but there is no evidence that he made a painting of either of them.

The degree of consent by Leda to the relationship with Jupiter seems to vary in different versions of the myth. For Leonardo, the union was positive, as he depicted Leda affectionately embracing the swan as their children play at their feet.

It is easy to miss the swan's wing where it is wrapped lovingly round Leda's naked form.

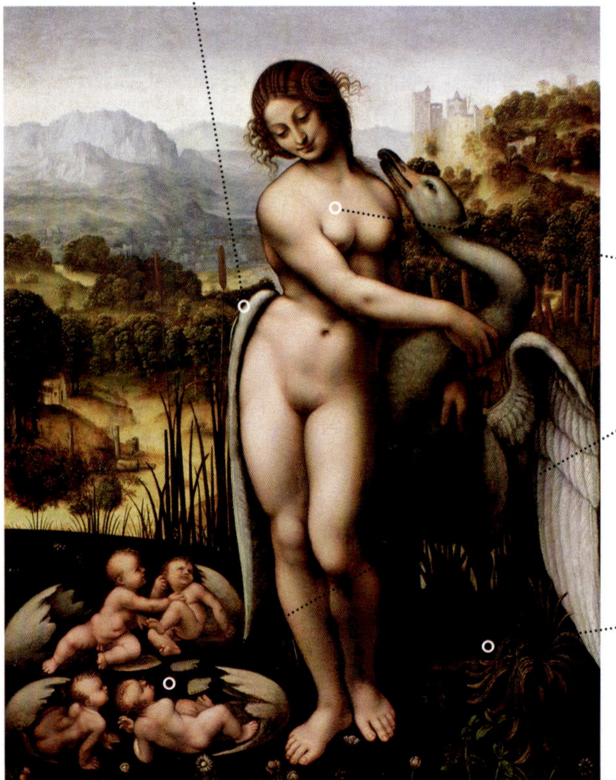

Did the model have breasts of different sizes? If so, da Sesto has conscientiously reproduced them.

According to the myth, each egg contained twins. Castor and Pollux, famed as the Dioscuri (sons of Jupiter), were born from the first egg and Helen and Clytemnestra from the second.

In the foreground, da Sesto has made careful copies of some of Leonardo's beautiful botanical studies: a bramble, a star of Bethlehem flower and bullrushes.

NIKLAUS MANUEL

The Judgement of Paris

c. 1516–28

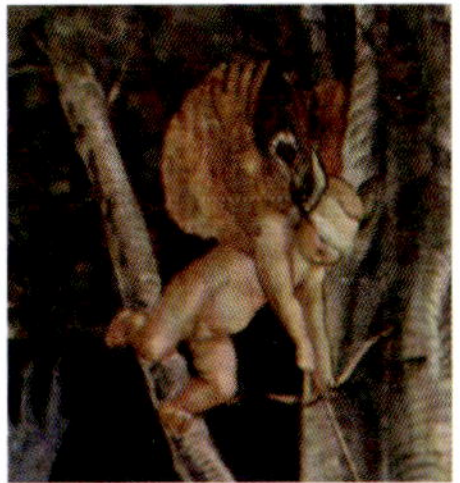

Venus's son, blindfolded Cupid – a symbol of love, which blinds – shoots an arrow at Paris.

In a dark and leafy wood, three women, two half-naked and one fully clothed, stand before a curly-haired gentleman seated under a tree. It is not immediately obvious that this painting depicts a critical moment in classical mythology, since Manuel (*c.* 1484–1530) has set the scene in his native Switzerland during the early sixteenth century. Originally a Greek myth, this is the Roman version featuring the goddesses Juno, Minerva and Venus. The artist has helpfully inscribed their names within the painting, but he has muddled them up. The lady on the left with the fantastic plumed headdress is not Juno but the war-like Minerva. Juno is the one in the ermine-trimmed gown. The man is Paris, who has been raised as a shepherd, unaware that he is actually a prince of Troy. He has been given the task of judging which of the three is the most beautiful, and the viewer of the painting is witnessing the moment when Paris awards the golden apple to Venus.

The contest was not in the least fair as all three ladies cheated. Juno offered Paris wealth and power, Minerva offered wisdom and strength and Venus promised him the most beautiful woman in the world, Helen, the wife of the King of Sparta. Paris promptly abducted Helen, thereby unleashing the war between the Greeks and the Trojans that would form the subject of Homer's *Iliad*.

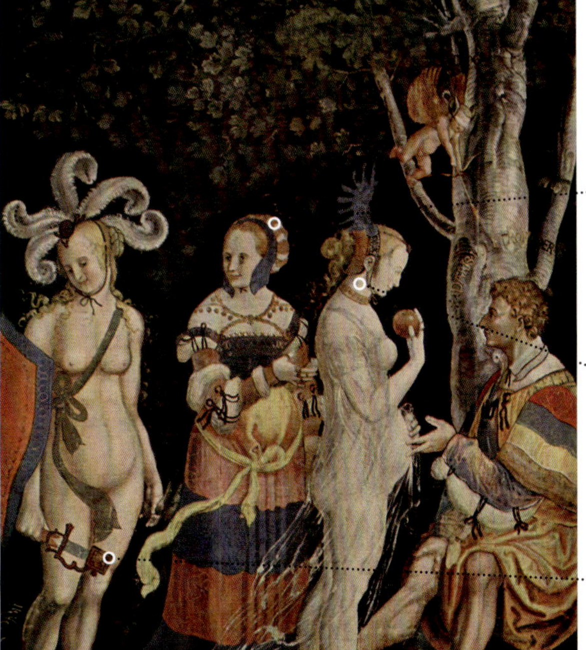

Juno's bonnet indicates that she is married – to Jupiter – and her dress of sumptuous velvet, bordered by an ermine train, is evidence of her wealth.

The snowy-white colour of Venus's skin testifies to her life of idle gentility. Her rounded belly does not indicate pregnancy but can be traced back to the influence of Dürer.

Manuel has modelled the sword on ones made in Milan. At this date, Switzerland's greatest export was mercenaries, and these Italian swords were much coveted by Swiss soldiers as war trophies.

TITIAN

Bacchus and Ariadne

1520–23

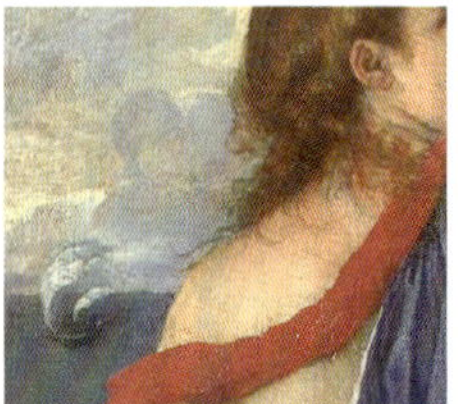

Is this Theseus' ship? Or is Ariadne desperately signalling to a passing vessel in the hope that it will rescue her?

In this image, Titian (*c.* 1485–1576) has captured both a moment of abandonment and one of enchantment. The grief-stricken Ariadne has just been deserted by her lover, Theseus, on the Greek island of Naxos. Bacchus, god of wine, returning from a triumphal visit to India, takes one look at Ariadne and, 'inflamed with love', leaps from his chariot. Bacchus is accompanied by his followers, a grotesque rabble that includes two nymphs clashing their cymbals and tambourines, a strutting satyr wreathed with vine leaves brandishing a calf's leg, and a wholly unloveable child satyr who is dragging the calf's head along the ground. Behind him, a horned man struggles with snakes. Among the trees, an obese and drunken Silenus, Bacchus's tutor, is slumped precariously on a donkey. According to the Roman poet Catullus, 'the bacchantes were jubilant' at the sight of their infatuated leader, 'whooping hurrah and wagging their heads'. Only the two cheetahs are indifferent to the clamour.

This story is told in different versions by several classical poets, principally Ovid and Catullus. The painting was commissioned by Alfonso I d'Este, Duke of Ferrara, for a small private room within the Ducal Palace at Ferrara. Titian has taken immense care over its creation, using the finest quality pigments available in Venice at the time – like the ultramarine that he has used so liberally on the sky.

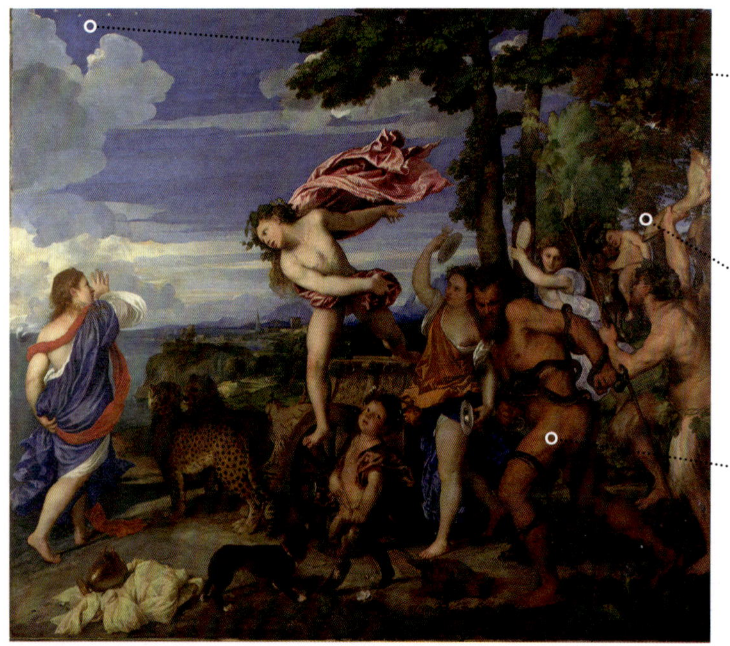

In one version of the myth, this ring of stars was created by Bacchus throwing Ariadne's wedding crown into the air, thus immortalising her as the Constellation Borealis.

Bacchic rites included frenzied, drunken orgies during which an animal was torn to pieces and its raw flesh consumed – a symbolic eating of the god himself.

Titian based this figure wrestling with snakes on the recently discovered and instantly famous ancient Roman sculpture of Laocoön, excavated in Rome in 1506.

PIETER BRUEGEL THE ELDER

Landscape with the Fall of Icarus

1558

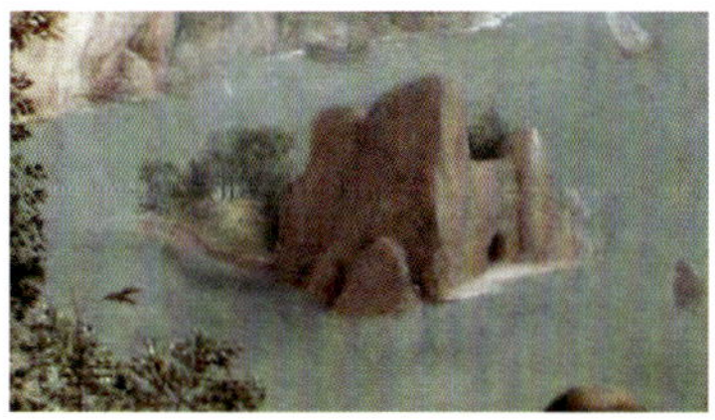

There is a supposition that the artist intended this ruined citadel to represent the Cretan Labyrinth where Daedalus and Icarus were imprisoned.

A farmer busy ploughing, sheep peacefully grazing guarded by a shepherd and his dog, a magnificent seascape and a ship setting sail for far horizons. But a distant splash and a desperate cry alerts the viewer that all is not as serene as it seems. On close examination, there are two legs thrashing about near the stern of the ship.

Bruegel is illustrating the Greek myth about Daedalus and his son Icarus who were imprisoned in the Labyrinth on the island of Crete. Determined to escape, Daedalus, who was a skilled craftsman, constructed two sets of wings using birds' feathers and wax. Before embarking on their flight, Daedalus warned his son not to fly too close to the sun, as the wax would melt. But, as Ovid described in his *Metamorphoses*, Icarus '... bold in vanity, began to soar,/ rising upon his wings to touch the skies ...'. The inevitable happens and the boy plunges to his death. This tragic event causes barely a ripple: the ploughman, shepherd and the fisherman down on the shore continue with their daily tasks. The painting can be read as an allegory of the dangers of youthful pride and ambition or the indifference towards other people's suffering.

In 1996, a technical examination of the painting aroused considerable doubt that it is by Bruegel, and it is now thought to be an early copy by an unknown artist of Bruegel's lost original.

This cargo ship has four decks and four masts and was one of the largest vessels of its day. Bruegel painted many ships during the course of his career and lived for ten years in the great trading port of Antwerp.

The sun is setting at the same time as Icarus is drowning. But the two are a great distance apart, so he has flown a long way before the wax holding his wings together has melted.

This fisherman is so intent on his task that he appears to neither see nor hear the disaster unfolding just across the water.

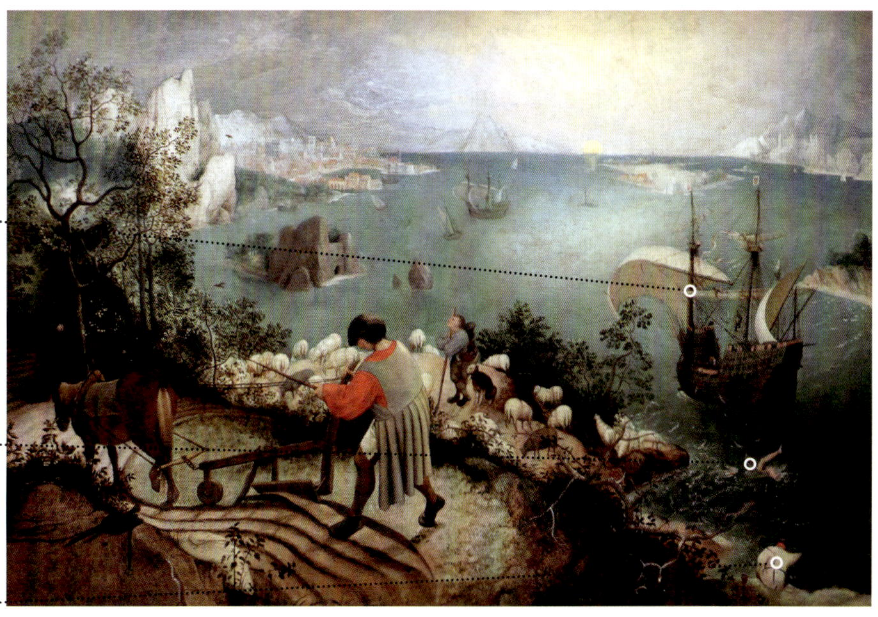

JACOPO TINTORETTO

The Origin of the Milky Way

c. 1575

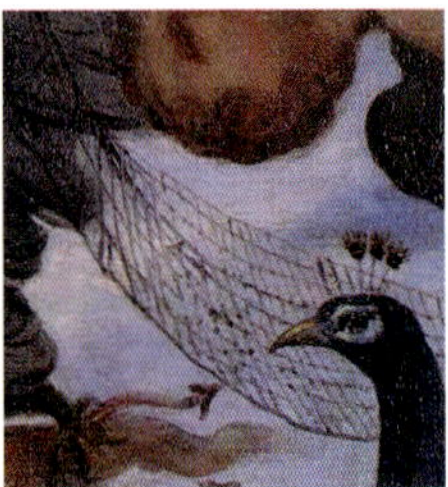

The net is a symbol of deceit and alludes to the trick Jupiter tried to play on Juno by giving her his illegitimate child to nurse.

Renaissance artists often used images of the pagan gods to represent the elements of the cosmos in their paintings. Tintoretto has produced this complex and richly coloured image in which Jupiter attempts to place his son Hercules on the breast of his sleeping wife, the goddess Juno, to drink her milk. By so doing, he hopes to immortalise the boy who was born out of wedlock to the mortal Alcmene. Juno, disturbed from her sleep and furious at Jupiter's deceit, brushes the infant away, and the milk from her left breast spurts heavenward in the form of golden stars that become the Milky Way. The lower half of the painting was cut off a long time ago, but a surviving sketch shows a reclining nude, possibly Alcmene, and lilies growing where milk from Juno's right breast fell to earth.

Tintoretto (1518–94) was a Venetian to his fingertips. His greatest achievement was his decoration of the city's Scuola Grande di San Marco. He produced this painting for Rudolf II, the Hapsburg emperor, for his castle in Prague. The legend of Hercules was already part of the Habsburg family tradition, and the emperor liked to have himself portrayed wearing a lion's skin and carrying a club, both attributes of Hercules. Rudolf struggled with ruling his troublesome empire, preferring instead to add to his art collection, especially with works that possessed erotic overtones.

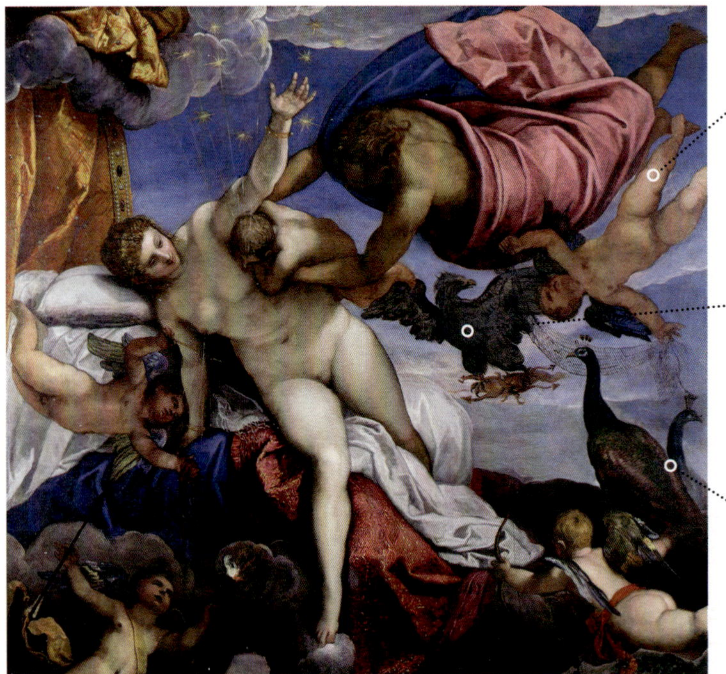

This is one of the four winged infants, or *putti*, who are romping about in the sky. One has a bow, another an arrow and a torch, all of which are erotic emblems. Another dangles a chain, which is a symbol of marriage.

While the eagle is one of Jupiter's principal attributes, what is it clutching in its talons? As Jupiter was supreme ruler of the gods and the sky, perhaps they are a supply of the thunderbolts that he used to destroy his enemies.

The two peacocks are the attributes of Juno. She used them to draw her chariot.

PAOLO VERONESE

Venus and Adonis

c. 1580

Venus and Adonis are lovers. Waking from sleep, Venus sees that her son, Cupid, is struggling to restrain one of Adonis' hounds from going hunting. With this image, Veronese is illustrating the passage in Ovid's *Metamorphoses* where Venus has warned her lover that 'boars have the force of lightning in their curving tusks', and is fearful that he will be gored. But, as Ovid relates, the dogs will pick up the scent of a boar and lead Adonis to it. The hunt will cost him his life. Unaware of his destiny, however, the handsome youth sleeps on.

This was a popular subject with artists. Titian and Rubens both produced versions of the story. Again taking as his theme love cut short by death, Veronese created a companion painting that illustrates the accidental killing by Cephalus of his wife Procris while out hunting. The two pictures were bought for the Spanish Royal Collection by Diego Velásquez during a trip to Italy.

Veronese (1528–88) was born in Verona but lived for much of his life in Venice. With Venus's gold bracelet, pearl necklace and carefully groomed hair, he has cast her in the guise of a fashionable Venetian temptress. The infinite care he has taken over the treatment of her skin illustrates his skill at depicting beauty, while his marvellous handling of the blue brocade and the orange of Adonis' garment confirms his fame as a painter of vibrant colours.

Barely visible at his feet is Cupid's bow that he dropped in order to have both hands free to restrain the hound. The strap across his shoulder leads to the quiver that he is gripping between his legs.

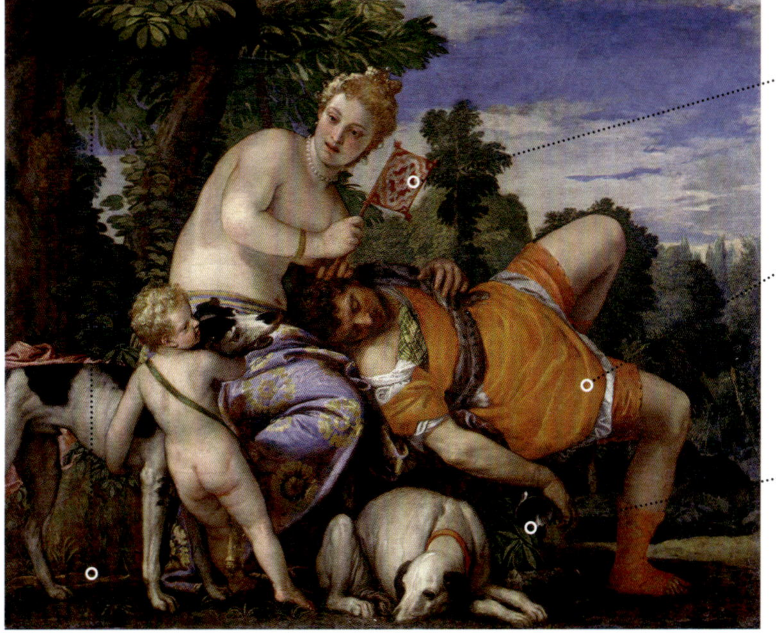

These hand-held fans were extremely popular in Venice throughout the sixteenth century. They were considered exotic ornaments rather than everyday accessories.

Veronese created this vivid colour by combining minium and the rare pigment realgar, the only pure orange pigment available at the time. It contained arsenic and another of its uses was to kill rats.

This is Adonis' hunting horn, but no art historian has been able to identify the strange object lying next to it, which appears to be a glass with a golden rim inserted in a fur sleeve.

PETER PAUL RUBENS

The Abduction of Ganymede

1611–12

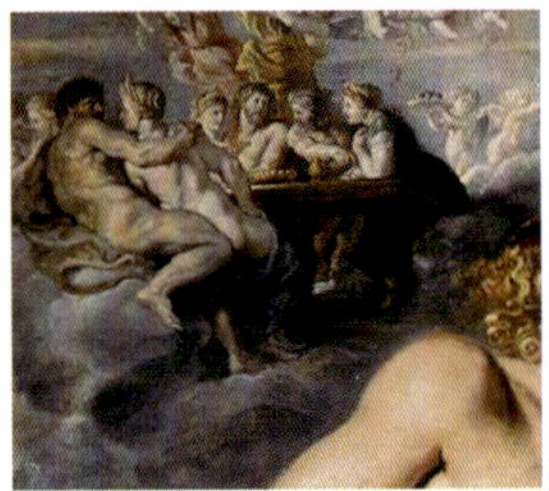

This reveller is Hercules, identifiable by the lion-skin over his shoulder. He is embracing Hebe, who seems able to be in two places at once.

Ganymede was a shepherd, the son of Tros, a legendary king of Troy. The youth was so beautiful that the god Jupiter fell headlong in love with him. In Ovid's great narrative poem, *Metamorphoses*, he describes how Jupiter (Zeus) transformed himself into an eagle, abducted Ganymede and carried him off to Mount Olympus, home of the Greek gods, where he made him his cup-bearer. The myth was approved of in ancient Greece because it appeared to provide religious sanction for homosexual love.

Rubens has shown the youth, enfolded in the wings of the eagle, accepting a cup from the woman in blue who may be Hebe, the daughter of Jupiter and Juno. Hebe was Jupiter's cup-bearer before Ganymede took her job. The woman in profile striding into the painting on the extreme right may be the wine-carrier. In the background a banquet is in full swing. Gods are being waited on by three flying *putti*, who hold the next course high above their heads, while two plump younger *putti* fetch more food and drink.

Classical scholar, diplomat and charmer, Rubens (1577–1640) was the greatest exponent of Baroque art in northern Europe. His gift for making his figures intensely alive and his skill at depicting flesh prompted this tribute from a fellow artist: 'This man must mix blood with his paint.' Here, Rubens' skill is apparent in the suppleness of the boy's body, the foreshortening of his legs and the tilt of his head.

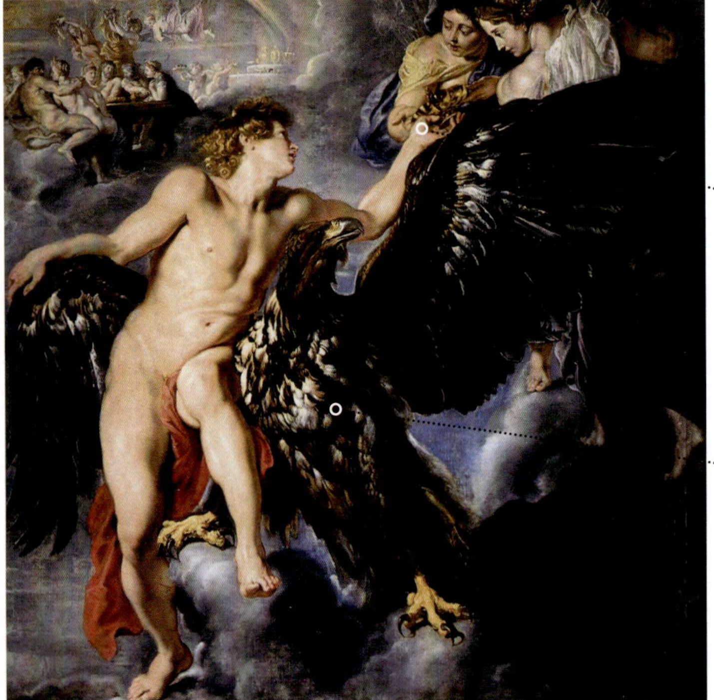

This gold cup will be used by Ganymede to pour Nectar into the cups of the gods. Called the divine drink, Nectar was able to confer immortality on any mortal.

The eagle was painted by Frans Snyders, one of the numerous assistants that Rubens employed to fulfil his many commissions. Such collaborations were considered perfectly acceptable at that date.

JOHANNES VERMEER

Diana and Her Companions

1655–56

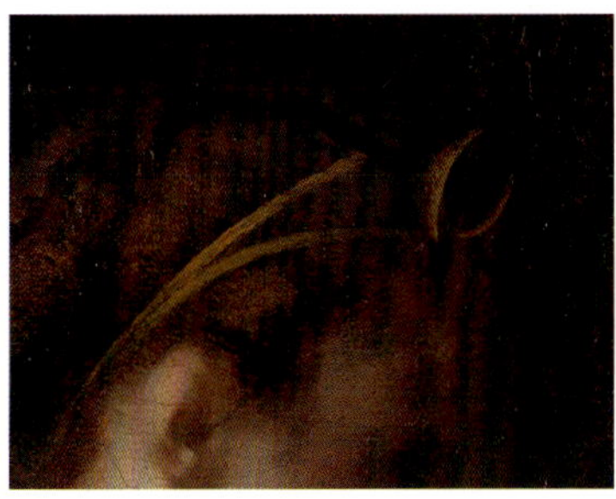

Diana's attribute as a moon goddess is the crescent moon. Among her many manifestations, she is also the personification of chastity.

This beautiful picture was created very early in Vermeer's career when he was producing history paintings rather than the interior scenes for which he has become famous. At that date history pictures were considered the highest form of art: an artist had to be so familiar with classical mythology, the Bible and history that he or she were able to decide which episodes to depict before even picking up a paintbrush.

Unusually, Vermeer has chosen to show Diana not as the vengeful goddess who changed Actaeon into a stag for seeing her naked, nor for turning the nymph Callisto into a bear as punishment for becoming pregnant. Neither has he shown Diana in her customary guise as a huntress striding through the forest with her bow and quiver at the ready and her dogs at her heels. Instead, he has chosen to depict her with her companions, peacefully at rest in a wooded glade. Although one of Diana's companions has her back to the viewer, and the woman in black is absorbed in her own thoughts, there is a sense of community about the group. They are old friends. Presaging his future style, Vermeer has conveyed a contemplative, dreamy and almost timeless atmosphere to the group.

Vermeer always spent a long time working on a painting. Today, only thirty-six are known to be by him. This picture could possibly be his earliest known work.

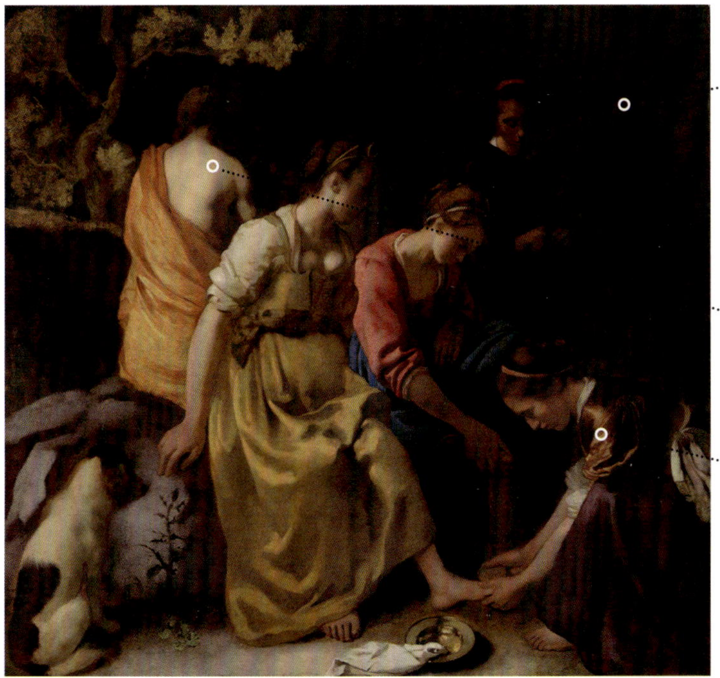

For years, this area was blue sky. During recent conservation it was found that it was painted with pigments that did not exist in Vermeer's day. So the area was given a film of dark paint, returning it to Vermeer's original conception of a moonlit scene.

This is the only known painting among Vermeer's surviving works that shows this much bare skin.

Conservators found that the right-hand side of the canvas had been cropped by approximately 12 cm, so this woman would have appeared in her entirety.

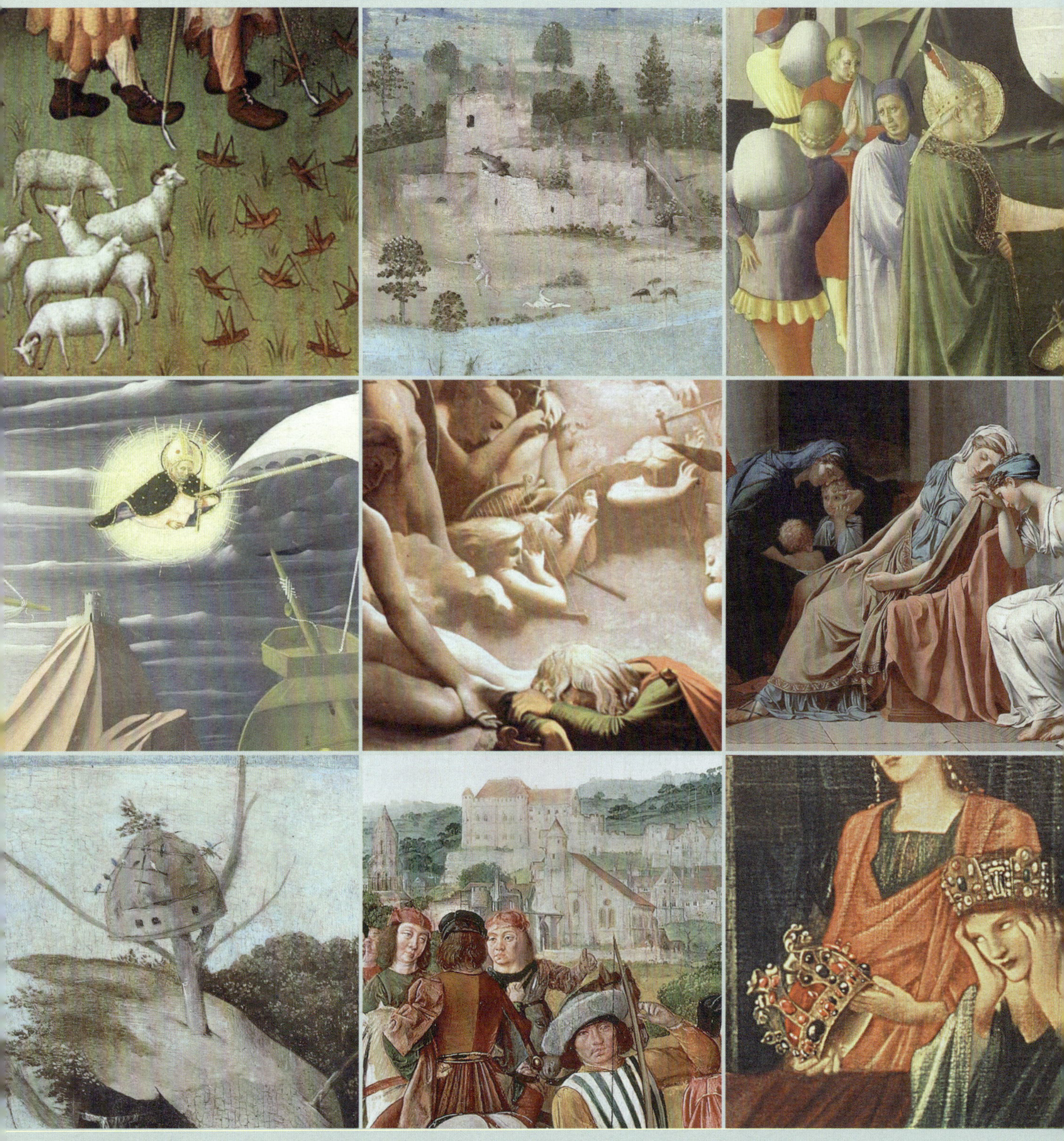

CHAPTER SEVEN

LEGEND

MASTER FRANCKE

The Pursuit of St Barbara

c. 1410–15

Little is known about this extraordinary artist except that he was probably born in the Netherlands in about 1380, was active at least until 1436 and is believed to have been a Dominican monk.

This is one of the eight panels that make up an altarpiece that relates the dramatic legend of St Barbara who wanted to convert to Christianity. Her father Dioscorus, depicted in the earlier panels as a dark, swarthy villain with a jutting beard and brandishing a scimitar, forbids her to convert and walls her up in a tower with two windows. She adds a third to symbolise the Holy Trinity. Barbara breaks out of the tower and is pursued by her father and his henchmen. A big white wall miraculously springs up in front of the pursuers, allowing Barbara to escape to the other side. This panel shows her fleeing through a dense forest. The wildly out of scale father, who retains his jutting beard but has lost his scimitar, asks two shepherds if they have seen his daughter. One shepherd denies all knowledge of her whereabouts but the other one indicates the direction she has taken.

The remaining panels of the altarpiece, painted in the same vivid colours and striking style, relate how Barbara is captured, accused by the emperor, tortured, has one of her breasts cut off and is finally beheaded by her father who is promptly consumed by a bolt of lightning.

Based on her father being struck by lightning, Barbara became the patron saint of artillerymen, armourers, military engineers, miners and others who work with explosives. One of her attributes is a canon.

One version of St Barbara's legend relates that she fled into a hilly landscape. This large orange shape is presumably Master Francke's portrayal of a hill.

As punishment for betraying St Barbara's location, the bad shepherd's flock has been turned into grasshoppers – or locusts – while the good shepherd's sheep remain woolly and intact.

St Nicholas of Bari

1437

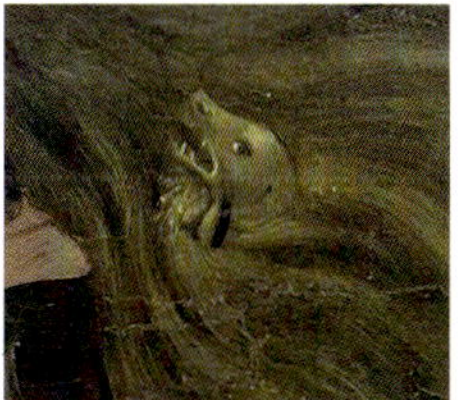

Almost invisible in the churning sea, a sea monster lurks in the hope that, should the ship founder, a drowning sailor may come his way.

The life of St Nicholas, the popular patron saint of mariners, is surrounded by numerous legends. In *The Golden Legend* he was credited with over a dozen pious and miraculous acts, two of which are depicted in this painting. On the right, the ship with the billowing sails is about to be driven by a storm-tossed sea on to the rocks of a mountainous coastline. The crew pray fervently to St Nicholas – conveniently floating on a cloud nearby – who touches the ship with his staff. This changes the direction of the wind and the ship is saved.

In the other half of the painting, the second miracle is being played out. Nicholas was also the patron saint of merchants, and of corn merchants in particular. At that date, famine was a constant threat: two failed harvests in succession were enough to empty a town's granaries. The picture shows sacks of corn on the quayside of the harbour at Myra. As the town's population was starving, Nicholas tries to persuade the ship's captain to increase the allowance, but he refuses on the grounds that supplies were strictly controlled by the emperor. So Nicholas multiplies the number of sacks.

Fra Angelico (1400–55) was a Dominican friar. For many years his painting was financed by Cosimo de' Medici, the most powerful merchant in Florence. In his *Lives of the Artists*, Vasari observed that the monk's figures 'are so exquisite that they really seem to be in Paradise'.

St Nicholas was the bishop of Myra, a town in Asia Minor. He is wearing his vestments, but as the Catholic Church never officially beatified him, his halo is illegitimate.

This is a measuring scoop, one of the most important pieces of equipment in the corn trade.

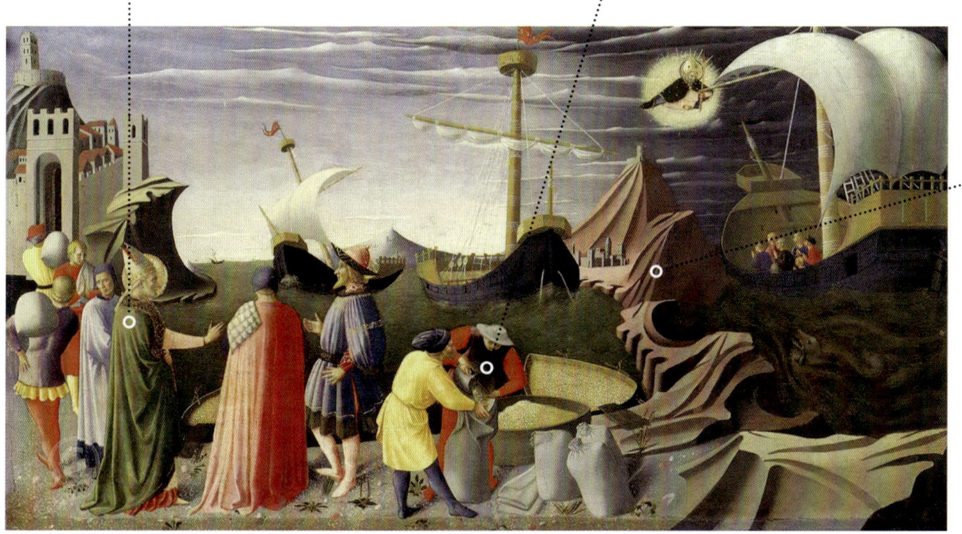

The mountainous ridge which threatens to sink the ship also serves to divide one of Nicholas's miracles from the other. It was common practice in the Middle Ages to portray several events unfolding within one and the same painting.

HIERONYMUS BOSCH

St Christopher Carrying the Christ Child

1490/96

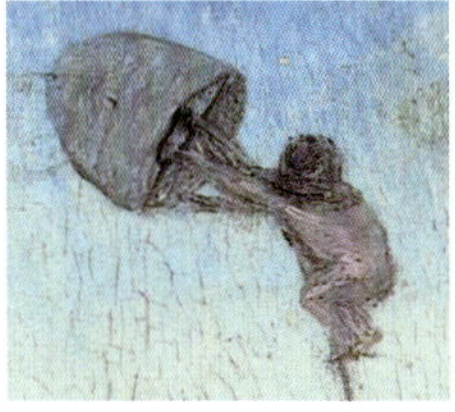

This naked figure scrambling up a tree branch towards a beehive is a symbol of drunkenness.

According to legend, St Christopher was a giant 'of terrifying appearance' who wanted to serve the most powerful king in existence. He entered the service of a local king, but on finding that he was terrified of the Devil, Christopher decided to serve the Devil instead. When the Devil avoided passing a wayside cross, he confessed to Christopher that whenever he saw one, he was 'seized with terror'. So Christopher left the Devil's service. He then met a hermit who instructed him in the Christian faith and suggested that he would find favour with Christ if he spent his life helping travellers across a deep and dangerous river. One day he carried a child across. In the middle of the river the child became so heavy that Christopher nearly drowned. He complained of the weight to the child who revealed himself to be Christ. St Christopher (Greek for 'Christ-Bearer') realised that he had actually carried the weight of the world on his shoulders.

So much for the legend. Bosch has embroidered it with countless weird and wonderful figments of his prolific imagination. St Christopher dwarfs everything around him as he gently carries the Child, but only Bosch could make their combined garments into a billowing sail, or hang a broken jug in a tree. And what was the bear's crime, seen hanging from a tree on the left?

Much to the distress of countless believers in the saintliness of Christopher, in 1969 he was demoted by the Roman Catholic Church.

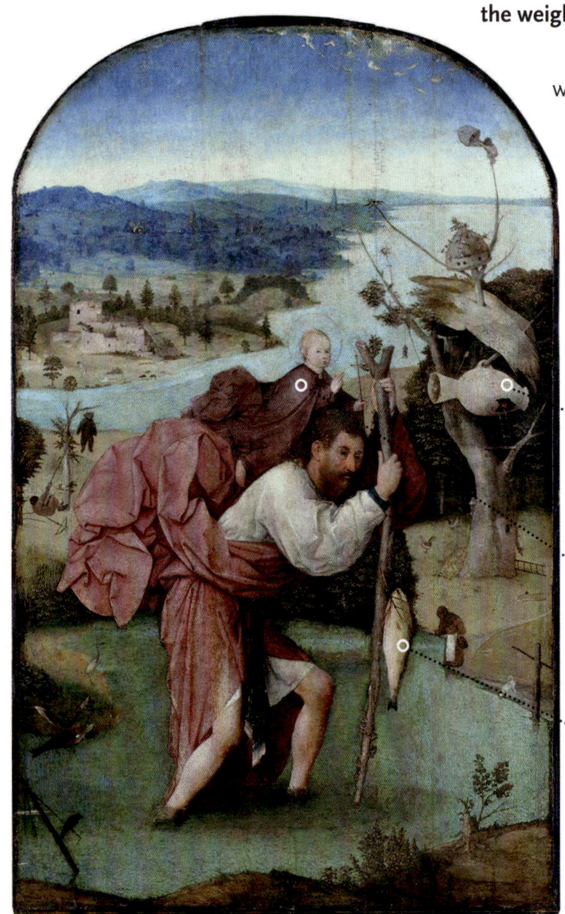

This strange jug-like object is the house that belongs to the hermit who advised Christopher to help travellers across the river. The hermit himself is standing at the edge of the water.

Perched on St Christopher's shoulders, the Christ Child can be identified by his halo, his cross-shaped staff and his gesture of blessing.

The fish has signified Christ from early Christian times onwards. Christ's Apostles are called the 'fishers of men'. It was also a very early symbol of Christian baptism. Believers were called *pisciculi*, or little fishes.

VITTORE CARPACCIO

Dream of St Ursula

1497–98

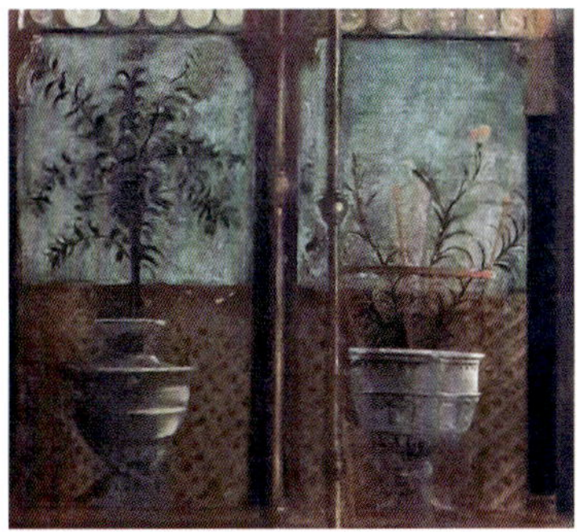

The two pots on the window ledge hold a myrtle and a carnation, both symbolic of fidelity in marriage.

This is the fifth in the cycle of nine extremely large paintings that recount the legend of St Ursula that Carpaccio adapted from *The Golden Legend*. Ursula, a fourth-century Christian princess, was betrothed to a pagan prince. She agreed to marry him on condition that he first accompanied her and eleven or 11,000 virgins (the accurate figure has been lost in translation) on a pilgrimage across Europe to Rome.

Carpaccio (*c.* 1460–1526) lived and worked in Venice and, understandably, chose to set this episode in the cycle in an early sixteenth-century Venetian house. Ursula is peacefully asleep in her room – presumably before she departs on her pilgrimage – in which the furnishings signal her aristocratic status. The ceiling is coffered, the floor covered with luxurious carpets imported from the East and the windows filled with costly glass. At the foot of the bed is a gold crown, an emblem of martyrdom. The room is suffused by a soft light, which is intensified by the arrival of an angel whose shadow leaves just a thin line on the floor. He is bearing a palm frond and informs Ursula of her impending martyrdom: she and her fellow pilgrims will be slaughtered by Huns when they reach Cologne.

Today this cycle of paintings is on display in the Accademia in Venice. John Ruskin, British art critic, writer, artist and philosopher, saw them there in 1878 and declared: 'I went crazy about Saint Ursula.'

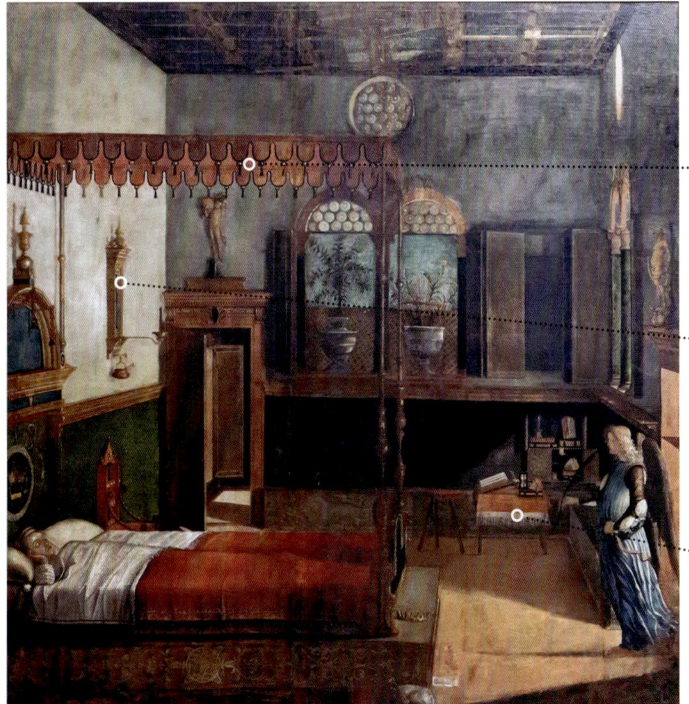

Ursula's bed is typically Venetian. It has a splendid ornate bedhead and is made of sturdy iron, decorated with a cloth canopy. The bed is raised on a base of painted chests.

Venetian society expected women to be consistent in their religious practices. Ursula would have frequently worshipped at this private altar. It is lit by a votive candle with a metal container filled with holy water beneath it.

Reading was another sign of a woman's religious piety. On the table is an open book, evidence that Ursula has been reading. Venice was an important centre of book production at the time, with Books of Hours and the Bible being among the most popular.

MASTER OF ST GILES

St Giles and the Hind

1500

Apart from the fact that he was active in Paris around 1500, little is known about the artist. In this painting he tells the story of the legendary St Giles who performed so many miracles that he became famous. Seeking solitude and anonymity, he retired to a cave where he lived as a hermit, his sole companion being his beloved hind, or female deer.

This image captures a defining incident in the saint's life. One day a king's hounds chased a beautiful deer in the forest near Giles's cave. The deer sought refuge with the saint. Giles prayed for her safety, whereupon the hounds fled howling back to their masters. When the king heard about it, he came the next day with his huntsmen. One of them fired an arrow into the thicket where the deer was last seen. The arrow missed her but seriously wounded St Giles. Mortified, the king offered him a doctor and compensation, but Giles refused. Eventually, with the king's support, Giles was persuaded to found a monastery at Saint-Gilles-du-Gard near Arles, which still exists today.

St Giles is one of the Fourteen Holy Helpers, a group of saints venerated by Catholics because of their intercession against various diseases. The group originated in the fourteenth century largely due to an outbreak of bubonic plague. Known as the Black Death, it killed up to 25 million people – almost one-third of Europe's population.

The town may be Saint-Gilles-du-Gard, near Arles, where the Benedictine monastery, founded by St Giles, is situated. It became an important stop on the pilgrimage route to Santiago de Compostela, Spain.

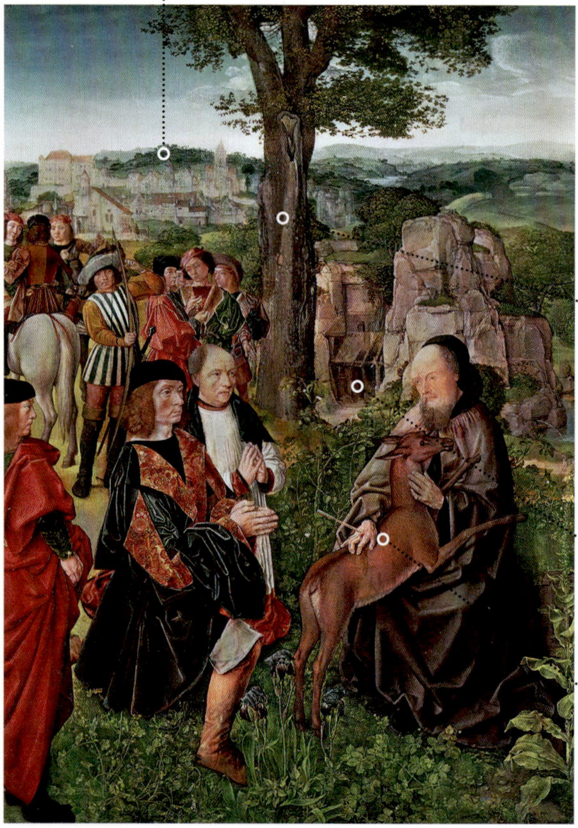

Typically for this artist, the painting's composition is split into two halves: the tree forms a vertical division between the solitary saint in his verdant wilderness on the right and the crowd of huntsmen and fashionably dressed courtiers on the left.

This is the entrance to St Giles's cave, where he is said to have subsisted on a diet of fruit, berries and milk from his deer.

In medieval art, the arrow and a female deer are the attributes associated with St Giles.

JACQUES-LOUIS DAVID

Oath of the Horatii

1784

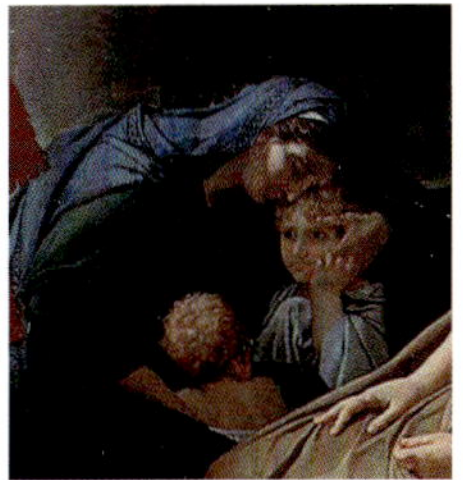

These are the children of Sabina, the wife of one of the Horatii brothers, who are accompanied by their nurse. One of the boys is watching the oath-taking ceremony with fascination.

David (1748–1825) was an exceptionally gifted artist. Considered the father of the Neoclassical art movement, he was also a moralist and a painter of political propaganda. Many of the images glorifying the French Revolution and Napoleon Bonaparte are painted by him.

David based this painting on the popular Roman legend, recounted by the Roman historian Titus Livius (Livy), about two warring cities in the first century BC, Rome and Alba Longa. It was decided that in order to save both cities further bloodshed, the dispute should be settled by three brothers from the Horatii family and three brothers from the Curiatii family. The tragedy inherent in this decision lay in the tangled relationships between the two families: one of the sisters of the Curiatii, Sabina, was married to one of the Horatii while one of the sisters of the Horatii, Camilla, was betrothed to one of the Curiatii. David has illustrated the moment when the Horatius brothers swear a sacrificial oath on their swords, which are held up before them by their father. The fact that they chose political ideals over personal safety and family ties made them role models at a time when France was on the brink of a cataclysmic revolution.

The painting was commissioned by the king, Louis XVI, in the belief that it would encourage loyalty to the monarchy. David, however, was deeply influenced by Enlightenment ideas and created an image that emphasised loyalty to the state rather than to the monarchy. The painting was first exhibited in Rome, where even the Pope asked to see it. It was not until 1785 that it was shown at the Paris Salon.

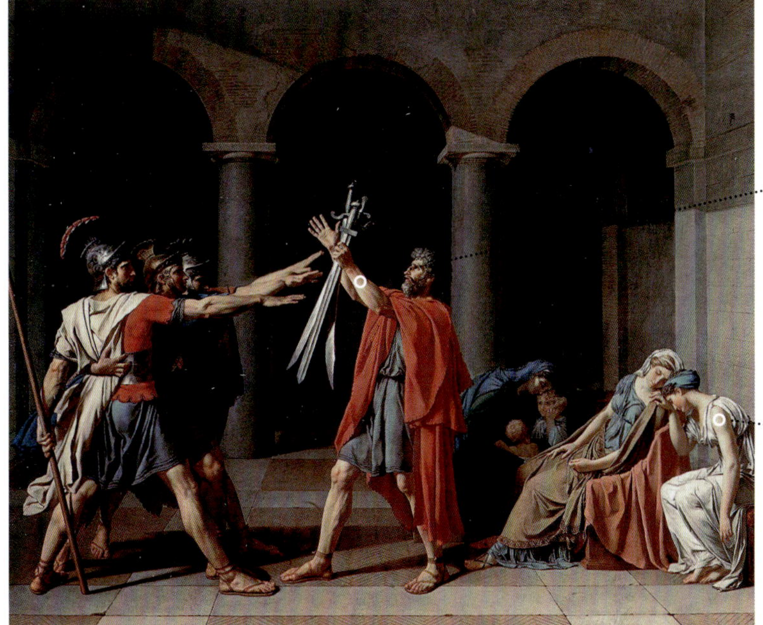

To show their courage and strength of purpose, David has deliberately painted all the men with rigid lines to mirror the Roman columns in the background, while the sorrowing women are soft and yielding.

Camilla, a sister of the Horatii, is weeping because she fears that in the coming contest she will lose either a brother or her betrothed. After the battle, the sole survivor is one of her brothers who kills her for shedding tears over the enemy.

JEAN-AUGUSTE-DOMINIQUE INGRES

The Dream of Ossian

1813

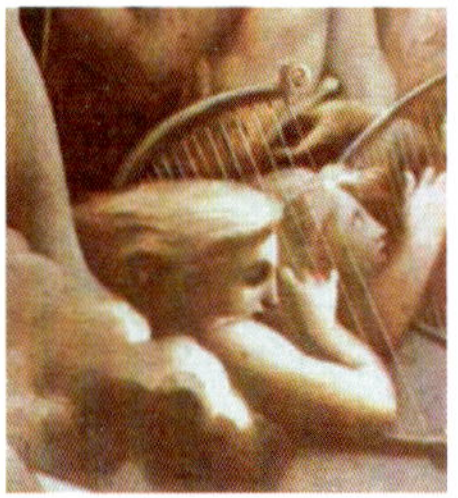

This is one of the four harpists in the painting. Their inclusion is a possible reference to the opera, Ossian, or The Bards, *which features a dreaming scene, armed warriors and their lovers.*

Ossian, the subject of this extremely strange painting, was purportedly a blind Irish or Scottish poet who lived in the third century. In the 1760s, the Scottish poet James Macpherson published texts, supposedly by Ossian, which he claimed to have rediscovered and translated from Gaelic into English. Ossian caused a sensation and was translated into every European language. Some declared it to be a Celtic equivalent of works by classical writers such as Homer. Napoleon Bonaparte carried his copy into battle and commissioned this painting for the ceiling of his bedroom in the Quirinal Palace in Rome. But Macpherson was accused of perpetrating a gigantic hoax by publishing poems of his own devising. Their authenticity is still a matter of dispute today.

The poems relate tales of endless battles. There is no single narrative, although the same characters reappear. They are prone to killing their loved ones by mistake, then dying of grief. Here, Ingres (1780–1867) has shown Ossian asleep in a rocky landscape. He is leaning on his harp, his orange cloak vivid against the muted colours in the background. He is dreaming of ghosts of the past: the relatives, warriors and deities who occupy two-thirds of the immense canvas. The drooping figures are ethereal, only the tips of the warriors' helmets and spears catching the light.

Ossian mania continued to provide a refreshing alternative to history and mythology, which had previously dominated European consciousness.

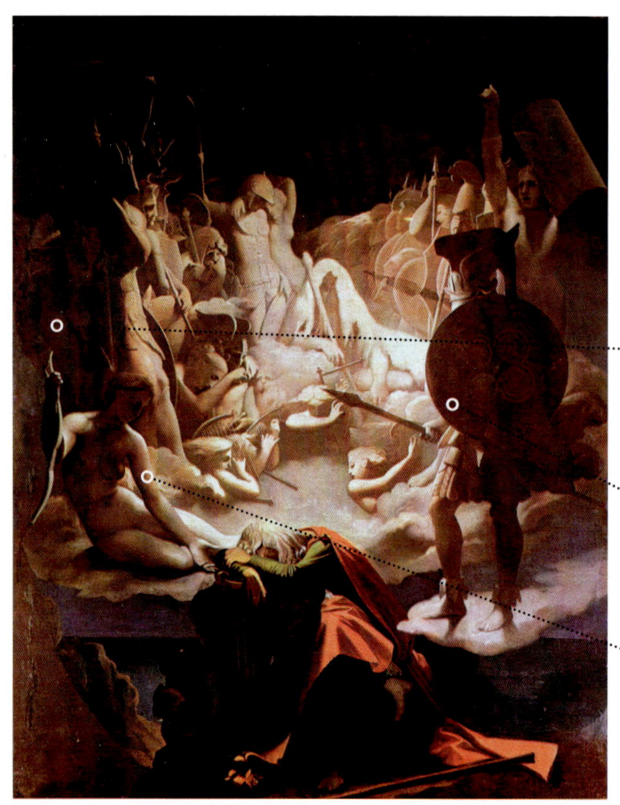

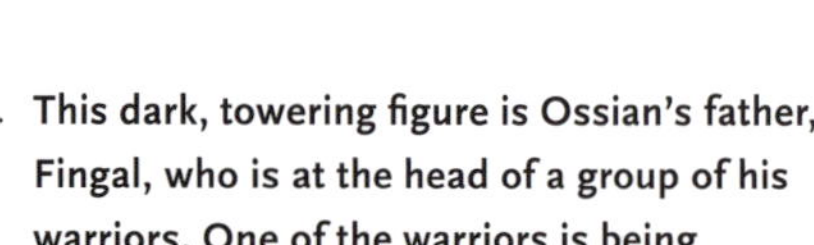

This dark, towering figure is Ossian's father, Fingal, who is at the head of a group of his warriors. One of the warriors is being embraced by a curvaceous, naked women.

The figure, balancing on a handy cloud and armed with a spear and shield, is Ossian's son, Oscar, who was treacherously slain in one of the battles.

The naked woman who holds a bow in one hand and extends the other towards Ossian has been identified either as Ossian's wife Evirallina or as Oscar's wife Malvina.

EDWARD BURNE-JONES

The Last Sleep of Arthur in Avalon (detail)

c. 1881–98

This monumental painting (6.4 m long) was commissioned from Burne-Jones by his patron George Howard, 9th Earl of Carlisle, to hang in the library of Naworth Castle. Howard approved the subject as he shared the artist's love for the Arthurian legends. Burne-Jones began work on the painting in 1881 and was still working on it within hours of his death seventeen years later. On the day before he died, he wrote to his intimate friend May Gaskell: 'And tomorrow I will go back to Avalon and try the experiment for bettering a weak place in the picture.' Although unfinished, the painting is considered the artist's masterpiece.

Burne-Jones (1833–98) based the painting on *Le Morte d'Arthur*, the first English-language prose version of the legend, completed by Sir Thomas Malory about 1470. Burne-Jones had come across Malory's tales about King Arthur when he was at the University of Oxford. William Morris, a life-long friend and co-member of the Pre-Raphaelite Brotherhood, was also inspired by all things Arthurian. It has been suggested that this painting is a hymn of grief for the relatively early deaths of Morris and Dante Gabriel Rossetti. The general breaking up of the Brotherhood left Burne-Jones experiencing increasing isolation and a painful awareness of his own mortality. Hence, his identification with Arthur who suffered a fatal wound in a battle against Mordred – said to be Arthur's son by his half-sister Morgause – and was taken to the magical island of Avalon where he fell into a deep slumber.

King Arthur's head lies in the lap of his sorceress half-sister, Queen Morgan le Fay. Burne-Jones's daughter, Margaret, was the model for the queen.

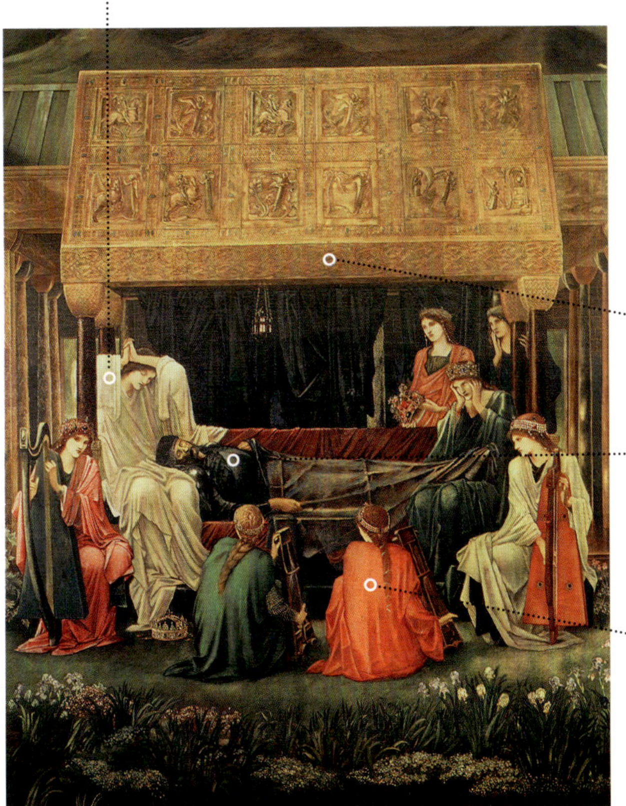

Arthur is lying in a Byzantine styled mausoleum beneath a canopy decorated with scenes from *Le Morte d'Arthur*.

Burne-Jones identified himself with Arthur and, according to his wife Georgiana, even adopted the king's pose when he slept. In his correspondence, too, he wrote as if he was already on the Isle of Avalon.

It is said that Burne-Jones's friend and confidante, May Gaskell, modelled for one of the queens, but it is not known which one. Apparently, it was she who suggested adding flowers to the foreground.

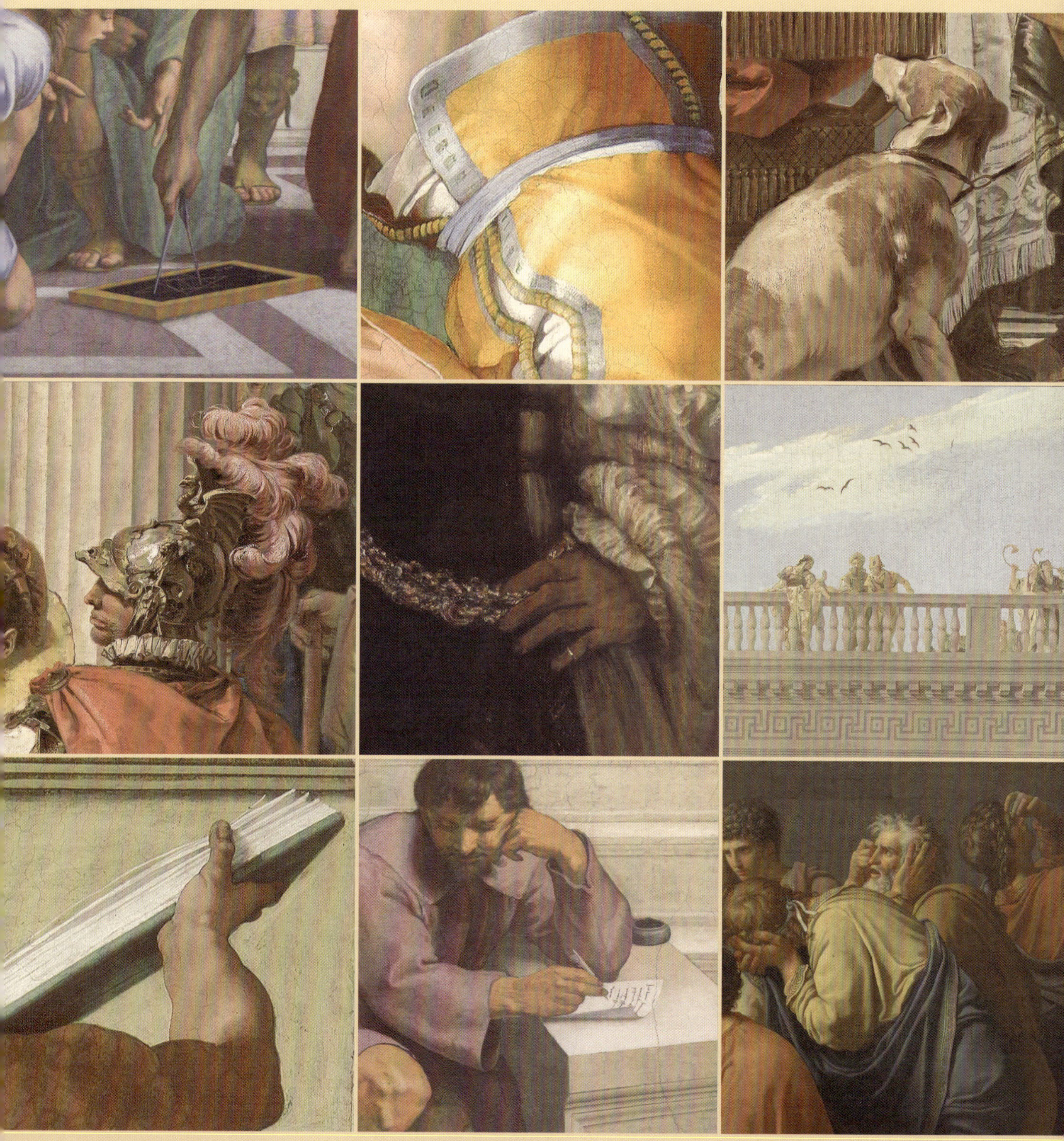

CHAPTER EIGHT

CLASSICAL ANTIQUITY

RAPHAEL

The School of Athens

1508–11

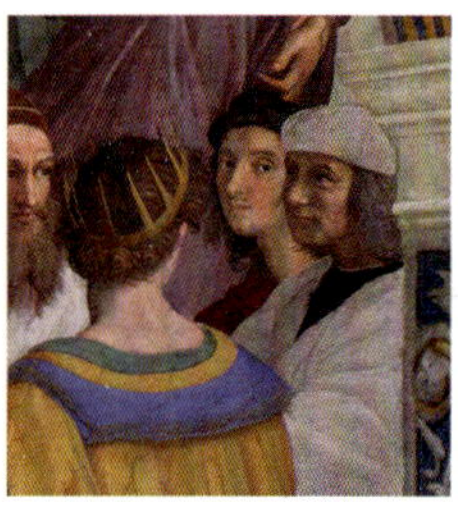

Looking directly out of the painting at the viewer, this young face belongs to Raphael, who has inserted his self-portrait among the philosophers.

It was a bold stroke of Pope Julius II (nicknamed the Fearsome Pope) to commission the twenty-seven-year old Raphael, who had little experience of painting large frescoes, to decorate the walls of his private library in the Vatican. *The School of Athens* is crowded with life-size figures of all the greatest mathematicians, philosophers and scientists from classical antiquity. These individuals all lived at different times, but Raphael has gathered them together under one glorious roof. The roof itself is reminiscent of the ceiling of the nave of the new St Peter's Basilica in Rome, which was under construction at the time.

In the centre, below the arch, are the two giants of antiquity: on the left Plato, the philosopher who is holding his *Timaeus*, and on the right Aristotle, founder of naturalist thought, with his *Ethics*. Plato, whose appearance is widely thought to be based on Leonardo da Vinci, is flanked by the philosophers who appealed to intuition and the emotions, Socrates among them. To the right of Aristotle are those individuals who represent rational activities: logic, grammar and geometry. The great brooding figure leaning his elbow on a marble block in the centre foreground is said to be the Greek philosopher Heraclitus, but Raphael has given him the likeness of Michelangelo in homage to the celebrated sculptor after he had seen his work on the Sistine Chapel ceiling. The cynic Diogenes, dressed in a sort of blue shift, sprawls untidily on the steps.

The title of both this fresco and the room in which it was painted were altered when Julius died in 1513. He was succeeded by Leo X, who changed its use from a library to a study in which he signed his official documents, and called it the Stanza della Segnatura (the room of the signature). When it was a library, the books would have been displayed flat on sloping shelves just below Raphael's frescoes. At that date a person would go to a book and read it *in situ*. The books themselves would have been beautiful and precious objects, exquisitely bound in leather and tooled with gold.

The other large frescoes created by Raphael in Julius's library include the *Disputa* and *Parnassus*, both concerned with the abstract world of literature and learning. Raphael was given further rooms to paint in the Vatican, displacing other artists who had been commissioned before he came to Rome. These rooms are now called Stanze di Raffaello. It seems incredible that an artist who was not yet thirty years old should devise such a balanced and harmonious composition, then fill it with figures – dressed in every hue imaginable – whose expressions and eloquent gestures are entirely credible. In the view of the eminent art historian Michael Levey: 'Raphael gives his [figures] a superhuman clarity and grace in a universe of Euclidian certainties.'

This sinuous figure is Apollo, one of the twelve gods of Olympus. The embodiment of the classical Greek spirit, he was seen as the god responsible for poetry and music.

The architecture, especially the coffered vault, is reminiscent of the new St Peter's that was being built at the same time that Raphael was working on the frescoes.

As the goddess of wisdom, Minerva is a natural patroness for the assembled philosophers. She was also the goddess of war, hence her helmet, shield and spear.

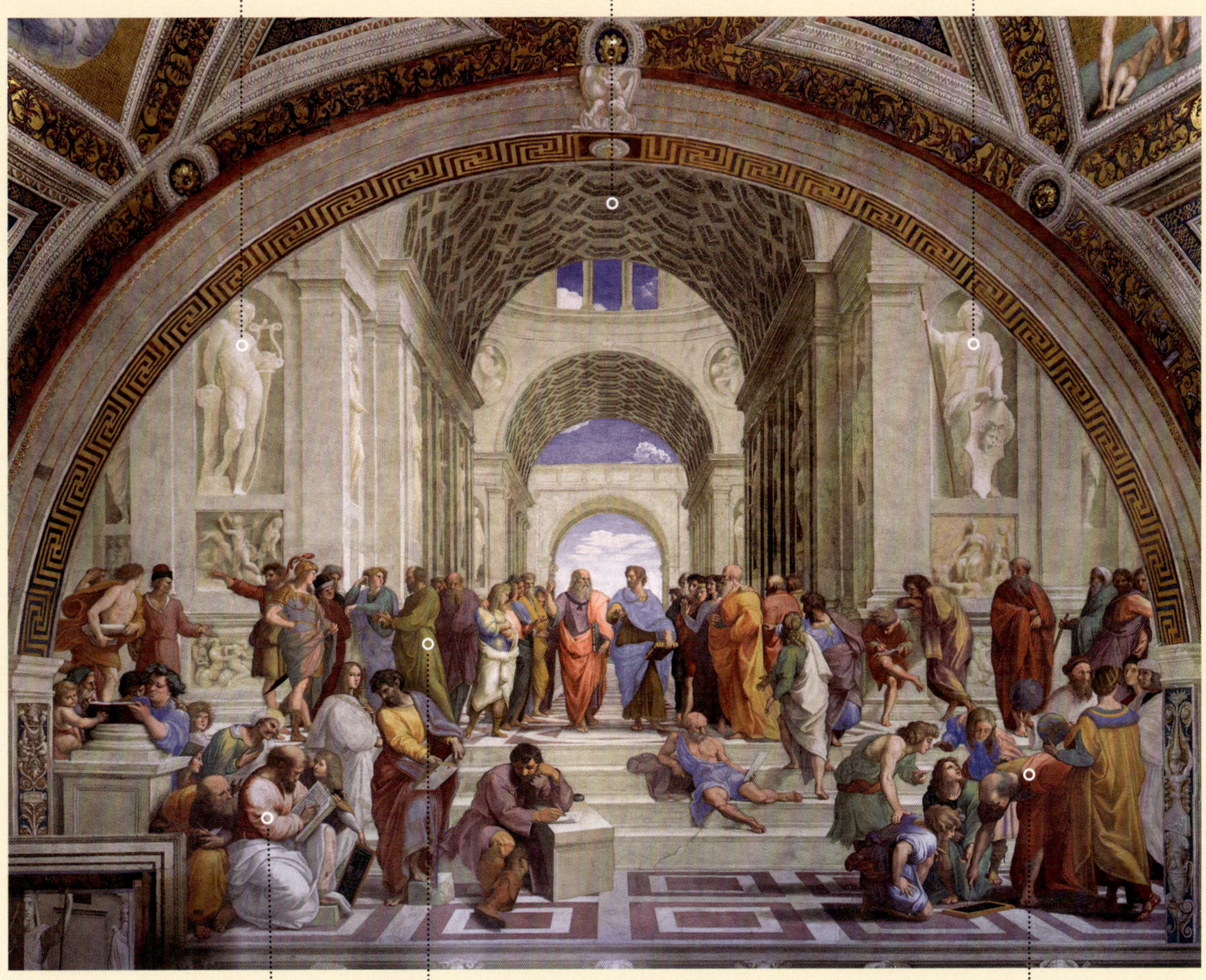

This is the Greek philosopher Pythagoras, who believed that the world operated according to mathematical laws. He is taking notes from a tablet that includes a formulation of his ideas on harmony and the musical scale.

Raphael used an antique sculpture for the features of the Greek philosopher Socrates, but it is said that he also captured his characteristic hand gestures.

This is probably the Greek mathematician Euclid, but Raphael has given him the face of Donato Bramante who designed the new St Peter's.

MICHELANGELO

The Libyan Sibyl

c. 1511

This magnificent figure, over 3.6 m high, is just one of the hundreds that Michelangelo created on the ceiling of the Sistine Chapel in Rome. Suspended on a creaking wooden platform nearly 21 m above the floor, his spine arched, his head craned backwards and in flickering candlelight, he worked swiftly in great sweeping brushstrokes. The Libyan Sibyl alone took him twenty *giornate* (days of work) to complete. Apart from a small team of assistants, who transferred his cartoons on to the wet plaster and ground his colours, he painted the entire ceiling himself.

Michelangelo (1475–1564) was reluctant to accept Pope Julius II's commission: as a sculptor he was sure of himself, but to tackle such a huge area in fresco, when he had limited experience in the medium, was a superhuman undertaking. Besides, he felt that Julius's scheme of painting the twelve apostles, and covering the rest of the ceiling simply with decorations, 'would be a poor affair'. The Pope acquiesced and gave him permission to do what he liked.

The Sibyls (prophetesses) owe their place on the ceiling to the tradition that they foretold the coming of Christ to the Gentiles. The Libyan Sibyl is a triumph of delicate colouring, foreshortening and sheer beauty. Michelangelo has feminised the male assistant who modelled for him and created a sublime profile, elaborately braided coiffure and an elegant twist to her body as she replaces the heavy book of prophecies on the shelf behind her.

Each of the five massive sibyls is accompanied by two *genii*, or guardian spirits. One of the Libyan Sibyl's *genius* is holding a tightly rolled scroll under his arm.

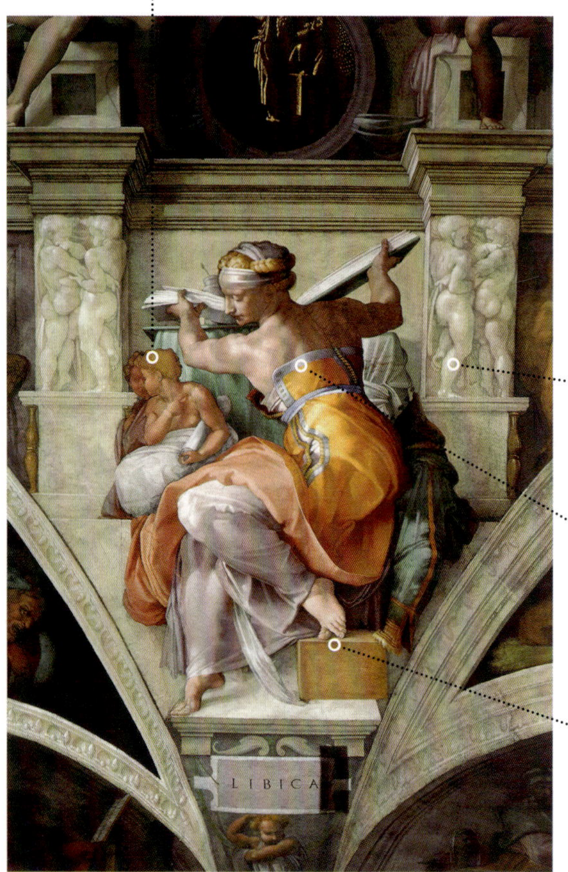

These *putti*, painted as if they were made of marble, serve as miniature Atlas figures supporting the imaginary cornice that runs all the way round the central rectangle of the ceiling.

One of Michelangelo's preparatory drawings for the ceiling includes an exquisite one of the male assistant who modelled for the Sibyl. It reveals the artist's determination to portray the rippling muscles before clothing them in silk.

On the same sheet as the drawing of the male model's muscles are studies of the Sibyl's big toe as it bends to support the weight of her turning body.

REMBRANDT VAN RIJN

Aristotle with a Bust of Homer

1653

In 1654, a merchant ship left the Netherlands on a month-long voyage to Messina in Sicily. In its cargo was a wooden crate containing this painting. It had been commissioned by Don Antonio Ruffo, a wealthy Sicilian nobleman to add to his spectacular collection of works of art. Ruffo assumed that the figure was Aristotle, the renowned fourth-century BC Greek philosopher. Rather than just painting a single figure, Rembrandt has ingeniously devised a way of including two more famous men of antiquity: a bust of Homer, the epic poet who had attained literary immortality with his *Iliad* and *Odyssey*, and the great military commander Alexander the Great, who is portrayed on the medallion on the gold chain.

Aristotle, dressed like a seventeenth-century Dutch burgher, lays his hand gently on Homer's head. In 343 BC, Philip II of Macedon had appointed the philosopher as tutor to his son Alexander. Both Aristotle and the young Alexander were known to have revered Homer. Following Alexander's death in 323 BC, anti-Macedonian sentiment in Athens resurfaced. Aristotle was accused of impiety and fled into exile on the Greek island of Euboea. His expression of profound melancholy could be interpreted as him contemplating the transience of fame.

There is another possible theory about the painting. It is not at all certain that Ruffo requested a painting of a philosopher. Perhaps this is not Aristotle but Apelles, the supreme painter of Greek antiquity who was also Alexander's favourite artist.

It is not known what Homer looked like. The bust is probably based on a Roman copy of a superb, although imaginary, ninth-century BC marble head of the poet. Rembrandt owned several Hellenistic busts.

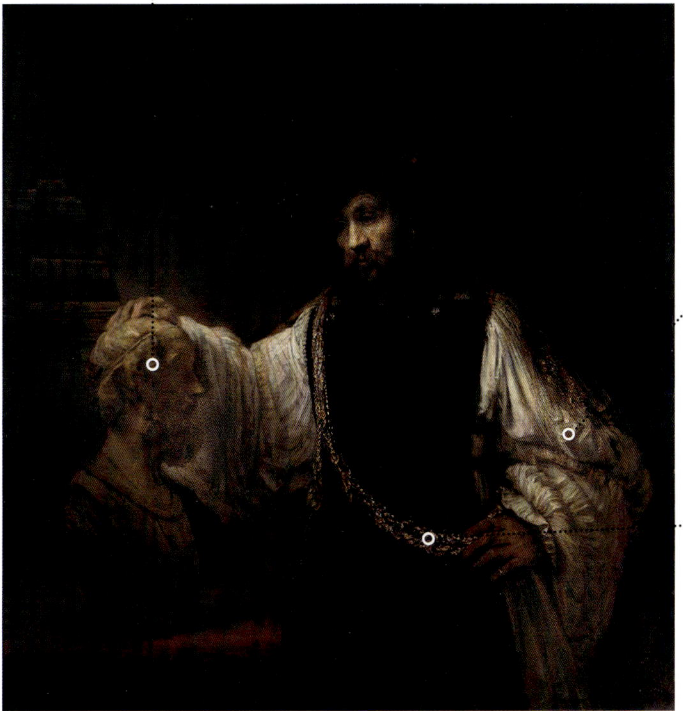

The voluminous ruched sleeves are painted with great slashing strokes. They are a perfect example of Rembrandt's 'rough' or 'unfinished' manner of painting which he increasingly adopted in his late works.

The gold chain is painted in dense impasto. In some places the clots, crusts and ridges of thickly mixed paint rise from the canvas by about 6 mm.

GIOVANNI BATTISTA TIEPOLO

The Banquet of Cleopatra

1743–44

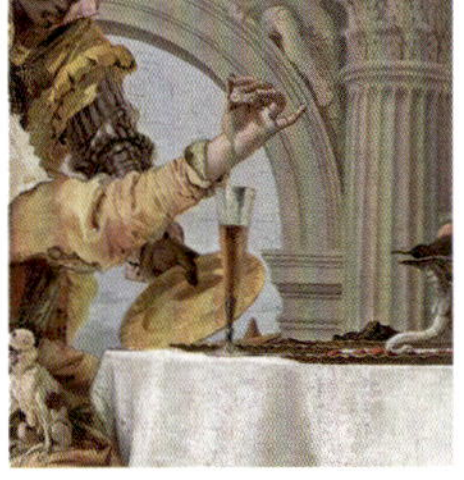

The goblet containing the vinegar in which Cleopatra dissolved her priceless pearl earring.

Described by Michael Levey as 'the greatest decorative painter of eighteenth-century Europe', Tiepolo has depicted a famous contest – as related by the Roman historian Pliny in his *Historia Naturalis* in AD 77 – between Cleopatra and her lover, the Roman consul Mark Antony.

Antony, who insists on wearing his plumed helmet, despite the heat, throws a lavish banquet to impress the Egyptian queen. The setting is a brightly lit loggia bordered by four classical pillars. Sumptuously robed in apricot silk, the queen is surrounded by a variety of attendants, some of whom are very bizarrely dressed. She is served an endless succession of expensive delicacies on what appear to be gold plates. Cleopatra, however, declares herself unimpressed by Antony's extravagance and wagers him that she can produce a dish a thousand times more costly than anything he has offered her. Removing one of her priceless pearl earrings, she dissolves it in a goblet of vinegar and drinks it. Antony is obliged to admit defeat.

Tiepolo created no less than three paintings of this subject. This particular one is much-travelled. Bought from the artist's Venice studio in 1744 for Augustus III, Elector of Saxony, it was dispatched to Dresden, then to the Elector's hunting lodge at Hubertusburg. However, by the turn of the nineteenth century it was off again, this time to decorate a ceiling in the Mikhailovsky Palace in St Petersburg. In 1801 it was transferred to the Hermitage Palace. There it remained until finally coming to rest in Australia's National Gallery in 1932.

With his bearded face in shadow and wearing the most curious garments beneath his blue cape, this tall man is a mystery. Is he a street vendor? If so, what is he doing hovering about the banquet?

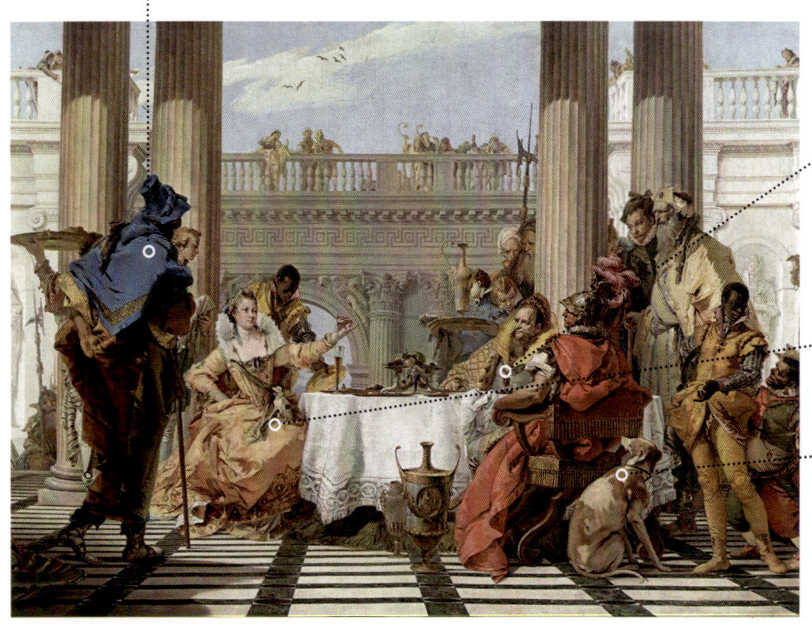

Lucius Plancus, a Roman senator, was invited to attend the banquet so that he could umpire the wager. He declared Cleopatra the winner and prevented her from destroying the second pearl earring.

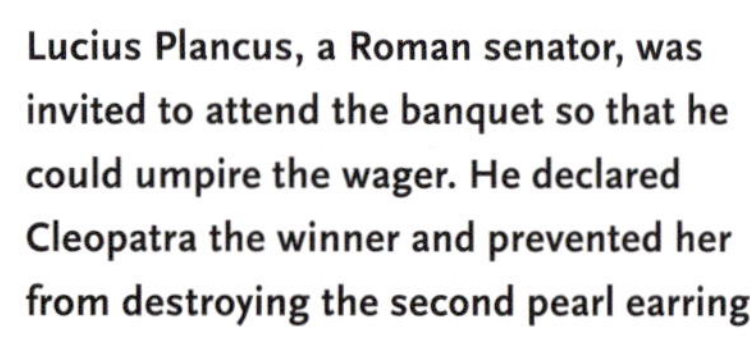

Sitting on the Egyptian queen's silken lap is an astonishingly small dog.

Mark Antony's greyhound is painted with Tiepolo's unrivalled fluency, although an x-ray of the picture demonstrates that he twice changed his mind about the position of its tail.

JACQUES-LOUIS DAVID

The Death of Socrates

1787

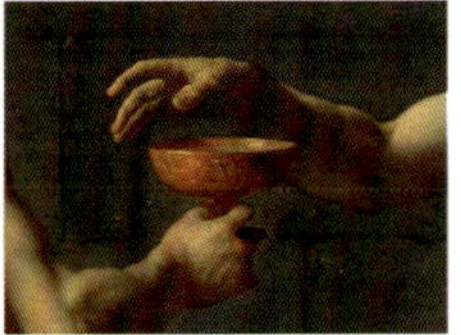

The cup containing the deadly poison. In ancient Greece, hemlock, made from the plant **conium maculatum*****, was used to execute condemned prisoners.***

This image was created two years before the beginning of the French Revolution. David sympathised with the revolution's aims and was imprisoned twice for his activities. His painting demonstrates that he shared the heroic ideals of the Greek philosopher Socrates. In 399 BC, Socrates was unjustly accused by the Athenian government of impiety and corrupting the minds of the young men of Athens. Found guilty, he chose to commit suicide rather than renounce his beliefs or live in exile.

The picture shows Socrates in his prison cell raising his hand to address his friends and disciples on the immortality of the soul before he accepts the cup of deadly poison from a mortified prison warder. These last moments of his life are known from *Phaedo*, one of Plato's Dialogues, in which he recounted the dignity and courage with which the philosopher met his death. Plato, although not present at the time, has been placed by David, bowed with grief, at the end of the bed. Another of Socrates's students, the seated red-robed Crito, grasps the philosopher's thigh as if beseeching him to change his mind. Other disciples weep and clasp their heads in distress at their teacher's impending death.

In his portrayal of Socrates, it seems probable that David copied a marble bust in the Louvre, dated to the first century AD, which in turn may be a copy of a lost fourth-century BC bronze statue. It is certainly very similar. David has faithfully reproduced the philosopher's rather snub and inelegant nose, but he has given him more hair.

According to Plato's *Phaedo*, Socrates sent away his family before he drank the poison. They are shown looking back as they leave the prison.

David has portrayed Plato as an old man, but he would have been only in his twenties. The philosopher's pen, inkwell and scroll lie on the floor beside him.

Snaking around under the bed is the heavy prison chain that Socrates was wearing. The open shackle shows that he was released to drink the poison.

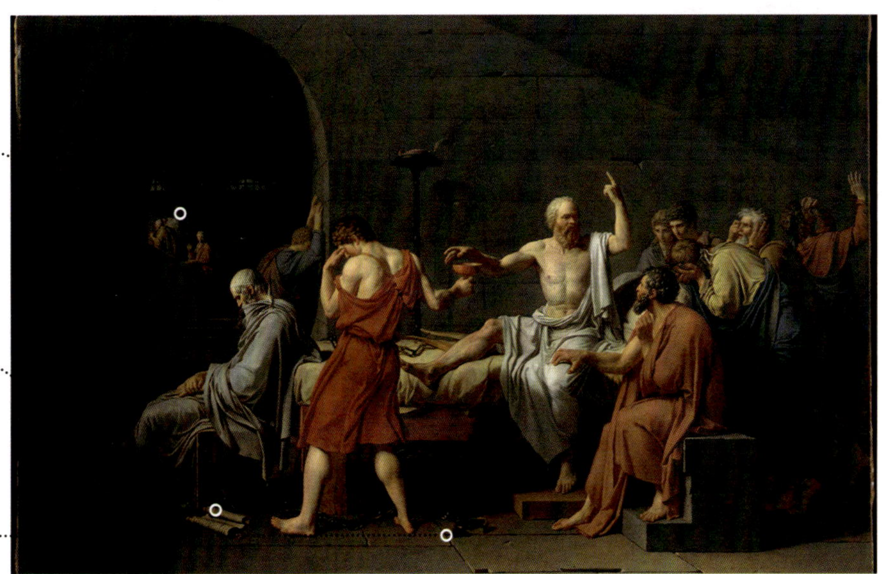

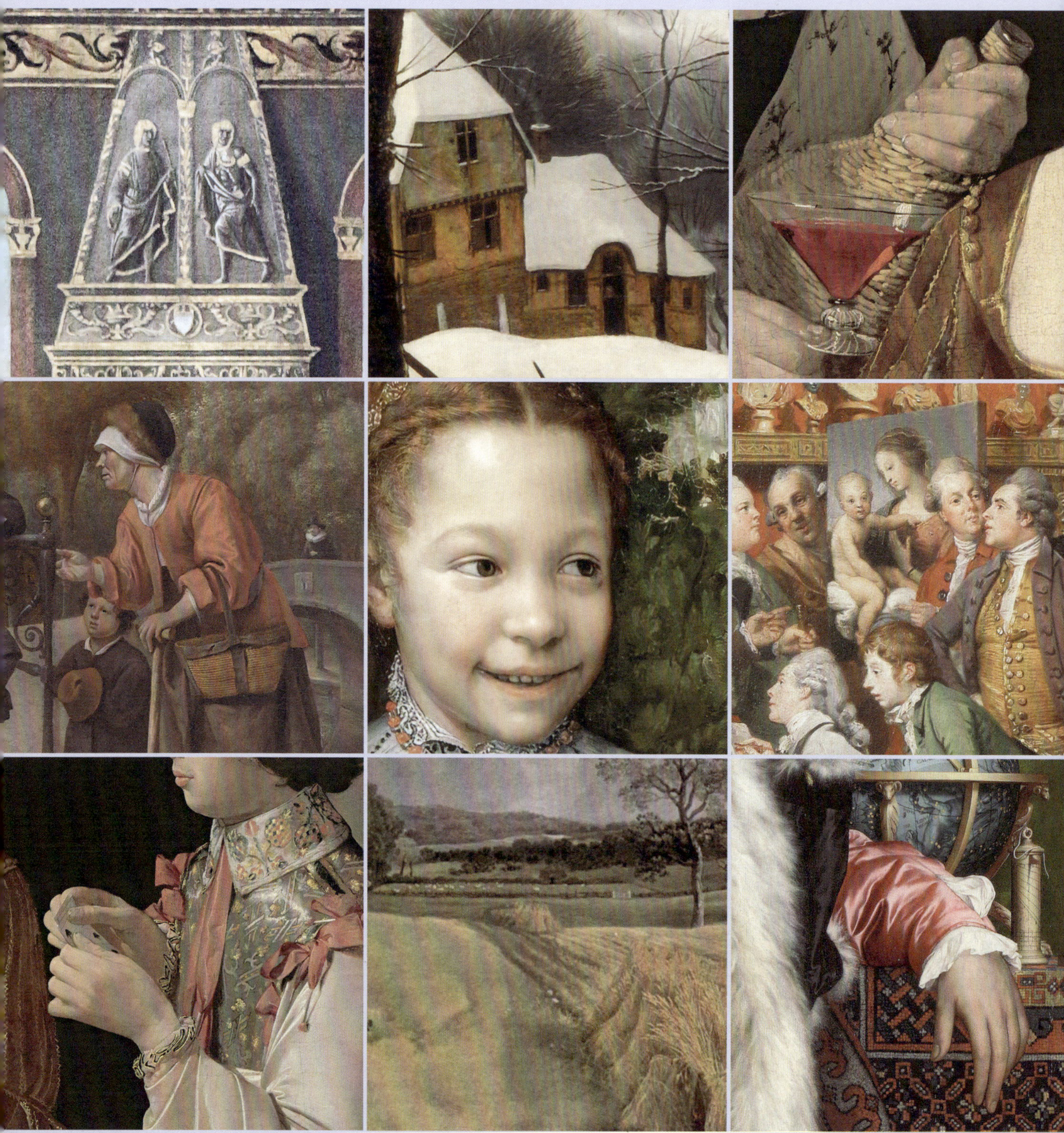

CHAPTER NINE

LIFE'S RICH TAPESTRY

Many outstanding paintings are rich in details – some symbolic, some representational – that tell us a great deal about how people lived. Whether it was the daily task of gathering wood in winter or hunting to fill the pot, or the more sophisticated trappings of international diplomacy or a gathering of Grand Tourists in Florence, the artists' powers of observation are both illuminating and fascinating.

February from *Les Très Riches Heures du duc de Berry*

c. 1416

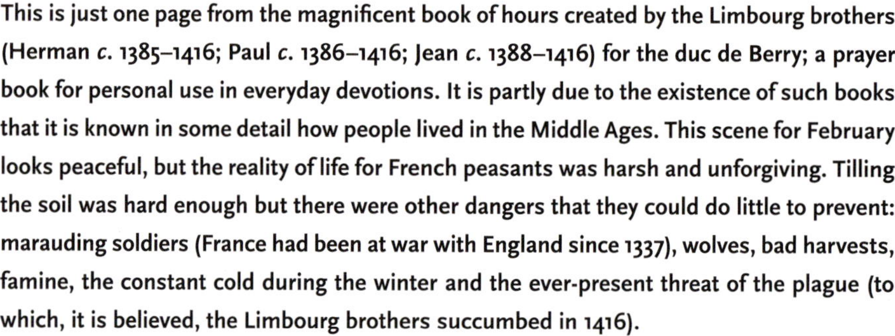

This is just one page from the magnificent book of hours created by the Limbourg brothers (Herman *c.* 1385–1416; Paul *c.* 1386–1416; Jean *c.* 1388–1416) for the duc de Berry; a prayer book for personal use in everyday devotions. It is partly due to the existence of such books that it is known in some detail how people lived in the Middle Ages. This scene for February looks peaceful, but the reality of life for French peasants was harsh and unforgiving. Tilling the soil was hard enough but there were other dangers that they could do little to prevent: marauding soldiers (France had been at war with England since 1337), wolves, bad harvests, famine, the constant cold during the winter and the ever-present threat of the plague (to which, it is believed, the Limbourg brothers succumbed in 1416).

Only a few of the buildings on a noble landowner's farm are depicted. The rest of his property would have consisted of a manor house, stalls for the animals, living quarters for the servants and labourers, and possibly a chapel. This image shows the corner of the farm manager's house, identified by the large bed and a fireplace against the wall. Peasants lived in huts with a fire in the middle of the single room, the smoke exiting through a hole in the roof. The blazing fire is being enjoyed by the manager's wife who raises her skirt daintily to the heat. The two farm labourers on her right are not so dainty in their enjoyment of the warmth.

This man is felling a tree to replenish the supply of firewood so essential in the winter. It is probably lengths of wood that are strapped to the donkey that the peasant is taking to the village in the distance.

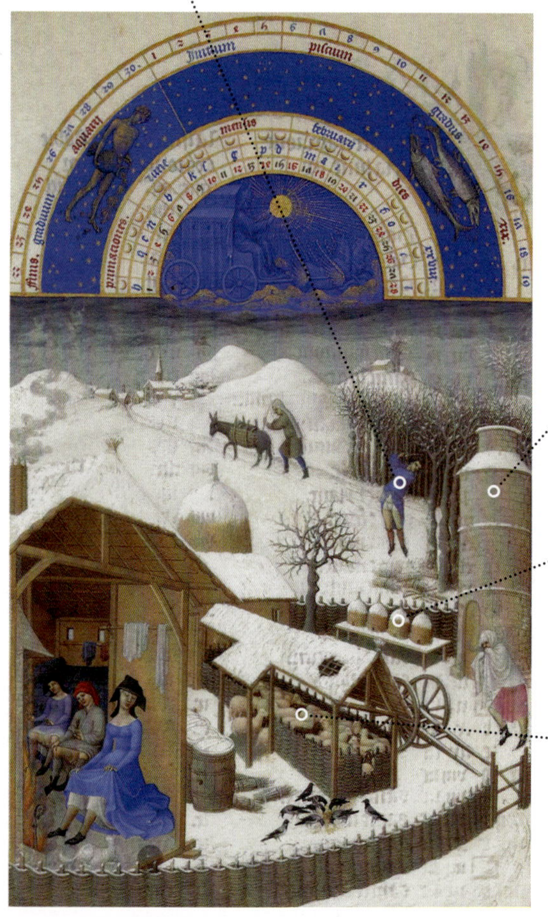

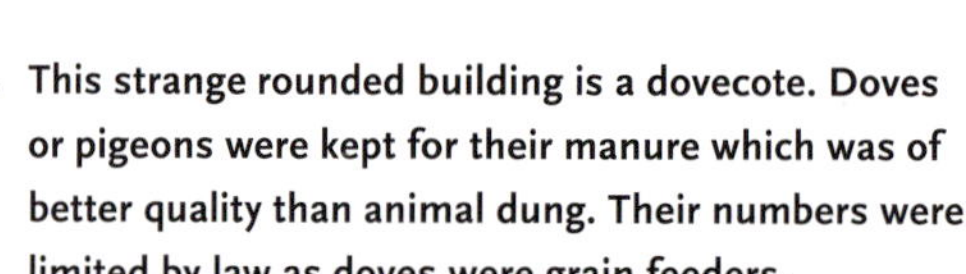

This strange rounded building is a dovecote. Doves or pigeons were kept for their manure which was of better quality than animal dung. Their numbers were limited by law as doves were grain feeders.

Bees were vital for their honey which was the only available sweetener at the time as only the rich could afford imported sugar. The beeswax, too, was essential as it was used to make candles that were far superior to the tallow variety.

The sheep are protected from the weather by their roofed enclosure. Sheep were the animals most commonly kept on a farm as they supplied meat, wool and milk. Also they were, unlike cows, able to exist on meagre grass.

GIOVANNI MANSUETI

The Miraculous Healing of the Daughter of Benvegnudo of San Polo

c. 1505

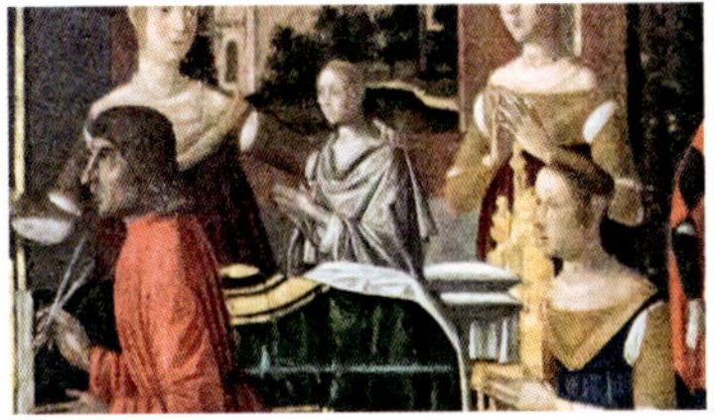

This diminutive figure is the daughter, sitting upright in her cot. Kneeling to the left of her is the proud father; kneeling behind him is her mother.

The subject of this picture demonstrates that religion dominated Renaissance life and society. The painting was one of a series of works commissioned by the Scuola of St John the Evangelist to show the miracles performed by its most precious relic, a fragment of wood from the Cross on which Christ was crucified. The healing of Benvegnudo's daughter, blind and paralysed from birth, had occurred when her father touched her head with three candles that had previously touched the relic.

Mansueti (active 1484–1526/27) has removed an outside wall of the Venetian palace to enable the viewer to join family, friends and various dignitaries to celebrate this miraculous healing. The ceremony takes place on the first floor in the *sala*, the grandest room in the palace and the site of the most significant events in a family's life. The tall windows are glazed, not made of waxed canvas or paper; the floor is marble. On the right is a high-backed bench set against the wall. At the foot of the impressive marble staircase is the public street. (There are no women in the street because they were confined to the domestic sphere and seldom left the house.) Although Venice was surrounded by water, the city was constantly short of water to drink. How to obtain water, how to preserve it and how to control it was an ever-present concern. The courtyard of the palace was frequently the site of the household well.

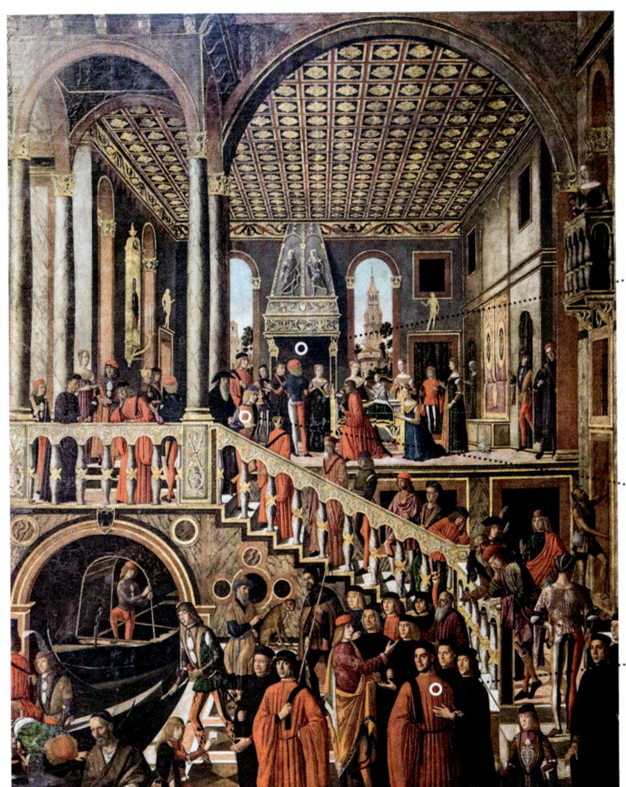

The fireplace was an essential element of the *sala*. It was a visual focus and a real source of warmth. A fifteenth-century priest described visiting a private palace in Venice: 'The fireplace was all of Carrara marble, shining like gold, and carved so subtly ...'

This man in the brightly coloured hose is a servant. He is wearing the livery of his master. There are several others among the throng of guests.

These two men in red with black stoles are high government officials called procurators. They worked closely with architects and engineers to ensure the historic preservation of St Mark's Basilica.

HANS HOLBEIN THE YOUNGER

The Ambassadors

1533

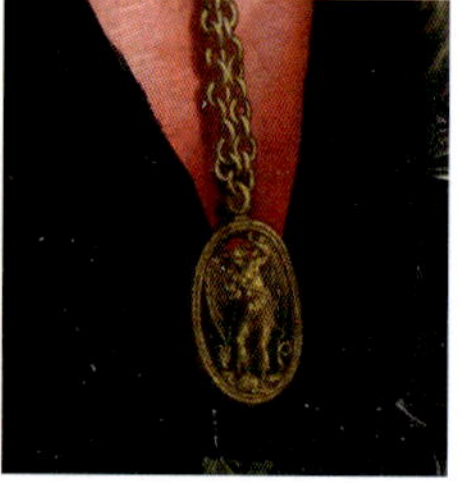

This is the Order of St Michael, the French equivalent to the English Order of the Garter. It was awarded to capable men in the hope of ensuring their devoted service to the throne.

Holbein's famous picture is full of ambiguities and symbols that still offer different interpretations to this day. It was painted at a time of religious upheaval in Europe. In 1533, the English king, Henry VIII, bypassed papal authority by secretly marrying his second wife, Anne Boleyn. He established the Church of England as independent from Rome and placed himself at its head. This break of religious and political ties with Catholic Europe was worrying for the French king, Francis I, who sent his ambassador Jean de Dinteville – the man on the left – to report on the situation. The other man is de Dinteville's close friend, Georges de Selve, Bishop of Lavaur. De Selve was also on a diplomatic mission, although its exact nature is unknown.

Holbein was a superlative artist. Every detail of de Dinteville's appearance is rendered to perfection: the folds in his pink satin doublet, the black velvet tunic, the coat lined with softest lynx fur and the tassel hanging from his dagger, every strand of which Holbein has picked out in gold. He has even brought de Selve's more sober clerical attire alive. The objects on the sideboard allude to their cultural, mathematical and scientific interests. The top shelf shows instruments used to measure time, altitude and the position of the stars. The lower shelf is devoted mainly to music: an exquisitely painted lute, a bag of flutes and an open hymnal. In the top left corner, almost hidden by the curtain, is a crucifix.

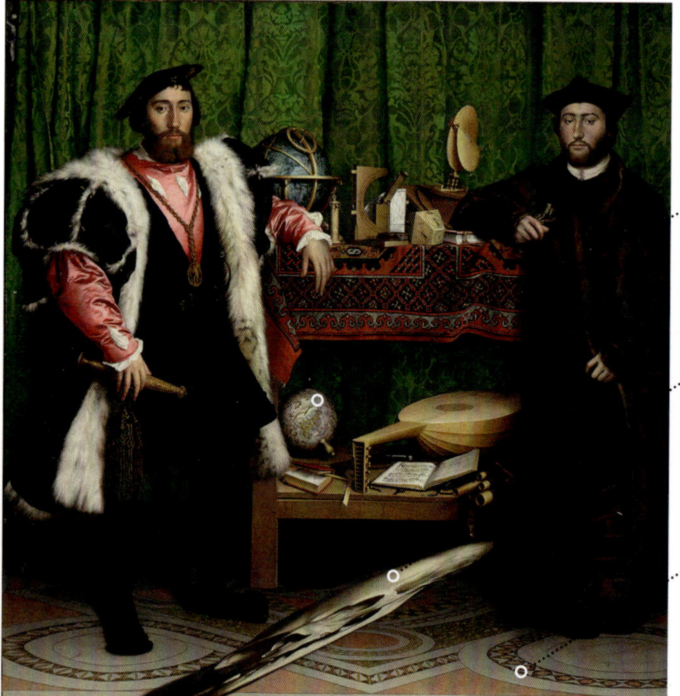

The globe is terrestrial and includes the hamlet of Polisy, about 200 km southeast of Paris, where de Dinteville had his chateau and where this painting was hung.

If viewed from the extreme right of the painting, this strange object reveals itself to be a large skull, a distorting effect called anamorphosis. Holbein has included it as a *memento mori*, a reminder of the brevity of life.

The beautiful medieval floor is based on the 'Cosmati' pavement in the sanctuary in Westminster Abbey. It was on this floor that Anne Boleyn was crowned Queen of England in the same year that this double portrait was painted.

SOFONISBA ANGUISSOLA

The Game of Chess

1555

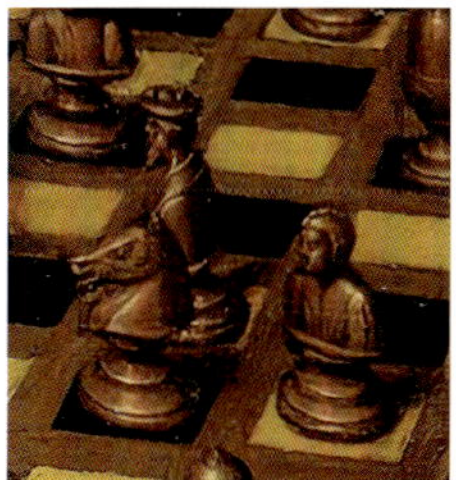

Luxury chess boards became common possessions among the elites and could even be incorporated into the design of gaming tables.

Over the course of the Renaissance the upper-class Italian house increasingly became a centre of social activity. Lavish entertainments, such as dinners, balls, recitals and theatrical performances, were held. Card games were very popular. Many such events saw the women taking a central role. While women taking part in games of chance was frowned upon, they were allowed to play games of skill like chess (*scacchi*).

Anguissola (*c.* 1532–1625) was born in Cremona in northern Italy to enlightened parents who gave their seven children a good education, including – most remarkably – their daughters. All the girls were taught to draw and paint, but it was forbidden for any woman to study a nude figure from life. Without this basic skill, it was difficult, if not impossible, for a woman to become a professional artist. But Anguissola overcame such obstacles and is today regarded as the most successful female artist of the Italian Renaissance. Her gentle, intimate, often humorous portraits earned her a place in Giorgio Vasari's *Lives of the Artists*. Her portraits, he wrote, are 'so lifelike that they lack only speech'.

In this image Anguissola has depicted three of her sisters, two of whom are playing chess. Accompanied by a maidservant, they have set up a table in the garden. Judging by her impish smile, the youngest sister, Europa, is enjoying the defeat of Minerva, on the right, by Lucia. Anguissola was only twenty-three when she painted this picture.

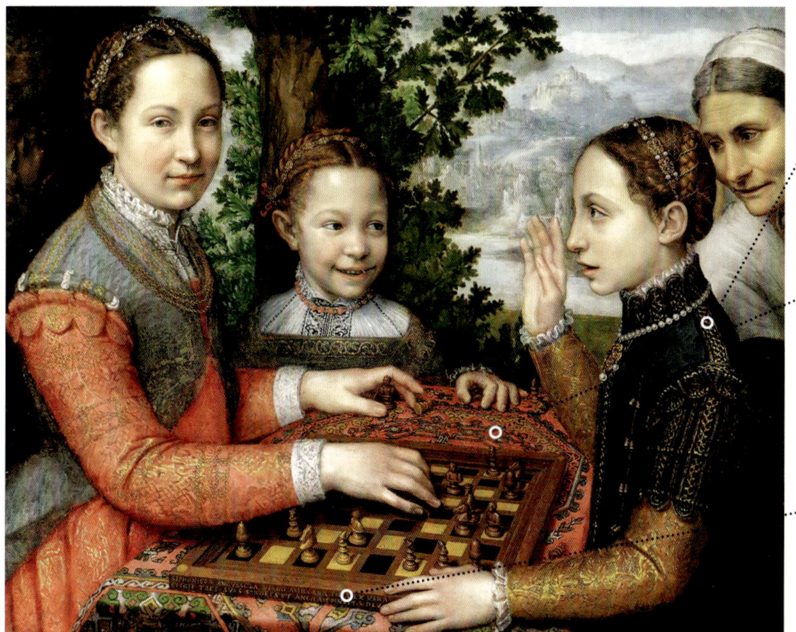

Anguissola has included a range of details that indicate her family's wealth and social status. All three sisters are wearing rich brocade dresses and their jewellery is made of gold or encrusted with pearls.

Venice had been importing carpets from the Middle East since at least the fourteenth century. This luxurious example is being used to cover a table rather than on the floor – another sign of the high status of the Anguissola family.

The artist signed her name along the edge of the chess board, adding the Latin term *ex vera* (from the truth), which suggests she painted the scene from life.

PIETER BRUEGEL THE ELDER

Hunters in the Snow

c. 1565

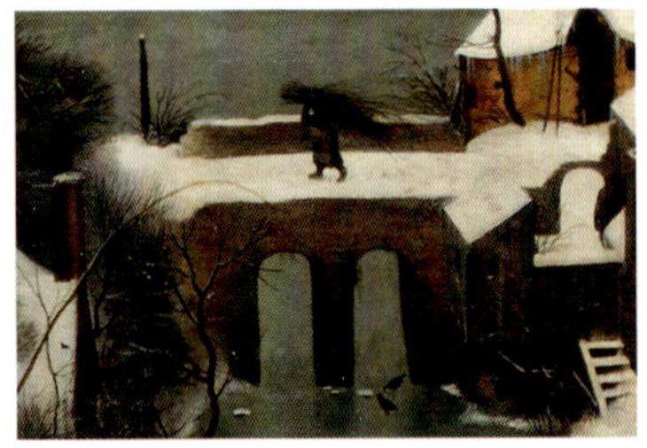

This woman, weighed down with a bundle of kindling on her back, is fulfilling one of the most urgent tasks of any householder in such weather.

Bruegel has skilfully manipulated the perspective of this painting so that the viewer enters the image *with* the tired, dejected hunters and their pack of dogs. As they thread their way through the trees and breast the rise, the village and the vast, snow-clad panorama opens up before them. Apart from the distant, muted cries of the people at play, a deep silence seems to pervade the scene. Yet there is so much going on: some sixty minute figures are skating, curling or playing ice hockey on the frozen lakes or going about their daily tasks, despite a lowering sky, pregnant with snow. At this date houses were so dark inside that people lived their lives outdoors, whatever the weather. The only colours in the scene are the russet coats of the hounds and the fire being stoked, possibly to roast a pig as winter was the season when pigs were slaughtered.

Bruegel's understanding of a landscape under snow came from experience, as he created the painting between 1564 and 1565, one of the hardest winters on record. Mountains in Belgium, one of the flattest countries in Europe, are entirely implausible. But Bruegel had crossed the Alps on his way to Italy and here he has recreated their appearance from sketches he made at the time.

Hunters in the Snow belongs to a series representing the months of the year. Bruegel painted only six of the months, but possibly intended to do all twelve. They are among the great landscape paintings of the age. The only landscapes previously had been in miniature form, such as the *Très Riches Heures du duc de Berry* (see page 118).

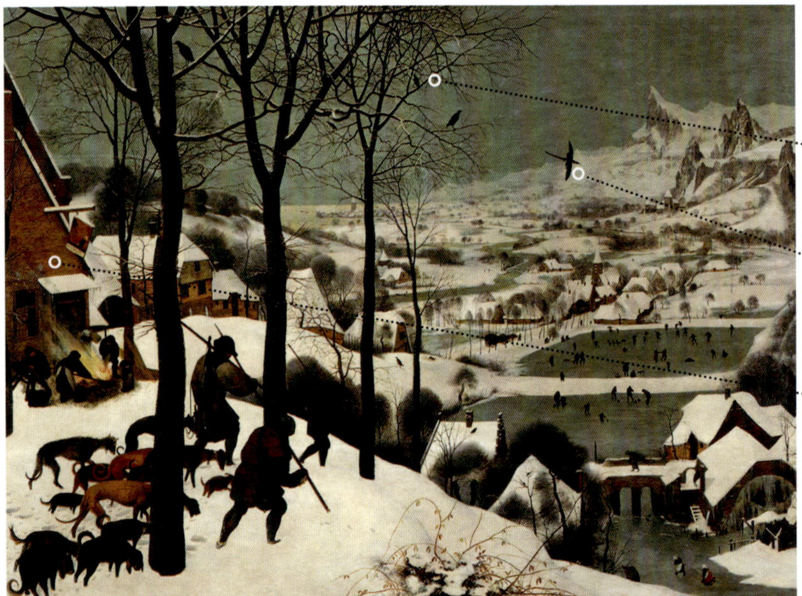

The several large black birds perched watchfully in the leafless trees add an ominous note to the scene.

This magpie, silhouetted against the snowy mountains, was associated with the Devil in Dutch culture.

Taverns were places of ill repute. They were for people passing through, like travelling salesman. The local, respectable townsfolk avoided them. The broken sign adds to the unsavoury, run-down atmosphere of the place.

GEORGES DE LA TOUR

The Card Sharp with the Ace of Diamonds

c. 1635–40

One glance at the boy on the right and it is at once apparent that he is in trouble, although he is blissfully unaware of it. Judging by his clothes, he is clearly of noble blood and he has gone out on the town, confident that he is smart enough to deal with any situation that arises. His rounded chin and chubby cheeks indicate that he is about fifteen years old and thus considered to be an adult by his contemporaries. He has dressed to impress: his jerkin is of pearl-grey satin, richly embroidered in gold and silver; his cravat and shoulder bands are of scarlet silk; the cuffs of his white shirtsleeves are trimmed with braided gold; his gleaming brown curls are topped off with a flamboyant ostrich feather.

But he is in bad company – or has been lured into it. He seems oblivious to the covert glances, the play of hands, as the other three plot his downfall. Judging by the piles of gold coins, they are playing for high stakes. Not only will the boy be fleeced of all he has – perhaps even his clothes – but the fleecers, if caught, might lose a thumb, a whole hand, or, at the worst, face execution. For the boy it is also a risky game: if he realises what his companions are up to, the rules of society dictate that he must draw his sword and fight them. So he may end up having to pay for his arrogance with his life.

Although normally associated with pious nocturnal subjects (see page 73), La Tour painted several cautionary tales of young men being cheated. One of his most famous paintings, *The Fortune Teller*, shows a youth being robbed while he has his fortune told.

The card sharp is trying to substitute the ace of diamonds for one of the low-denomination cards he holds in full view.

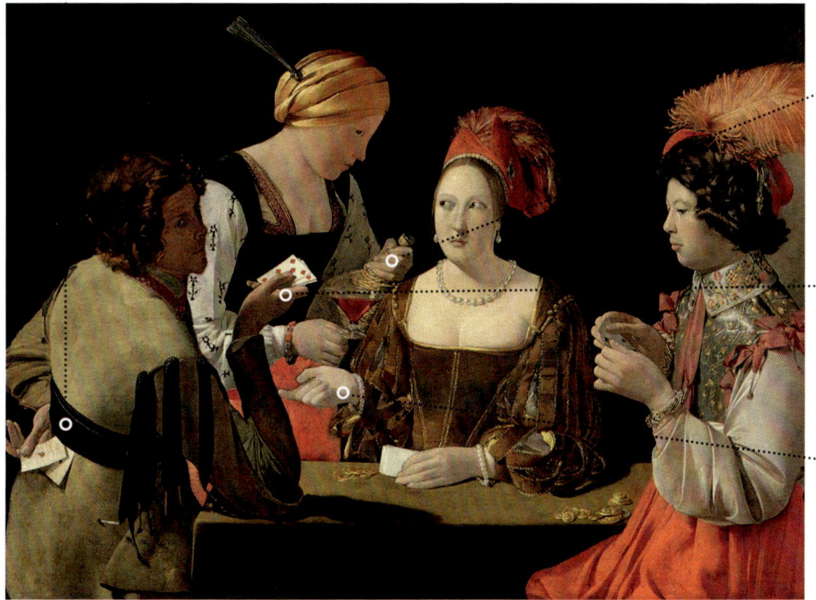

The maid is pouring wine into a Venetian crystal glass. In La Tour's native Lorraine, wine was a supplement to meagre victuals: one or two litres a day were considered normal.

To the skilful man with good nerves, card-sharping was a good way to make money. But a pack of cards was popularly known as 'the devil's prayer-book'.

This woman's hand is signalling to the man that he should play the ace of diamonds. As can be seen by the cards in her other hand, cards did not yet have printed backs.

JAN STEEN

The Burgher of Delft and his Daughter

1655

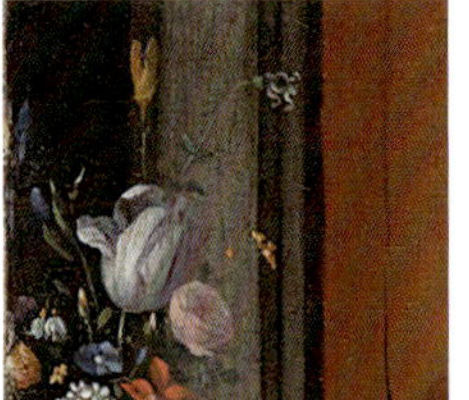

Tulips frequently featured in Dutch flower paintings. They had been brought to the Netherlands from Constantinople in the seventeenth century. Their arrival caused 'tulip mania', during which fortunes were won and lost.

Recent research has established that the commanding figure seated on the *stoep* of his house is not the burgher of the title but the wealthy corn merchant Adolf Croeser. That Steen was inclined to use people from his own milieu as models, and that he actually lived opposite Croeser on the Oude Delft, aided the identification. The girl is Croeser's thirteen-year-old daughter, Catharina, the only one to survive out of the five children his first wife gave birth to before she herself died. The *stilleven* (still life) of flowers on the windowsill is probably a reference to the wife's death and also symbolises the transience of life.

A *stoep* was a popular addition to a house: it encouraged conversation with the neighbours and was also a good place to transact business, although on occasion it rendered the householder vulnerable to unwanted approaches. Croeser seems to be contemplating giving money to the old lady and her little boy, but the prim and proper Catharina appears to be hurrying away. She holds up her underskirts daintily and the manner in which she carries her fan indicates that she has been taught courtly deportment as dictated by the etiquette books of the period.

Jan Steen (1626–79) was a prolific and versatile artist. His subjects often depict scenes from every day life. In 1657, just two years after this portrait was painted, Croeser stood surety for Steen, who was seriously in debt.

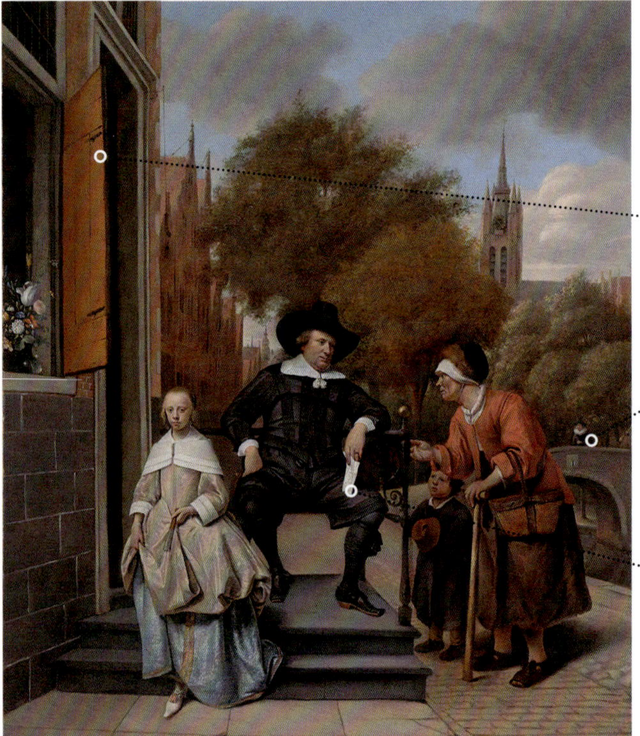

The red shutters are still a feature of Delft today. The town has changed very little since the time of Vermeer and Jan Steen.

Steen has located his subject precisely. This is the west bank of the Oude Delft canal. The man wearing a stiff ruff is crossing the canal by a bridge. In the background is the Oude Kerk Church.

The paper Croeser holds may be the old lady's licence to beg for alms. Every town had to be on its guard against itinerant tramps such as discharged mercenaries, landless peasants or criminals fleeing justice.

FRANÇOIS BOUCHER

The Breakfast

1739

At first glance, this appears to be a perfectly normal scene of two women, a man and two small children having breakfast together – a repast that was said to have been invented by the French. But with this painting Boucher is recording several major developments in the way in which a wealthy bourgeois family lived in early eighteenth-century France.

Apartments were changing: instead of one room leading into the next, there were corridors with smaller rooms leading off them. Glass was cheaper now, so people could afford large mirrors and windows that made the rooms feel lighter and more extensive. Small fireplaces kept rooms warmer. Rooms had specific uses, such as the dining room, the salon, the bedroom and the boudoir. These cosy rooms were more private and encouraged a growing sense of family.

It is thought that the woman in the white morning gown may be Boucher's wife. She was known to be very beautiful and often modelled for him. The children, too, may be Boucher's, as they are the right age. It is remarkable that they are with their mother: some 80 per cent of children were sent at birth to wet nurses in the country and remained there for several years. The way both the mother and the nurse are paying loving attention to the children is also highly unusual. The children even have toys to play with. This was the era when the nuclear family was born and Boucher was one of the first artists to record it.

This young man is not the husband, as he is wearing an apron, but has probably just delivered breakfast. At this date, drinks like coffee, tea and hot chocolate were more likely to be brewed in the local public house than in the home.

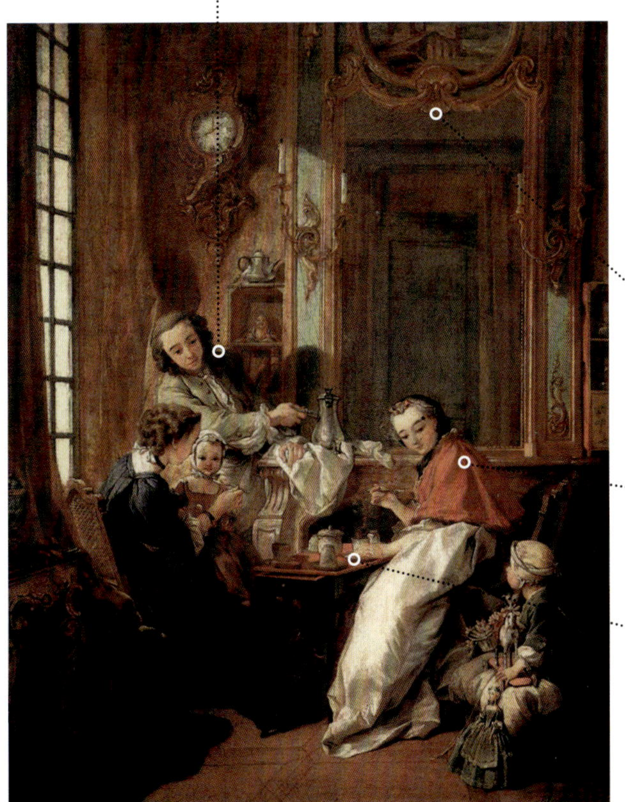

The scallop shell was a decorative motif throughout the rococo era. Boucher has used one here to link the landscape to the mirror. Venus stepped out of scallops in many of his paintings.

The mother is still wearing her négligé and red make-up cape. The hairdresser will arrive after breakfast to powder and dress her hair.

The mother's delicate cup and saucer appear to be decorated with a Chinese motif. Very few people could afford porcelain, as it had to be imported from China. The Sèvres china factory was not founded until 1740.

THOMAS GAINSBOROUGH

Mr and Mrs Andrews

c. 1750

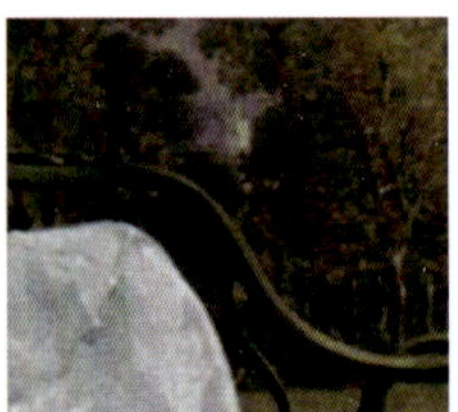

This is All Saints Church in Sudbury where the couple were married. Robert was twenty and Frances barely seventeen years old at the time.

Although, strictly speaking, this is a portrait – commissioned and paid for as such – the inclusion of Mr Andrews' spreading acres and the information it gives about farming practices in the mid-eighteenth century adds a narrative aspect to the painting. It is the masterpiece of Gainsborough's early career.

The picture celebrates the coming together in marriage of two local families, the Andrews and the Carters, to ensure the cohesion of an extensive property near Sudbury in Suffolk. Both Gainsborough and Robert Andrews were natives of the town and had been to school together. With his muzzle-loading shotgun under his arm, bags of powder and shot dangling from his pocket, and his devoted gun dog at his feet, Robert looks very proprietorial, not only of his wife but of his acres. His wife, Frances, sitting bolt upright, looks a trifle dyspeptic. Wearing a blue silk gown over hooped pale-yellow petticoats, she is hardly dressed for the country.

The woods, meadows and fields belong to their estate. The stubble reveals the modern practice of 46cm-wide planting. Robert was a good farmer: the famous agriculturist Arthur Young, a native of Sudbury, asserted that Robert's 'husbandry is excellent'. The sheaves and ripe ears of corn are fitting fertility symbols for a wedding portrait. Gainsborough (1727–88) earned a healthy income from painting portraits – referring to his profession as 'picking pockets in the portrait way' – but what he always longed for was to take up his 'Viol da Gamba and walk off to some sweet Village where I can paint Landskips ...'.

An oak tree symbolises stability and continuity. This particular tree was measured in 1786 by Young and found to be nearly 3.4 m in circumference. It was still flourishing in 2017.

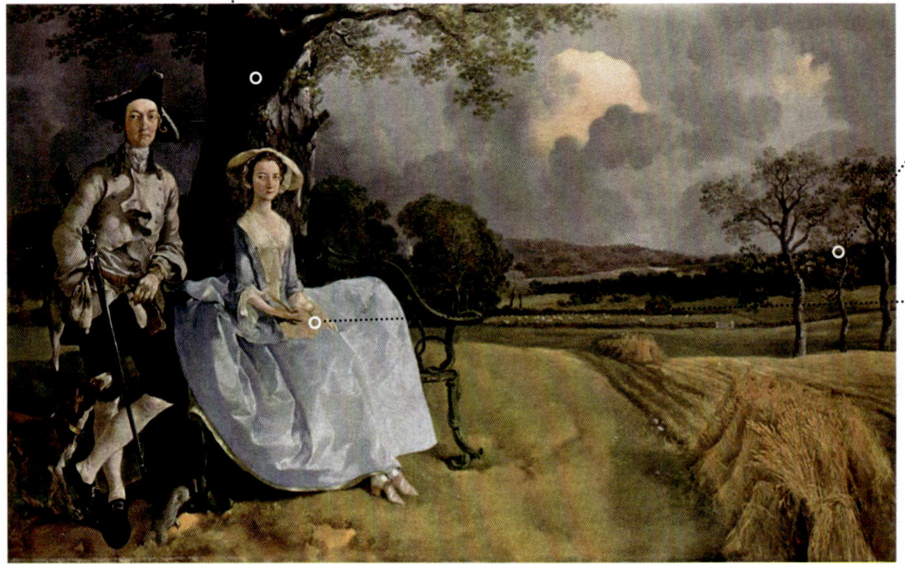

For those who see symbols everywhere, the small tree between the two larger trees is said to stand for the hoped-for son and heir.

This blank in Frances's lap has long been a source of speculation. Is that the tail of a dead pheasant, shot by Robert? Some scholars think Gainsborough reserved the space for a baby. The first one of eight arrived after this portrait was painted.

JOHAN ZOFFANY

Tribuna of the Uffizi

1772–77

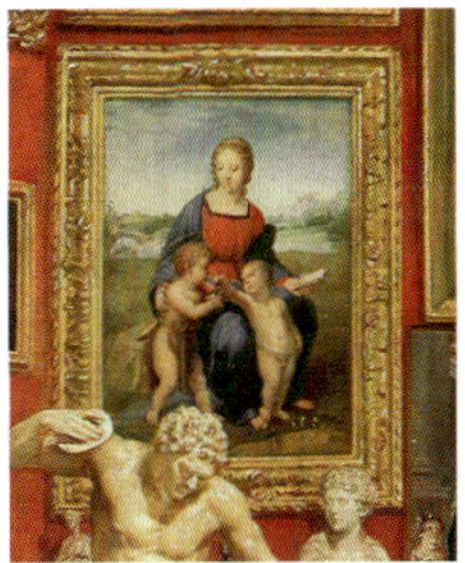

Faithfully copied by Zoffany, Raphael's **Madonna of the Goldfinch** *is just one of five paintings by the artist in the Tribuna. A detail of the Christ Child holding the goldfinch can be seen on page 141.*

In 1772 German-born Zoffany (1733–1810) set off from London for Florence with a commission in his pocket from the Queen of England to paint the highlights of the Duke of Tuscany's collection, which was housed in the Tribuna at the very heart of the Uffizi Palace. If he had kept to the commission, all would have been well, but for some reason Zoffany chose to add numerous people, some of whom were youthful Grand Tourists and not worth including.

Unfortunately, George III and Queen Charlotte were not pleased to have some of the most revered works of art in the world cluttered up with travelling Englishmen, a view that was foreseen by Sir Horace Mann, the British Consul in Florence. Mann had been *en poste* for years and knew everybody and everything that went on in Italy, much of which he communicated in letters to his close friend, the politician, writer and historian Horace Walpole. 'The one-eyed German, Zoffany' (Mann is alluding to the artist's squint) has 'too much crouded' the painting with spectators he told Walpole. Apparently, the king's response was: 'The Queen wd. not suffer the picture to be placed in any of her apartments.' Zoffany never worked for the royal family again. Later, he made a fortune in India painting the English and the native princes.

This painting remains a painstakingly accurate record of the fabulous works of art housed in the Tribuna in the eighteenth century.

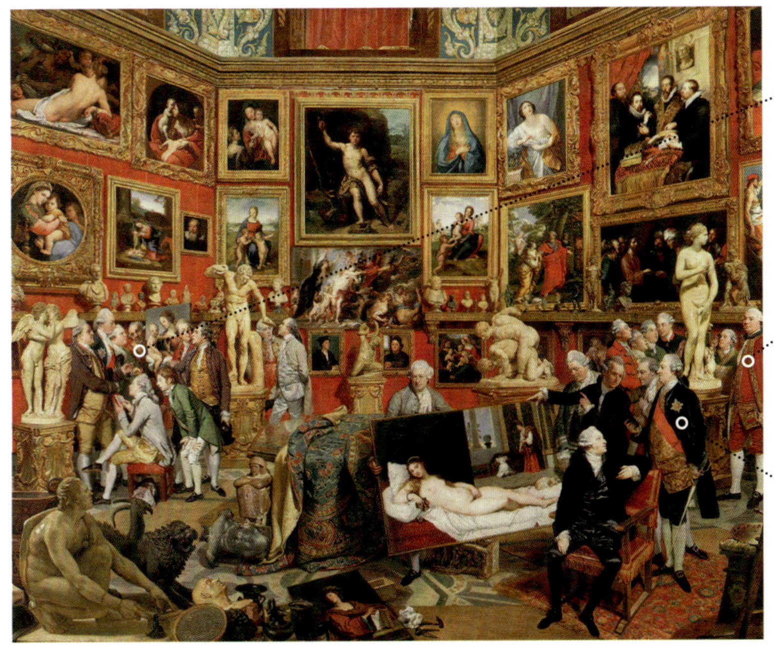

Although barely visible, this is Zoffany. He is surrounded by Grand Tourists and connoisseurs, all contemplating a *Madonna and Child* by Raphael. The boy in green is Richard Edgcumbe, sent abroad aged thirteen.

The group of men closely examining the *Medici Venus* consists of connoisseurs and Grand Tourists. The large man in red on the extreme right is the famous African explorer James Bruce.

The imperious and portly figure with his toes turned out is Sir Horace Mann. He is discussing Titian's *Venus of Urbino* with his friend, the artist and caricaturist Thomas Patch.

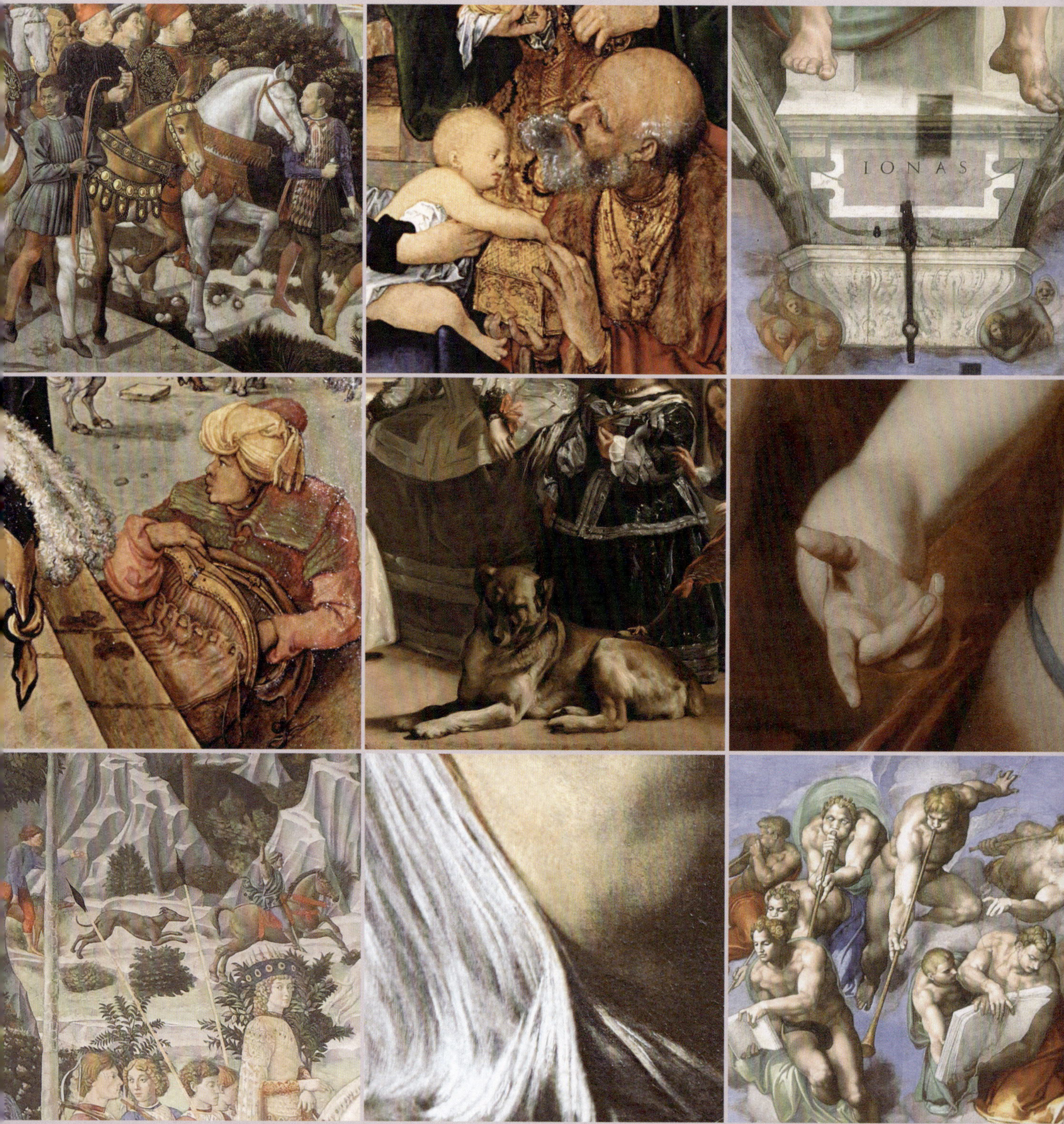
IONAS

CHAPTER TEN

ENTER THE ARTIST

Artists paint themselves for several reasons: for self-promotion, to save paying a model, to show their skill, for practise. Rembrandt depicted himself with various facial expressions, such as laughing, open-mouthed and frowning. Caravaggio's particularly gruesome self-portrait was a plea for his life. One artist's self-portrait went undiscovered for centuries. Others use their likeness to masquerade as a character from history or the Bible. In some paintings, the face looking out of the crowd is doubling as a signature: 'Here I am. I painted this.'

BENOZZO GOZZOLI

The Procession of the Magi

1459–63

Today the practice of taking selfies has become such an obsession that it has been dubbed a 'culture of narcissism'. Artists, however, have been painting themselves from time immemorial. Better and cheaper mirrors facilitated the genre. Rembrandt painted nearly eighty self-portraits in his lifetime. This chapter is not about self-portraits per se but about artists who have smuggled themselves into a commissioned work. In a group scene they are frequently the only individual who is looking straight out of the painting at the viewer – as if to catch their eye. Some artists hide themselves in very unexpected places. Others use their likeness to portray a legendary figure, like Jan van Eyck who is thought to have painted himself as St Luke, the patron saint of artists.

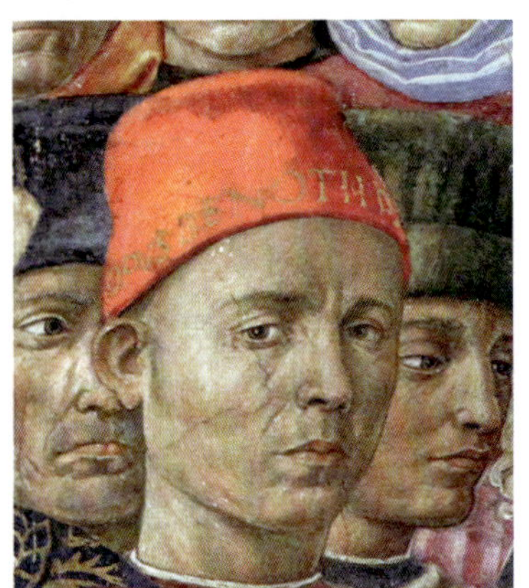

Gozzoli (*c.* 1420–97) covered three sides of the Medici family chapel with a series of frescoes, each wall depicting one of the three kings accompanied by his train of servants. Confronted with depicting hundreds of different faces, it was understandable if Gozzoli made use of some of his friends and acquaintances as models. And there, amid the youngest king's retinue, is Gozzoli himself. To ensure that he is recognised, he is not only looking out of the picture but has carefully inscribed his name on the brim of his red hat.

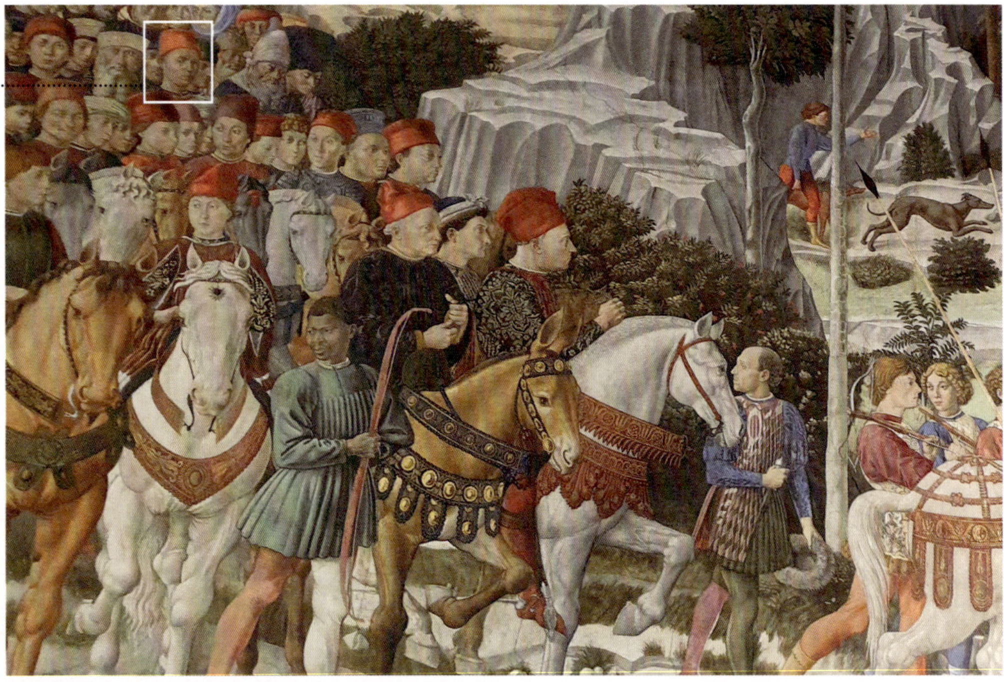

ALBRECHT DÜRER

The Adoration of the Magi

1504

In this painting Dürer takes centre stage as one of the three kings. Festooned with jewels and wearing a fabulous cape over emerald green sleeves, he has removed his fur hat to reveal the full glory of his luxurious hair. It is the hair more than any other feature that identifies him. It had appeared to full effect in the most famous of his self-portraits, painted in 1500, in which he is looking straight at the viewer, his bronze ringlets cascading to his shoulders. (It is said that the ringlets had to be waved and curled every day.) It is a mesmerising, almost Christ-like image and confirms him as the most celebrated and inventive painter of self-portraits during the Renaissance.

Dürer has set the scene against a background of architectural ruins that are based on ones he had seen during his visit to Italy. As is so often the case, Joseph is nowhere to be seen. The Virgin Mary, who holds the Christ Child out to the oldest king, is more substantial and matronly than the slender and beautiful Madonnas so beloved by Renaissance artists. The cow looks fat and peaceful but the donkey is in full bray. The gentleman in a turban, seated below the steps, could be a servant to one of the kings and is perhaps carrying more gifts in his voluminous bag. But why the enormous stag beetle on the steps on the right?

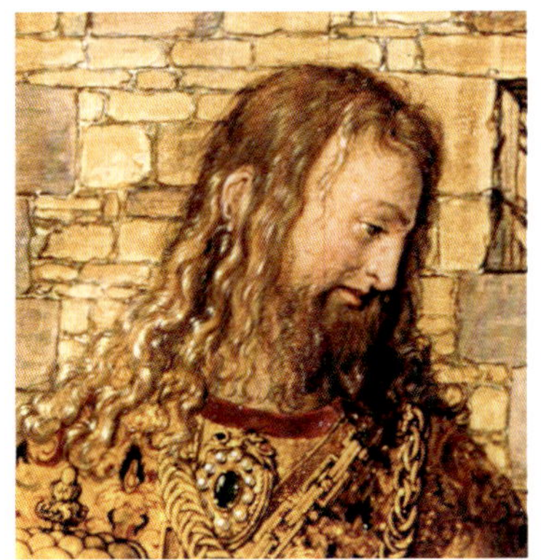

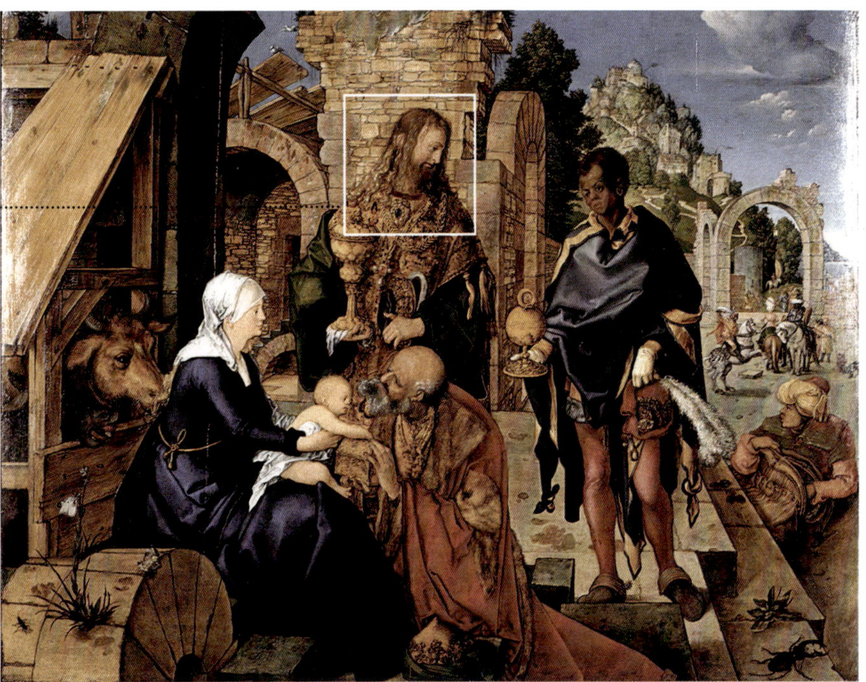

MICHELANGELO

The Last Judgement, Sistine Chapel, Rome (detail)

1536–41

In late 1533, Pope Clement VII persuaded Michelangelo to paint a huge new mural depicting *The Last Judgement* on the wall above the altar in the Sistine Chapel. Clement died soon afterwards and the pope who was to see this great project completed was Paul III. At the age of sixty-two, Michelangelo was reluctant to cover a vast surface of *c.* 167 sqm with frescoes. The scaffolding alone must have been some seven storeys high. This formidable task was to take Michelangelo over five years to complete.

At the centre of the mighty fresco is Christ, his arm raised as he judges who to consign to heaven and who to hell. Most of the figures were very scantily clad, many of them stark naked. Just below and to the right of Christ is St Bartholomew, who was martyred by being flayed alive. Dangling from his left hand, directly over the abyss, is his skin on which is painted the most astonishing image: the anguished features and broken nose of Michelangelo himself. This enigmatic self-portrait remained unnoticed for centuries. When the fresco was unveiled it caused a sensation. Opinion was divided. It was eventually decreed that some of the figures were indecent and should be covered up. The addition to the nudes' nether regions of wisps of cloth, underpants and jockstraps continued until the 1760s.

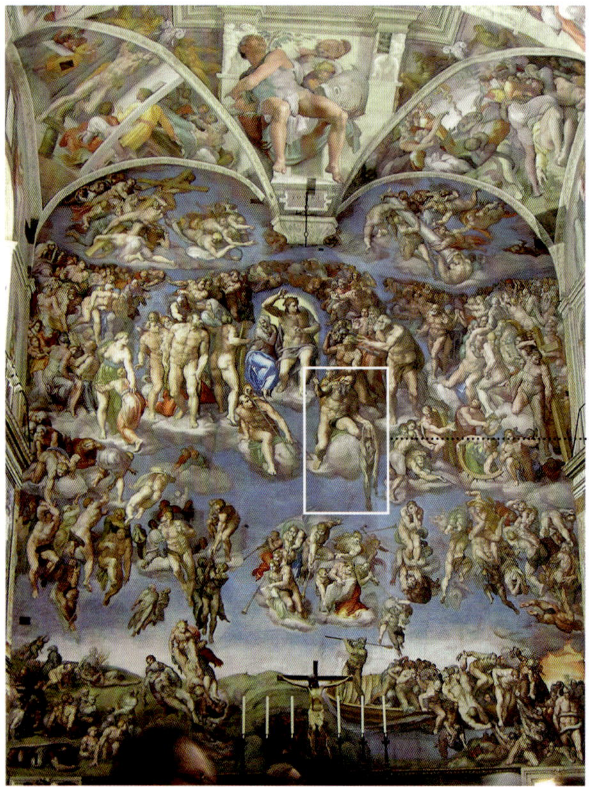

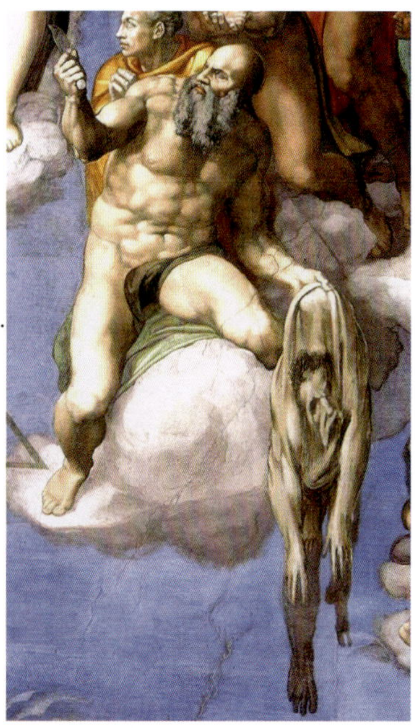

DIEGO VELÁSQUEZ

Las Meninas

1656

The painting shows an artist poised with his brush and palette before an enormous canvas, its back turned frustratingly to the viewer. The location is the studio in the palace at Madrid that the Spanish king, Philip IV, gave the artist when he became Court Painter in 1623. In the centre of the painting is the little Infanta Margarita, flanked by two *meninas* (maids of honour), her tutors, page, dwarf and a large dozing mastiff. But, if Margarita is having her portrait painted, why is she standing beside the artist and not in front of him?

The artist, of course, is Velásquez (1599–1660) who has portrayed himself splendidly attired in a silk doublet. The red cross pinned to his breast signifies his posthumous knighthood and was added later. A mirror on the rear wall shows Philip, accompanied by his wife Mariana, caught in the act of visiting the artist. Or are they? What if the royal couple were in front of Velásquez – where the viewer is standing – and the mirror reflects them posing for their double portrait? This would explain why the Infanta is beside Velásquez: she is watching him paint her parents. Or is she? This is Velásquez's only known self-portrait, and it is posing puzzling questions to this day.

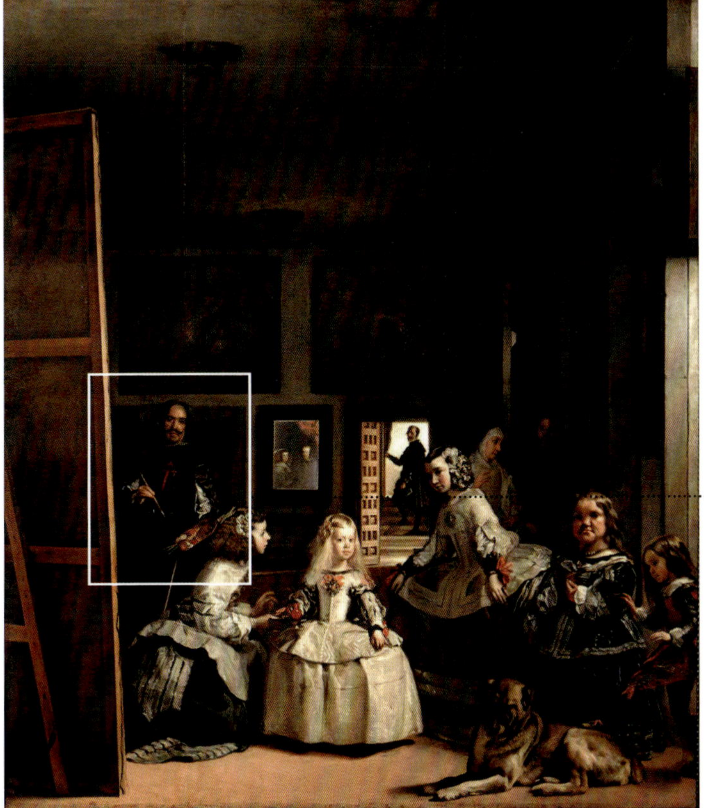

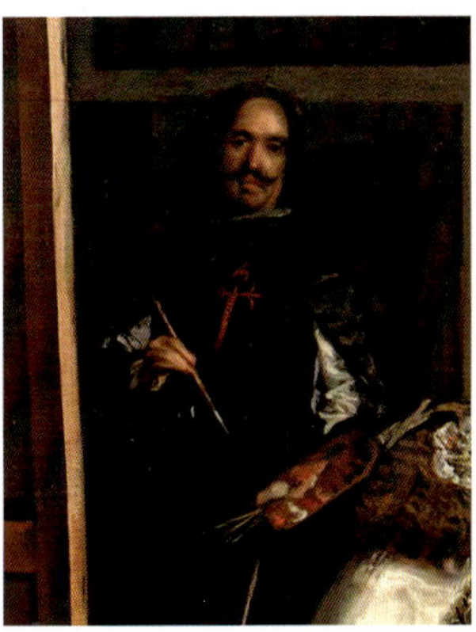

CARAVAGGIO

David with the Head of Goliath

1606

This shocking image was painted in Naples a few months after Caravaggio had killed a man in a duel and had fled from Rome. The Papal Authority had declared a *bando capitale* (capital sentence) on the artist that allowed anyone to take his life and collect a reward on presentation of his head. It is thought that Caravaggio created this picture as a plea to Cardinal Scipione Borghese, an avid art collector, an admirer of Caravaggio's work and the only man who had the power to pardon the artist's crime. Since the head of the Philistine general Goliath is a self-portrait of Caravaggio, his message to Borghese is clear: pardon me or the severed head will be mine.

Caravaggio had painted several self-portraits during his career, including a queasy Bacchus and, in 1598, a monstrous Medusa, the head a mass of writhing snakes. For Caravaggio to paint a portrait of his own head, dripping with blood, and with eyes that still retain some signs of life, is evidence of a very desperate state of mind. He was a convicted murderer, in exile, longing to return to Rome.

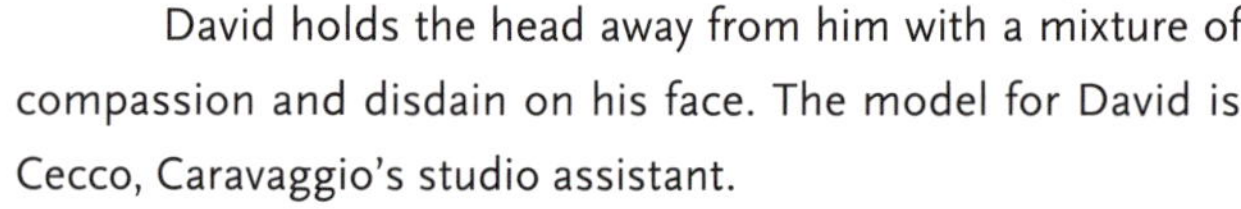

David holds the head away from him with a mixture of compassion and disdain on his face. The model for David is Cecco, Caravaggio's studio assistant.

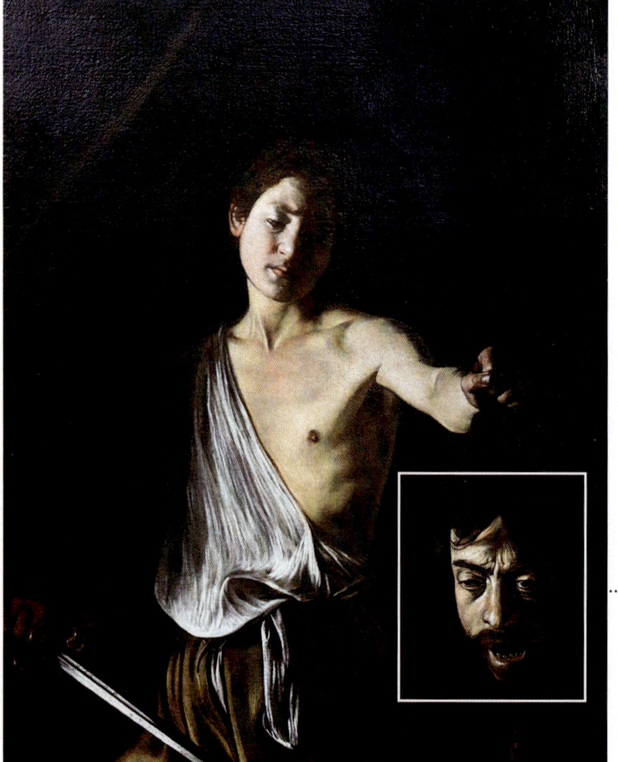

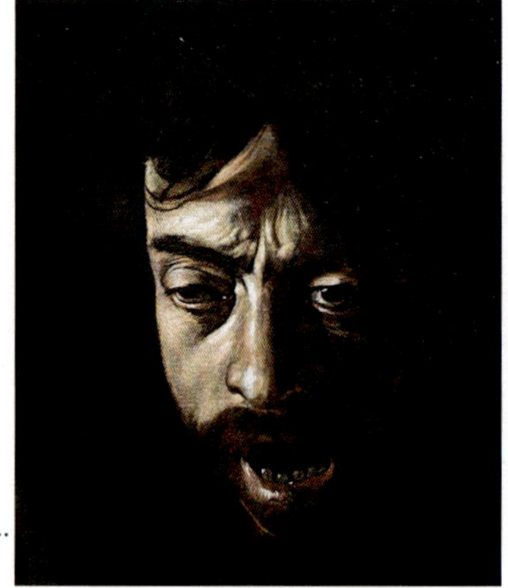

ANTHONY VAN DYCK

Daedalus and Icarus

1615–25

In the sixteenth and seventeenth centuries, there was a fashion for paintings that were based on episodes from myths or religious stories. In this unusual image, this fresh-faced youth with the golden curls is Van Dyck himself, playing the part of Icarus. In the Greek myth (told on page 93), Daedalus, the father of Icarus, fashioned wings of beeswax and feathers that he then attached to his son's back to enable him to fly. Daedalus is pointing to the sky but the boy is not heeding his father's warnings to avoid going too close to the sun; he is confident that he knows better.

Several artists have tackled this subject, and the same blue ribbon features in a surprising number of their paintings. Why is the ribbon blue, and why fix heavy wings in such a rudimentary fashion?

During the course of his career Van Dyck painted a series of self-portraits, although not as many as Rembrandt, who was possibly subjecting himself to painful self-examination. In Van Dyck's case it was said that he painted himself out of pure vanity. The date of this painting is vague, but the young artist may have been on the cusp of embarking for London where he would become painter to James I, King of England.

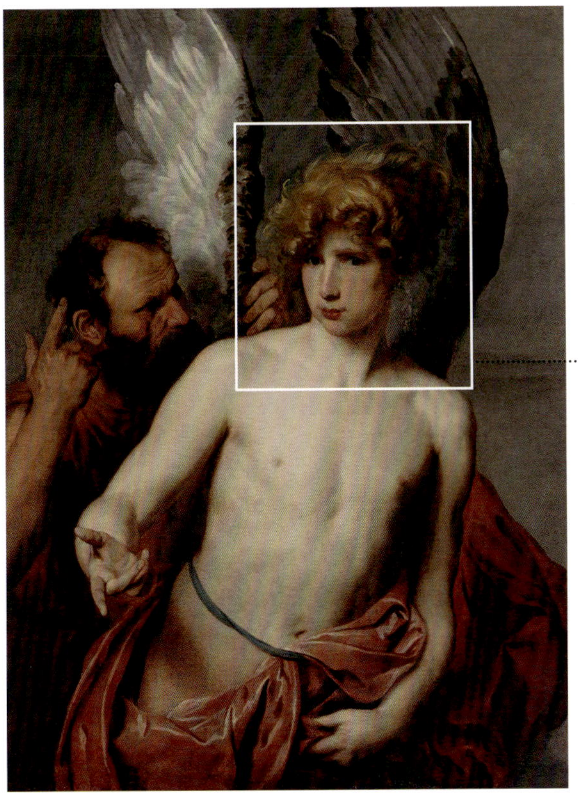

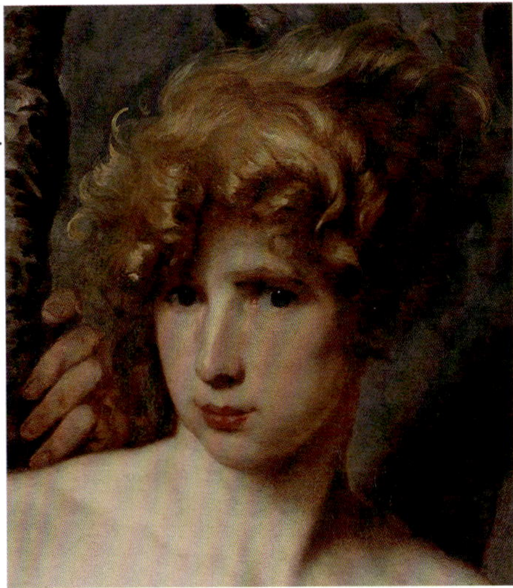

GLOSSARY

A SELECTION OF THE MOST COMMON SYMBOLS AND ATTRIBUTES

The choice of symbols has been restricted to those used by European artists in their paintings and to those that appear in this book.

Angels Messengers of God; intermediaries between God and man, heaven and this world. There are nine choirs of angels: Seraphim, Cherubim, Thrones, Dominions, Virtues, Powers, Principalities, Archangels, Angels.

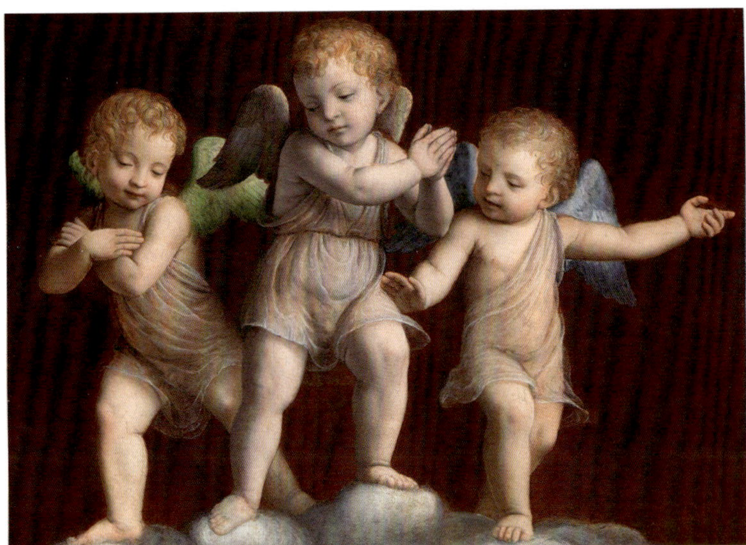

Angels: Bernardino Luini, *Three Angels on Clouds*, *c.* 1515–18

Apple Eve ate the forbidden fruit from the Tree of Knowledge in the Garden of Eden. Although the fruit is not specified in the Bible, it was taken to be an apple, perhaps because *malus* is Latin for both apple and evil. An apple thus represents original sin and the Fall of Man. However, if held by the Christ Child it signifies salvation and redemption.

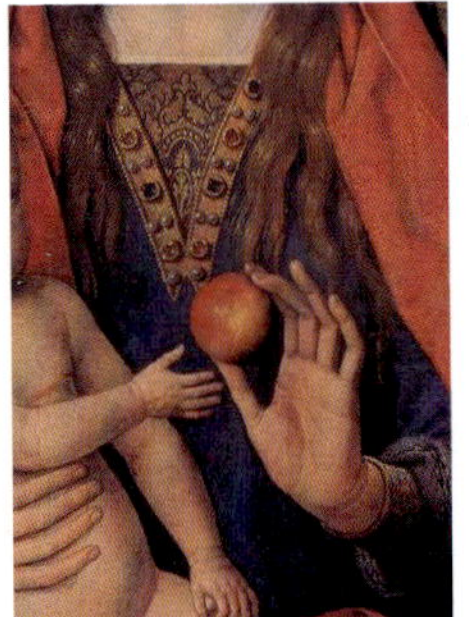

Apple: Hans Memling, *Diptych of Maarten Nieuwenhove*, 1487 (detail)

Archangel The order of angels that most frequently interact with humanity. The three most important ones are: Michael, messenger of divine judgement, who is depicted with a sword or a pair of scales with which he weighs the souls on Judgement Day; Gabriel, messenger of divine mercy, holds a lily at the Annunciation; Raphael is particularly associated with healing.

Book An attribute that represents intelligence and the contemplative life. In portraits, it is a sign that the sitter is educated and learned. The Virgin Mary is often reading a book at the Annunciation.

Butterfly: Antonio Pisanello, *A Princess of the House of Este*, 1433 (detail)

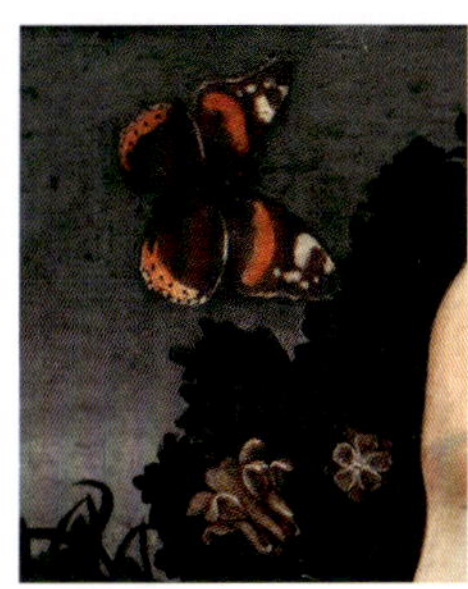

Butterfly Because the caterpillar transforms itself into a pupa, then a butterfly, it symbolises life, death and resurrection. It can also be a symbol of the resurrected human soul. Butterflies sometimes appear in still-life paintings as a reminder of the transience of life.

Candle The eternal light that burns in churches symbolises the presence of God or the Holy Ghost. A recently snuffed-out candle can also signify that God is present. A lit candle can refer to the transience of life.

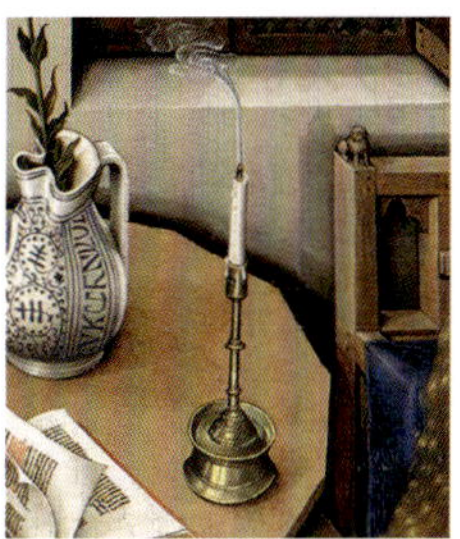

Candle: Robert Campin, *The Mérode Triptych*, *c.* 1427–32 (detail)

Carnation A symbol of Christ since its Greek name, *dianthus*, means 'the flower of god'. Red ones refer to a betrothal or marriage, and are also symbolic of maternal or compassionate love as they were said to grow on the ground where the Virgin Mary's tears fell at the Crucifixion. Three red carnations together recall the three nails with which Christ was hammered to the cross. The carnation's symbolism, although changed, has survived into the present day. (See page 53.)

Cat A symbol of satanic mischief, lust, darkness and laziness. Cats are not mentioned once in the Bible. In art, they feature as mediators between the human and animal kingdom.

Cat: William Hogarth, *The Graham Children*, 1742 (detail)

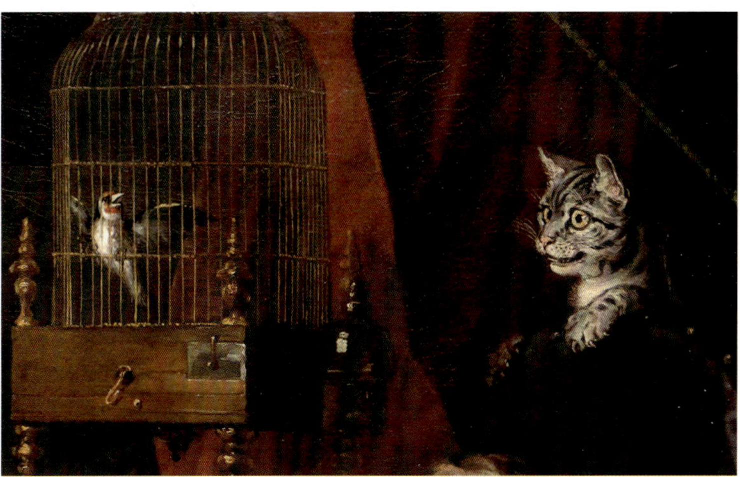

Cherry Called the Fruit of Paradise, they are given as a reward for virtuousness. They also symbolise heaven. In paintings, they are sometimes held by the Christ Child.

Columbine It was so named because the flower was thought to resemble doves in flight. Hence, the flower is a symbol of the Holy Ghost. Seven blue columbines are symbolic of the Seven Sorrows of Mary.

Corn The combination of wheat and grapes is symbolic of the bread and wine of the Eucharist, which themselves symbolise the body and blood of Christ's sacrifice. A sheaf of wheat is a reference to Bethlehem, as the name means 'house of bread'.

Crane These long-legged wading birds symbolise vigilance. It was believed that in a group of cranes one would act as a sentry, keeping itself awake by holding a stone in its claw; if it dozed off, it would be woken by the sound of the stone dropping.

Deer Represented in art as ethereal, mystical creatures. In Greco-Roman myth they are an attribute of Diana the Huntress.

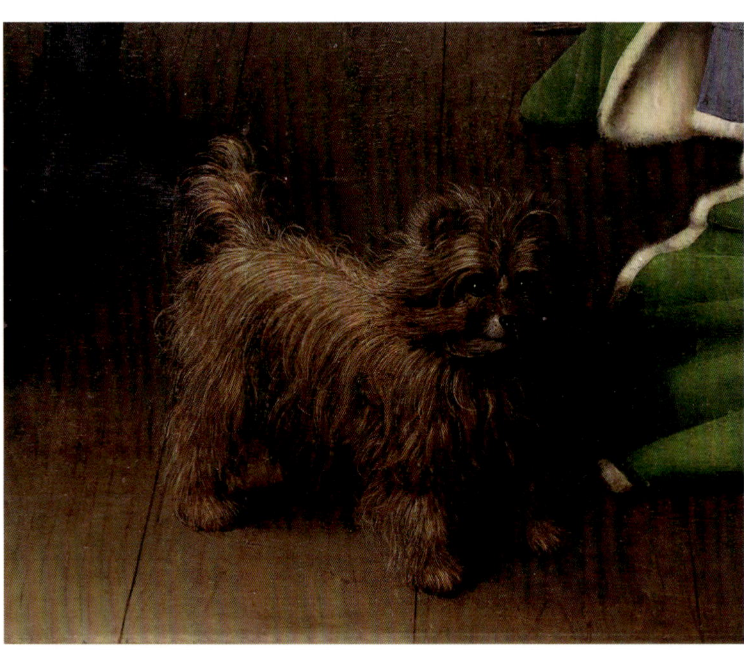

Dog: Jan van Eyck, *The Arnolfini Portrait*, 1434 (detail)

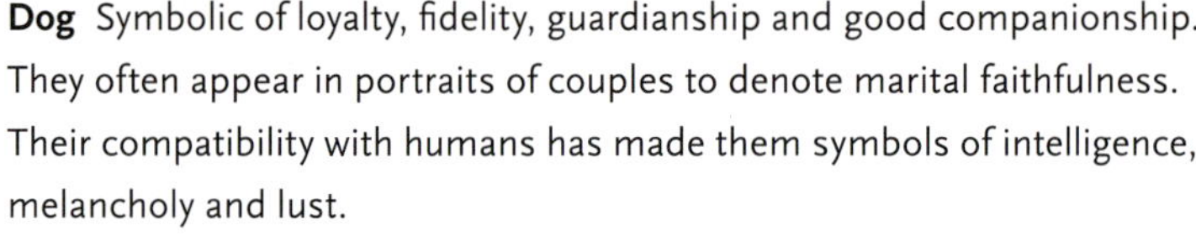

Dog Symbolic of loyalty, fidelity, guardianship and good companionship. They often appear in portraits of couples to denote marital faithfulness. Their compatibility with humans has made them symbols of intelligence, melancholy and lust.

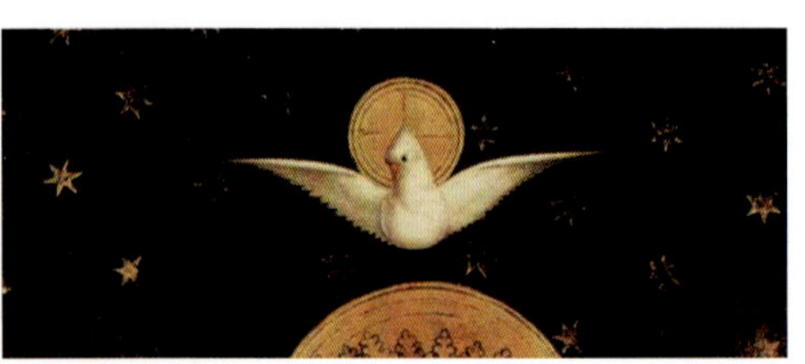

Dove: Anonymous, *Madonna on a Crescent Moon in Hortus Conclusus*, 1450 (detail)

Dove One of Christianity's oldest symbols. Associated with positive qualities like purity, peace and the human soul. A divine messenger. In later Christian iconology, the dove became a symbol of the Holy Spirit or Holy Ghost and thus makes up the third part of the Holy Trinity. The dove sent out by Noah returned to the Ark with an olive branch in its beak, signifying a new peace between God and man (see page 51). An attribute of Venus.

Dragon A symbol of Satan. *Draco* in Latin means both dragon and snake (or serpent), hence the two are sometimes interchangeable. It is slain by Archangel Michael and St George, among others. A dragon chained or trodden underfoot symbolises the conquest of evil.

Eagle Symbol of power and supreme leadership. It was represented on the standards of the Roman legions. Sacred to Jupiter and his attribute. Also the attribute of St John the Evangelist.

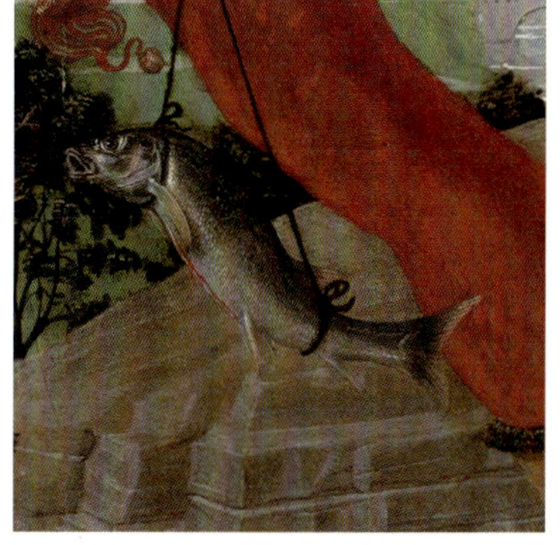

Fish An early symbol of Christianity because the Greek word for fish, *ichthus,* forms the initial letters Jesus, CHristos, THeou Uios, Soter (Jesus Christ, Son of God, Saviour). Christ's Apostles are called the 'fishers of men'. The biblical story of Jonah and the Whale symbolises the Resurrection.

Goldfinch A symbol of Christ's passion, the splash of red around its beak is said to be a drop of Christ's blood when the bird plucked a thorn from his brow on the road to Calvary. The bird, a favourite pet with children, is generally seen in the hand of the Christ Child.

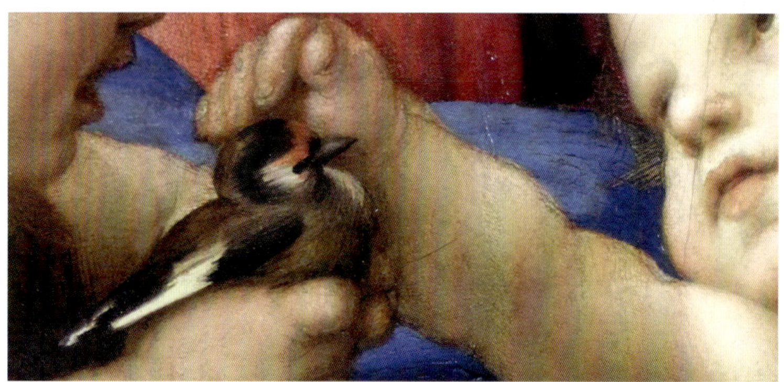

Fish: Workshop of Andrea del Verrocchio, *Tobias and the Angel*, *c.* 1470–75 (detail)

Goldfinch: Raphael, *Madonna of the Goldfinch*, *c.* 1505–06 (detail)

Gourd A symbol of Christ's resurrection, of forgiveness and pilgrimage. An attribute of the Archangel Gabriel. Dried and hollowed out, it was used to carry water and became a symbol of pilgrimage. Mentioned in the story of Jonah, who was swallowed by a whale and then disgorged, it can be seen as a symbol of Christ's Resurrection.

Grapes Fundamental to Christian iconography. The fruit most mentioned in the Bible, where they consistently allude to fertility. When grapes are shown together with corn they represent the wine and bread of the Eucharist. The vine symbolises loyalty. In mythology, grapes are linked to Dionysus, god of wine.

Halo The halo or nimbus is the light shining around the head of a divine person. It was not used in Christianity until the fifth century. It can be a symbol of power. An aureole denotes the radiance that appears to emanate from the whole figure, not just the head (see page 19). Artists depicted haloes in very different ways. Their shape was often governed by date and who was wearing them. It fell out of favour in post-Renaissance art.

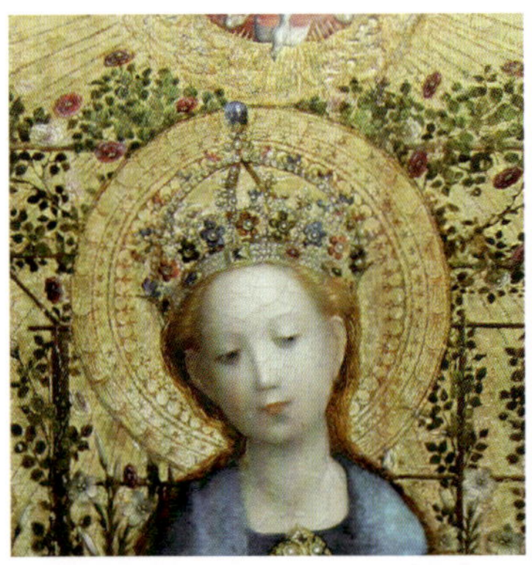

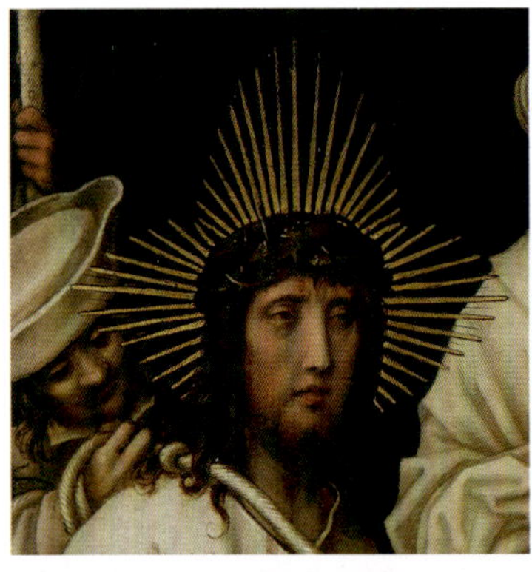

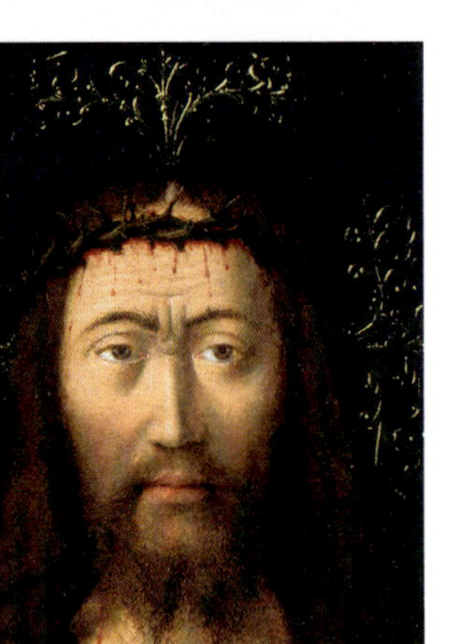

Haloes, clockwise from top left: Stefan Lochner, *Madonna of the Rose Bower*, *c.* 1440–42 (detail); Hans Holbein the Elder, *Grey Passion: Christ before Pilate*, 1494–1500 (detail); Petrus Christus, *Head of Christ*, *c.* 1445; Attrib. Master of San Miniato, *Virgin and Child with Goldfinch*, 1450–1500 (detail)

Iris Shares its symbolism with that of the lily. A white iris represents purity, the purple iris royalty. As the 'sword lily' it depicts the sorrow of the Virgin.

Lamb Symbolises innocence, gentleness, patience and humility. Adopted by early Christians as the symbol of Christ in his sacrificial role. It has different meanings when combined with other elements, such as a cross. Christ carrying a lamb is the Good Shepherd caring for his flock, or searching for and finding the lost lamb or sinner. It is the principal attribute of John the Baptist.

Laurel The evergreen leaves of the laurel or bay tree symbolise eternity or immortality. A laurel crown is a mark of political leadership, victorious Roman generals and poetic genius – hence Poet Laureate. Sacred to Apollo, Greek god of poetry.

Lily The white lily, *lilium candidum*, is a symbol of purity and innocence. It is the Virgin Mary's key attribute and is frequently present at the Annunciation either in a vase or carried by the Archangel Gabriel. It is also associated with the virgin saints.

Lion The attribute of the Evangelist Mark and of many others. A lion symbolises authority and the wise rule of mighty monarchies. A lion's skin is the attribute of Hercules.

Mirror Symbolises truth (a mirror does not lie), wisdom and the soul. A spotless mirror depicts the Virgin Mary. Can also symbolise pride, lust and vanity because it encourages self-obsession.

Monkey Often represents the Devil, also the baser human instincts: vanity, lust, folly, mischief, desire for luxury, inquisitiveness.

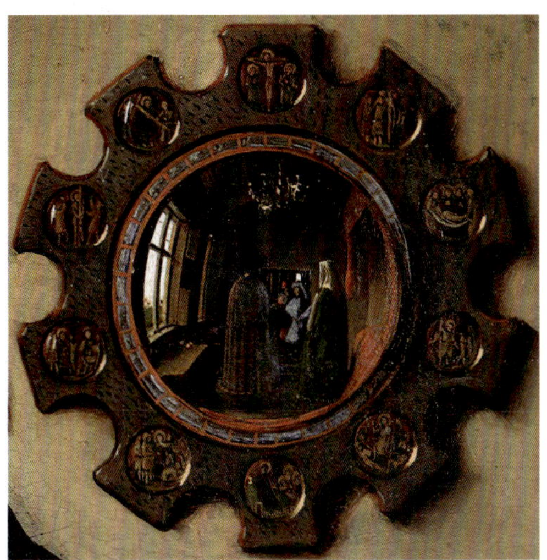

Moon A crescent moon is the attribute of the goddess Diana. If beneath the feet of the Virgin Mary it symbolises chastity, notably in paintings of the Immaculate Conception.

Myrtle An evergreen shrub, it is sacred to Venus and her companions, the Three Graces. A symbol of joy, peace and victory. To Renaissance artists it symbolised everlasting love and fidelity in marriage.

Owl In the ancient world it was associated with ignorance, dirt, evil and disease, but in the West it represented wisdom, possibly because it was the attribute of Minerva, the Greco-Roman goddess of tactical warfare. In Renaissance art it represented sleep and night.

Mirror: Jan van Eyck, *The Arnolfini Portrait*, 1434 (detail)

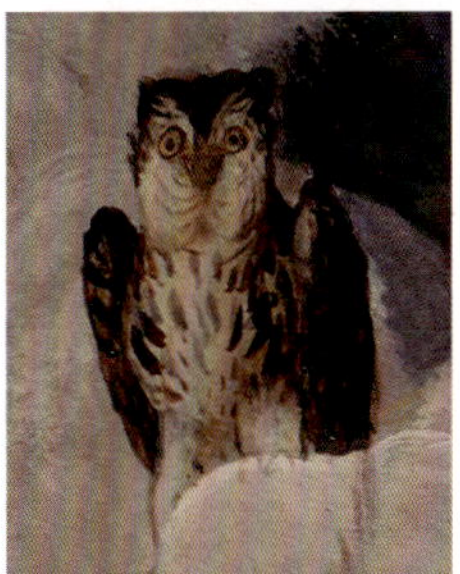

Owl: Giovanni Mannozzi, *The Night with Aurora and Cupid*, *c.* 1635 (detail)

Palm As an attribute of the goddess of Victory, it was a symbol of military success and fame for the Greeks and Romans. For Christians it represented Christ's triumphal entry into Jerusalem. It also symbolised victory over death, and thus martyrdom.

Partridge In medieval bestiaries the bird is reputed to be a thief, lustful and remarkably fertile. But it is also cunning in defence of its young. It can detect the Devil.

Peacock In Christian iconography it was linked to immortality and to Christ's Resurrection because its flesh was rumoured never to decay. The 'hundred eyes' in its tail symbolise the all-seeing Church. It was the attribute of Juno, queen of the gods.

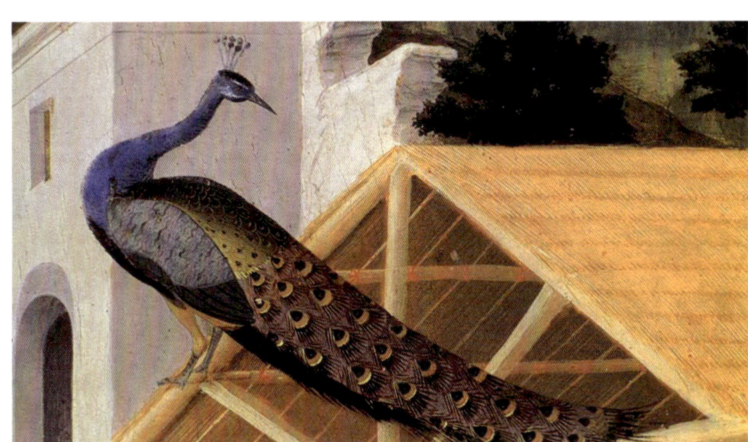

Peacock: Fra Filippo Lippi, *Adoration of the Magi*, *c.* 1445 (detail)

Pig A symbol of fertility, but also of gluttony, greed, lust, anger and the unclean. Attribute of St Anthony the Great, who overcame gluttony.

Pomegranate Symbol of eternal life. When held by the Christ Child it is a symbol of the Resurrection. Because it has many seeds in one body, it is also a symbol of the Church, which contains many souls.

Poppy Symbol of sleep, oblivion, degeneracy and death. Poppies seldom appear in Christian art, apart from occasions where the deep red variety represents the blood of Christ. A poppy's properties have evolved into the present day, but still include death (see page 50).

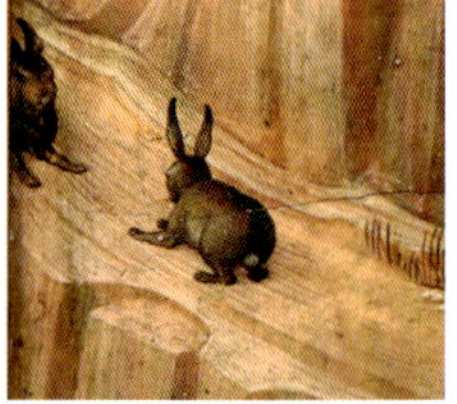

Rabbit: Andrea Mantegna, *The Agony in the Garden*, *c.* 1455 (detail)

Snake/Serpent: Lucas Cranach the Elder, *Adam and Eve*, 1528 (detail)

Rabbit A byword for fecundity and hence a symbol of lust. They are one of the many attributes of Venus. If sitting at the Virgin's feet, a rabbit symbolises the victory of chastity. The rabbit and hare are interchangeable.

Raven Symbol of ever-present death. Because it is able to talk, it represents prophecy. The first bird to be sent by Noah from the Ark to see if the waters had receded.

Rose Particularly associated with the Virgin Mary who is called the 'rose without thorns', i.e. sinless. A red rose symbolises martyrdom and references Christ's forthcoming Passion. The white rose represents innocence and purity. The rose can also symbolise eroticism and sensuality. It is closely associated with Venus.

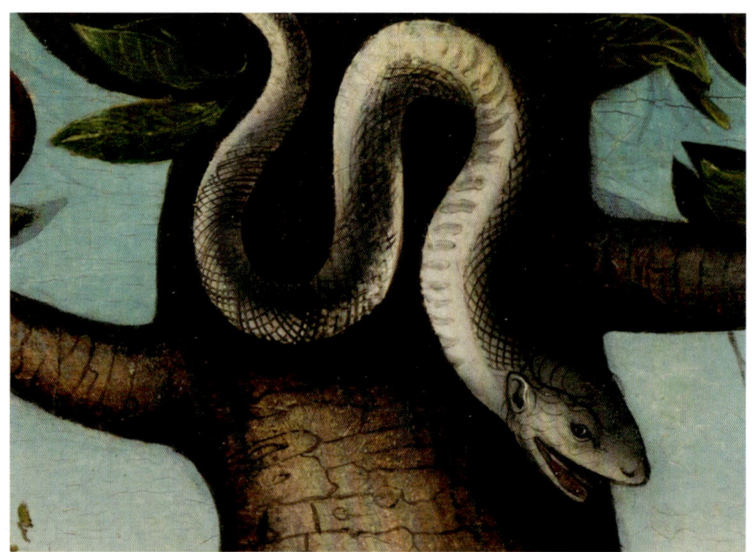

Skull A *memento mori* (reminder of death), the brevity of life and the vanity of worldly possessions. An attribute of St Francis and Mary Magdalene. In portraiture a sitter's hand resting on a skull indicates piety.

Snake/Serpent Seen as either good or bad. Because of its temptation of Eve in the Garden of Eden, it is seen as a symbol of sin and Satan. In the classical world it was associated with wisdom. (See **Dragon**)

Swastika For millennia it remained true to its Sanskrit meaning of 'well-being' or 'good fortune' in almost every culture in the world. To the Romans it was a symbol of good luck. In Germany in the late nineteenth and early twentieth centuries, it was seen by early right-wing groups as the visual equivalent of the 'Aryan' language. (See page 52.)

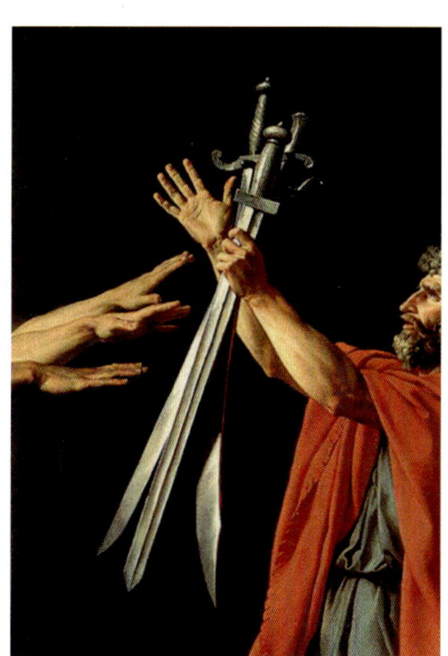

Sword A symbol of strength, masculine courage and authority. Associated with heroic virtue and action. When wielded by the Archangel Michael, it is a symbol of divine justice. The attribute of a Christian martyr and, as such, the emblem of St Paul.

Unicorn Symbol of purity, feminine chastity and virginity, thus it is associated with the Virgin Mary. In the late Middle Ages and the Renaissance its horn was said to be an antidote to poison, which symbolised Christ's power to destroy sin. Seen as both a symbol of Christ and of worldly love.

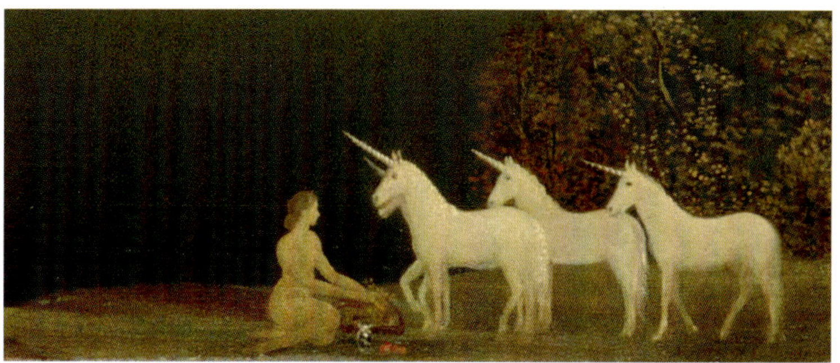

Sword: Jacques-Louis David, *Oath of the Horatii*, 1784 (detail)

Unicorn: Arthur Bowen Davies, *Unicorns (Legend–Sea Calm)*, *c.* 1906

Wheel: Caravaggio, *St Catherine of Alexandria*, *c.* 1598

Violet Symbol of modesty, humility and submission to God's will.

Wheel A symbol of oppression when it appears as the instrument of St Catherine's martyrdom.

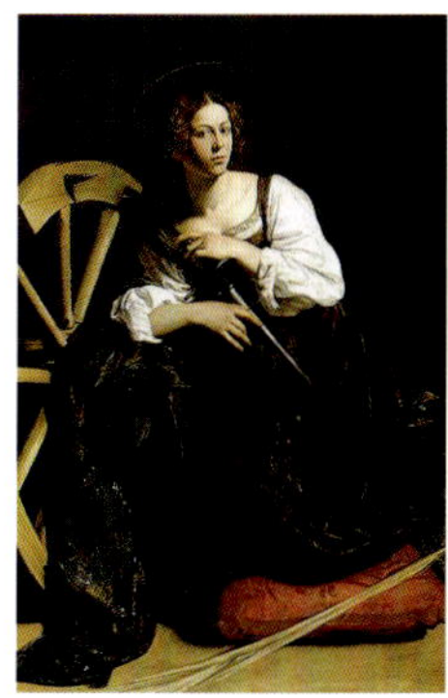

BIBLIOGRAPHY

Ajmar-Wollheim, A. and F. Dennis, *At Home in Renaissance Italy*, exhibition catalogue, Victoria & Albert Museum, London, 2006

Battistini, M., *Symbols and Allegories in Art*, (trans.) S. Sartarelli, Los Angeles, 2005

Bergström, I., *Dutch Still-Life Painting in the Seventeenth Century*, London, 1956

Beyer, A., *Portraits: A History*, (trans.) S. Lindberg, Munich, 2003

Cannon-Brookes, P. and C. Sterling, *Still Life Painting from Antiquity to the Twentieth Century*, Oxford, 1984

Carr-Gomm, S., *Dictionary of Symbols in Art*, London, 1995

––––––, *The Secret Language of Art*, London, 2001

Cherry, J. (ed.), *Mythical Beasts*, London, 1995

Clark, K., *Civilisation*, London, 1971

Cooper, J.C., *An Illustrated Encyclopaedia of Traditional Symbols*, London, 1978

Dimbleby, J., *A Profound Secret*, London, 2004

Farthing, S. (ed.), *1001 Paintings You Must See Before You Die*, London, 2018

Frick, C.C., *Dressing Renaissance Florence*, Baltimore & London, 2002

Gascoigne, Laura, 'The Devil's in the Detail', *The Spectator*, 16–30 December, 2023

Gayford, M., *Michelangelo: His Epic Life*, London, 2013

––––––, *The Pursuit of Art*, London, 2018

Gombrich, E.H., *The Story of Art*, Oxford, 1989

––––––, *Symbolic Images: Studies in the Art of the Renaissance*, London, 1972

Graham-Dixon, A., *Caravaggio: A Life Sacred and Profane*, London, 2011

Grovier, K., *A New Way of Seeing: The History of Art in 57 Works*, London, 2018

Hagen, R-M. and R., *What Great Paintings Say*, London, 2005, Vols I & II

Hall, J., *Hall's Dictionary of Subjects and Symbols in Art*, London, 1989

––––––, *The Self-Portrait: A Cultural History*, London, 2014

Harrison, C., *An Introduction to Art*, Newhaven & London, 2020

Impelluso, L., *Gods and Heroes in Art* (ed.) S. Zuffi, (trans.) T.M. Hartmann, Los Angeles, 2002

Jones, C.P., *Great Paintings Explained*, Leamington Spa, 2021

––––––, *Great Paintings That Tell Stories*, Leamington Spa, 2023

––––––, *How to Read Paintings*, Leamington Spa, 2020

––––––, *Masterpieces of Art Explained*, Leamington Spa, 2023

––––––, *What Great Artworks Say*, Leamington Spa, 2022

Jones, J., *Earthly Delights: A History of the Renaissance*, London, 2024

Jones, R., and N. Penny, *Raphael*, New Haven & London, 1983

Mancoff, D., *The Secrets of Art*, London, 2021

Millar, O., *The Queen's Pictures*, London, 1977

Moyle, F., *The King's Painter: The Life and Times of Hans Holbein*, London, 2021

Mullins, E. (ed.), *Great Paintings: Fifty Masterpieces, Explored, Explained and Appreciated*, New York, 1981

Nicholl, C., *Leonardo da Vinci: Flights of the Mind*, London, 2004

Noble, B., *Lucas Cranach the Elder: Art and Devotion of the German Reformation*, Plymouth, 2009

Panofsky, E., *Early Netherlandish Painting: Its Origins and Character*, Cambridge, Mass., 1953, Vol. I

——————, *Meaning in the Visual Arts*, London, 1983

Pietrangeli, P., et al., *The Sistine Chapel: The Art, the History, and the Restoration*, London, 1986

Roelofs, P. and G.J.M. Weber, *Vermeer*, exhibition catalogue, Rijksmuseum, Amsterdam, 2023

Rynck, P. de, *How to Read a Painting*, London, 2004

———————, *Understanding Paintings: Bible Stories and Classical Myths in Art*, (trans.) Y. Rosenberg, London, 2009

Rubens: A Master in the Making, exhibition catalogue, National Gallery, London, 2005

Schama, S., *Rembrandt's Eyes*, London, 2000

Stemp, R., *The Secret Language of the Renaissance: Decoding the Hidden Symbolism of Italian Art*, London, 2018

Still Life Paintings from the Netherlands, 1550–1720, exhibition catalogue, Rijksmuseum, Amsterdam, *c.* 1999

The Story of Painting: How Art was Made, Dorling Kindersley, London, 2019

Strong, R., *Artists of the Tudor Court: The Portrait Miniature Rediscovered*, 1520–1620, London, 1983

Vasari, G., *Lives of Painters, Sculptors and Architects*, (trans.) G. du C. De Vere, London, 1996, Vols I & II

Voragine, J. de, *The Golden Legend* (trans.) C. Stace, London, 1998

Wittkower, R., *Allegory and the Migration of Symbols*, London, 1977

Wilson, M., *Hidden Language of Symbols*, London, 2022

—————, *Symbols in Art*, London, 2022

Woodford, S., *Looking at Pictures*, London, 2020

LIST OF ILLUSTRATIONS

Illustrations are listed by page number.

T = top | C = centre | B = bottom | TL = top left
TR = top right | BL = bottom left | BR = bottom right

Front cover: Giovanni di Paolo, *Paradise*, 1445. Tempera and gold on canvas, transferred from wood, 47 x 40.6 cm. Metropolitan Museum of Art, New York /Rogers Fund, 1906

Back cover: TL Andrea Mantegna, *San Luca Altarpiece*, 1453–54 (detail). Panel, overall dimensions 177 x 230 cm. Brera, Milan; TR Caravaggio, *Supper at Emmaus*, *c.* 1601 (detail); BL Albrecht Dürer, *Lot and His Daughters*, *c.* 1496–99 (detail); BR Sofonisba Anguissola, *The Game of Chess*, 1555 (detail)

Half title: Raphael, *Sistine Madonna*, 1513-14 (detail). Oil on canvas, 265 x 196 cm. Gemäldegalerie Alte Meister, Staatliche Kunstsammlungen Dresden, Germany

Title page: Peter Paul Rubens, *The Raising of Lazarus*, 1625. Oil on canvas, 177 x 160 cm. Galleria Sabauda, Turin

4. Giovanni Bellini, *Madonna with the Child (Greek Madonna)*, 1460–64. Tempera on wood, 82 x 62 cm. Brera Milan

6. Titian, *The Madonna of the Rabbit*, *c.* 1520–30. Oil on canvas, 71 x 85 cm. Louvre Museum, Paris.

8. Sandro Botticelli, *Madonna of the Eucharist*, *c.* 1470 (detail). Tempera on panel, 85.2 x 65 cm. Isabella Stewart Gardner Museum, Boston, USA

12. Anonymous, *The Wilton Diptych*, 1395–99. Tempera on panel, 53 x 57 cm. National Gallery, London

14. Upper Rhenish Master, *The Little Garden of Paradise*. *c.* 1410. Mixed technique on oak panel, 26.3 x 33.4 cm. Städel Museum, Frankfurt

16. Robert Campin, *The Mérode Triptych*, *c.* 1427–32. Oil on oak panel, central panel, 64.1 x 63.2 cm. Metropolitan Museum of Art, The Cloisters Collection, New York, 1956

18. Stefan Lochner, *Madonna of the Rose Bower*, *c.* 1440–42. Oil and tempera on panel, 51 x 40 cm. Wallraf-Richartz Museum, Cologne, Germany

19. Antonio Pisanello, *The Virgin and Child with Saints Anthony Abbot and George*, *c.* 1435–41. Egg tempera on wood, 46.5 x 29 cm. National Gallery, London

20. Andrea Mantegna, *The Agony in the Garden*, *c.* 1455. Tempera on panel, 62.9 x 80 cm. National Gallery, London

21. Sandro Botticelli, *The Virgin and Child and Eight Angels*, 1478. Tempera on wood, diameter: 136.5 cm. Gemäldegalerie der Staatlichen Museen zu Berlin

22. Hugo van der Goes, *The Portinari Triptych*, 1476–78. Oil on panel, 253 x 586 cm. Uffizi Gallery, Florence

26. Carlo Crivelli, *The Annunciation, with Saint Emidius*, 1486. Egg tempera and oil on canvas, 207 x 147 cm. National Gallery, London

27. Geertgen Tot Sint Jans, *The Holy Kinship*, 1495. Oil on oak panel, 137.2 x 105.8 cm. Rijksmuseum, Amsterdam

28. Giovanni Bellini, *Madonna of the Meadow*, *c.* 1505. Oil, originally on wood, transferred to board, 67.3 x 86.4 cm. National Gallery, London

29. Raphael, *The Miraculous Draught of Fishes*, *c.* 1515–16. Cartoon, 360 x 400 cm. Royal Collection/ Victoria and Albert Museum, London

30. Raphael, *Ezekiel's Vision*, *c.* 1518. Oil on panel, 41 x 30 cm. Galleria Palatina, Florence

31. Giovanni Battista Tiepolo, *The Immaculate Conception*, 1767. Oil on canvas, 281 x 155 cm. Prado Museum, Madrid

34. Antonio Pisanello, *A Princess of the House of Este*, 1433. Tempera on wood, 43 x 30 cm. Louvre Museum, Paris

35. Jan van Eyck, *The Arnolfini Portrait*, 1434. Oil on wood, 82 x 59.5 cm. National Gallery, London

36. Lorenzo Lotto, *Portrait of a Gentleman in his Study*, 1528–30. Oil on canvas, 98 x 116 cm. Gallerie dell'Accademia, Venice

37. Agnolo Bronzino, *Portrait of a Lady in Red*, *c.* 1533. Mixed technique on poplar panel, 89.8 x 70.5 cm. Städel Museum, Frankfurt

38. Nicholas Hilliard, *George Clifford, 3rd Earl of Cumberland*, *c.* 1590. Watercolor and gouache on vellum, 19 x 27 cm. National Maritime Museum, Greenwich, London, Caird Collection. akg-images / De Agostini Picture Library.

39. Isaac Oliver, *The Rainbow Portrait*, *c.* 1600. Oil on canvas, 127 x 99.1 cm. Hatfield House, Hertfordshire, UK

40. Anthony Van Dyck, *Venetia, Lady Digby*, *c.* 1633–34. Oil on canvas, 101.1 x 80.2 cm. National Portrait Gallery, London

41. William Hogarth, *The Graham Children*, 1742. Oil on canvas, 160.5 x 181 cm. National Gallery, London

42. Pompeo Batoni, *Francis Basset*, 1778. Oil on canvas, 221 x 157 cm. Prado Museum, Madrid

43. François Boucher, *Madame de Pompadour*, 1756. Oil on canvas, 212 x 164 cm. Alte Pinakothek, Munich

46. Caravaggio, *Supper at Emmaus*, *c.* 1601. Oil on canvas, 141 x 196.2 cm. National Gallery, London

47T. Francisco de Zurbarán, *Still Life with Lemons, Oranges and a Rose*, 1633. Oil on canvas, 62.2 x 109.5 cm. Norton Simon Museum, Pasadena, CA, USA /Bridgeman Images

47C. Jan Davidsz. de Heem, *A Vanitas Still Life with a Skull, a Book and Roses*, *c.* 1630. Oil on panel, 23.2 x 34.6 cm. Nationalmuseum, Stockholm, Sweden

47B. Maria van Oosterwijck, *Vase of Tulips, Rose and Other Flowers with Insects*, 1669. Oil on canvas, 46 x 37.1 cm. Cincinnati Art Museum, USA

48. Sandro Botticelli, *Minerva and the Centaur*, *c.* 1482. Tempera on canvas, 207 x 148 cm. Uffizi Gallery, Florence

49T. Paolo Uccello, *Saint George and the Dragon*, 1470. Oil on canvas, 55.5 x 74 cm. National Gallery, London

49L. Henry Fuseli, *Thor Battering the Midgard Serpent*, 1790. Oil on canvas, 26.7 cm x 37.8 cm. Royal Academy of Arts, London

49R. Domenichino, *Virgin and the Unicorn*, *c.* 1602. Fresco, 21.3 x 16.9 cm. Palazzo Farnese, Rome

50T. Poppies at the Cenotaph, London. Wikimedia / Sergeant Steven Hughes, RLC/MOD

50B. Giovanni da San Giovanni, *The Night with Aurora and Cupid*, *c.* 1635 (detail). Fresco, 26.5 x 41.1 cm. Museo Bardini, Florence

51T. Fra Filippo Lippi, *Adoration of the Child with St Bernard*, 1463 (detail) Tempera on panel, 140 x 130 cm. Uffizi Gallery, Florence

51B. 'The Dove that Goes Boom!', anti-communist poster, 1952–53. Colour litho. Private Collection / © Succession Picasso/DACS, London 2025 / Bridgeman Images

78. Sandro Botticelli, *Spring*, *c.* 1480. Tempera on poplar, 203 x 314 cm. Uffizi Gallery, Florence

80. Gherardo di Giovanni del Fora, *The Combat of Love and Chastity*, *c.* 1475–1500. Tempera on panel, 43 x 35 cm. National Gallery, London

81. Hieronymus Bosch, *The Ship of Fools*, *c.* 1494–1510. Oil on oak wood, 58 x 33 cm. Louvre Museum, Paris

82. Raphael, *The Dream of a Knight*, *c.* 1504. Oil on poplar wood, 17.1 x 17.3 cm. National Gallery, London

83. Lorenzo Lotto, *Allegory of Virtue and Vice*, 1505. Oil on panel, 56.5 x 43.2 cm. National Gallery of Art, Washington, DC / Samuel H. Kress Collection

84. Agnolo Bronzino, *An Allegory with Venus and Cupid*, *c.* 1540–45. Oil on wood, 146.5 x 116.8 cm. National Gallery, London

85. Johannes Vermeer, *Woman Holding a Balance*, *c.* 1664. Oil on canvas, 40.3 x 35.5 cm. National Gallery of Art, Washington, DC

88. Lorenzo Costa, *The Expedition of the Argonauts*, 1484–90. Tempera on oak panel, 46 x 53 cm. Civic Museums of Padua, Italy

89. Andrea Mantegna, *Parnassus*, 1497. Tempera on canvas, 160 x 192 cm. Louvre Museum, Paris

90. Follower of Leonardo da Vinci (Cesare da Sesto?), *Leda and the Swan*, 1505–10. Oil on panel, dimensions unknown. Collection of the Earl of Pembroke, Wilton House, Wilts. / Bridgeman Images

91. Niklaus Manuel, *The Judgement of Paris*, *c.* 1516–28. Tempera on canvas, 223 x 160 cm. Kunstmuseum Basel, Switzerland

92. Titian, *Bacchus and Ariadne*, 1520–23. Oil on canvas, 176.5 x 191 cm. National Gallery, London

93. Pieter Bruegel the Elder, *Landscape with the Fall of Icarus*, 1558. Oil on canvas, 73.5 x 112 cm. Royal Museums of Fine Arts of Belgium, Brussels

94. Jacopo Tintoretto, *The Origin of the Milky Way*, *c.* 1575. Oil on canvas, 18 x 165 cm. National Gallery, London

95. Paolo Veronese, *Venus and Adonis*, *c.* 1580. Oil on canvas, 162 x 185 cm. Prado Museum, Madrid

96. Peter Paul Rubens, *The Abduction of Ganymede*, 1611–12. Oil on canvas, 203 x 203 cm. Schwarzenberg Palace, Vienna

97. Johannes Vermeer, *Diana and Her Companions*, 1655–56. Oil on canvas, 98.5 x 105 cm. Mauritshuis, The Hague

100. Master Francke, *The Pursuit of St Barbara*, *c.* 1410–15. Tempera on wood, 91 x 54 cm. National Museum of Finland, Helsinki

101. Fra Angelico, *St Nicholas of Bari*, 1437. Tempera on panel, overall dimensions 128 x 88 cm. National Gallery of Umbria, Perugia, Italy

102. Hieronymus Bosch, *St Christopher Carrying the Christ Child*, 1490/96. Oil on panel, 113 x 71.5 cm. Museum Boijmans Van Beuningen, Rotterdam

103. Vittore Carpaccio, *Dream of St Ursula*, 1497–98. Tempera and oil on canvas, 273 x 267 cm. Gallerie dell'Accademia, Venice

104. Master of St Giles, *St Giles and the Hind*, 1500. Oil and egg tempera on oak wood, 61 x 45 cm. National Gallery, London / Bridgeman Images

105. Jacques-Louis David, *Oath of the Horatii*, 1784. Oil on canvas, 330 x 401.5 cm. Louvre Museum, Paris

106. Jean-Auguste-Dominique Ingres, *The Dream of Ossian*, 1813. Oil on canvas, 348 x 275 cm. Musée Ingres, Montauban, France

107. Edward Burne-Jones, *The Last Sleep of Arthur in Avalon*, *c.* 1881–98 (detail). Oil on canvas, 282 x 645 cm. Museo de Arte de Ponce, The Luis A. Ferre Foundation, Inc., Puerto Rico / Bridgeman Images

110. Raphael, *The School of Athens*, 1508–11. Fresco, width at base, 770 cm. Vatican Museums and Galleries, Vatican City, Rome

112. Michelangelo, *The Libyan Sibyl*, *c.* 1511, The Sistine Chapel Ceiling, Rome

113. Rembrandt van Rijn, *Aristotle with a Bust of Homer*, 1653. Oil on canvas, 143.5 x 136.5 cm. Metropolitan Museum of Art, New York / Purchased by the Metropolitan Museum of Art with support of friends of the Museum

114. Giovanni Battista Tiepolo, *The Banquet of Cleopatra*, 1743–44. Oil on canvas, 250.3 x 357 cm. National Gallery of Victoria, Melbourne, Australia

115. Jacques-Louis David, *The Death of Socrates*, 1787. Oil on canvas, 130 x 196 cm. The Metropolitan Museum of Art, New York

118. The Limbourg brothers, February from *Les Très Riches Heures du duc de Berry*, *c.* 1416. Tempera on vellum, 22.5 x 13.6 cm. Condé Museum, Paris

119. Giovanni Mansueti, *The Miraculous Healing of the Daughter of Benvegnudo of San Polo*, *c.* 1505. Tempera on canvas, 369 x 296 cm. Gallerie dell'Accademia, Venice

120. Hans Holbein the Younger, *The Ambassadors*, 1533. Oil on oak panel, 207 x 209.5 cm. National Gallery, London

121. Sofonisba Anguissola, *The Game of Chess*, 1555. Oil on canvas, 72 × 97 cm. National Museum, Poznań, Poland.

122. Pieter Bruegel the Elder, *Hunters in the Snow*, *c.* 1565. Oil on panel, 117 x 162 cm. Kunsthistorisches Museum, Vienna

123. Georges de la Tour, *The Card Sharp with the Ace of Diamonds*, *c.* 1635–40. Oil on canvas, 106 x 146 cm. Louvre Museum, Paris / Bridgeman Images

124. Jan Steen, *The Burgher of Delft and his Daughter*, 1655. Oil on canvas, 82.5 x 68.7 cm. Rijksmuseum, Amsterdam

125. François Boucher, *The Breakfast*, 1739. Oil on canvas, 81.5 x 65.5 cm. Louvre Museum, Paris

126. Thomas Gainsborough, *Mr and Mrs Andrews*, *c.* 1750. Oil on canvas, 70 x 119 cm. National Gallery, London

127. Johan Zoffany, *The Tribuna of the Uffizi*, 1772–77. Oil on canvas, 123.5 x 154.9 cm. Royal Collection, London

130. Benozzo Gozzoli, *The Procession of the Magi*, 1459–63 (detail). Fresco, Palazzo Medici, Florence

131. Albrecht Dürer, *Adoration of the Magi*, 1504. Oil on wood, 99 x 113.5 cm. Uffizi Gallery, Florence

132. Michelangelo, *The Last Judgement*, Sistine Chapel, Rome, 1536–41 (detail)

133. Diego Velásquez, *Las Meninas*, 1656. Oil on canvas, 320 x 276 cm. Prado Museum, Madrid

134. Caravaggio, *David with the Head of Goliath*, 1606. Oil on canvas, 125 x 101 cm. Galleria Borghese, Rome

135. Anthony van Dyck, *Daedalus and Icarus*, 1615–25. Oil on canvas, 115.3 x 86.4 cm. Art Gallery of Ontario, Canada

138T. Bernardino Luini, *Three Angels on Clouds*, *c.* 1515–18. Oil on panel, 57.7 x 75.6 cm

138B. Hans Memling, *Diptych of Maarten Nieuwenhove*, 1487 (detail). Oil on oak wood, 52 x 41.5 cm. Sint-Jan de Bruges, Belgium

139T. Antonio Pisanello, *A Princess of the House of Este*, 1433 (detail). Tempera on wood, 43 x 30 cm. Louvre Museum, Paris

139C. Robert Campin, *The Mérode Triptych*, *c.* 1427–32 (detail). Oil on oak panel, central panel, 64.1 x 63.2 cm. Metropolitan Museum of Art, The Cloisters Collection, New York, 1956

139B. William Hogarth, *The Graham Children*, 1742 (detail). Oil on canvas, 160.5 x 181 cm. National Gallery, London

140T. Jan van Eyck, *The Arnolfini Portrait*, 1434 (detail). Oil on wood, 82 x 59.5 cm. National Gallery, London

140B. Anonymous, *Madonna on a Crescent Moon in Hortus Conclusus*, 1450 (detail). Oil on oak wood, 95 x 62 cm. Gemäldegalerie. Staatliche Museen zu Berlin

141T. Workshop of Andrea del Verrocchio, *Tobias and the Angel*, c. 1470–75 (detail). Egg tempera on poplar wood, 83.6 x 66 cm. National Gallery, London

141B. Raphael, *Madonna of the Goldfinch*, *c.* 1505–06 (detail). Oil on panel, 107 x 77 cm. Uffizi Gallery, Florence

142TL. Stefan Lochner, *Madonna of the Rose Bower*, *c.* 1440–42 (detail). Oil and tempera on panel, 51 x 40 cm. Wallraf-Richartz Museum, Cologne, Germany

142TR. Hans Holbein the Elder, *Grey Passion: Christ Before Pilate*, 1494–1500 (detail). Oil on spruce wood, 89.4 x 87.4 cm. Staatsgalerie Stuttgart

142BL. Attrib. Master of San Miniato, *Virgin and Child with Goldfinch*, 1450–1500 (detail). Tempera on panel, 61 x 44.7 cm. Musée de Tessé, Le Mans, France

142BR. Petrus Christus, *Head of Christ*, *c.* 1445. Oil on parchment, laid down on wood, 14.9 x 10.8 cm. Metropolitan Museum of Art / Bequest of Lillian S. Timken, 1959

143T. Jan van Eyck, *The Arnolfini Portrait*, 1434 (detail). Oil on wood, 82 x 59.5 cm. National Gallery, London

143C. Giovanni da San Giovanni, *The Night with Aurora and Cupid*, *c.* 1635 (detail). Fresco, 26.5 x 41.1 cm. Museo Bardini, Florence

143B. Fra Filippo Lippi, *Adoration of the Magi*, *c.* 1445 (detail). Oil on wood, diameter, 137.3 cm. National Gallery of Art, Washington / Samuel H. Kress Collection

144T. Andrea Mantegna, *The Agony in the Garden*, *c.* 1455 (detail). Tempera on panel, 62.9 x 80 cm. National Gallery, London

144B. Lucas Cranach the Elder, *Adam and Eve*, 1528 (detail). Oil on panel, 56.6 x 34.9 cm. Detroit Institute of Arts, USA

145T. Jacques-Louis David, *Oath of the Horatii*, 1784 (detail). Oil on canvas, 330 x 401.5 cm. Louvre Museum, Paris

145C. Arthur Bowen Davies, *Unicorns* (Legend – Sea Calm), *c.* 1906 (detail). Oil on canvas, 46.4 x 102.2 cm. Metropolitan Museum of Art, New York / Bequest of Lillie P. Bliss, 1931

145B. Caravaggio, *St Catherine of Alexandria*, *c.* 1598. Oil on canvas, 173 x 133 cm. Thyssen-Bornemisza Museum, Madrid

GODS AND GODDESSES

Most Roman gods and goddesses are renamed counterparts of their Greek predecessors, with similar attributes and powers. In order to avoid confusion, the form of name used for prominent deities has been chosen to reflect contemporary usage and the artists' own titles for their works. The list is limited to those gods and goddesses in this book.

Greek	Roman
Aphrodite	Venus
Artemis	Diana
Athena	Minerva
Eros	Cupid
Dionysus	Bacchus
Hermes	Mercury
Heracles	Hercules
Hera	Juno
Leda	Leda

Greek	Roman
Medea	Medea
Mount Olympus	Capitoline Hill
Odysseus	Ulysses
Paris	Paris
Perseus	Perseus
Psyche	Psyche
Silenus	Silenus
Theseus	Theseus
Zeus	Jupiter

INDEX

Page numbers indicate both text and artworks, those in bold are for main featured artworks.

D

E

F

G

ACKNOWLEDGEMENTS

This has been a complicated book to put together. That it looks as good as it does is entirely due to the skills and ingenuity of the designer Nicola Liddiard. That the text is coherent, logical and with all my infelicities ironed out is thanks to the incomparable editor, Liz Wyse. Ramona Lamport's eagle eye has ensured that every t is crossed and every i dotted. Lucy Duckworth, Unicorn's Publishing Director, has held all the disparate parts together. Finally, I am very grateful to Unicorn's Chairman, Ian Strathcarron, for accepting the book for publication.

Painted Mysteries would never have come to fruition without the staunch support of my family: the monumental patience and forbearance of my husband Roger, the incredible generosity of my sister-in-law Jan Conway, and the interest and advice of my daughters, Catherine and Jessy.

Published in 2025 by Unicorn
an imprint of Unicorn Publishing Group
Charleston Studio
Meadow Business Centre
Lewes BN8 5RW
www.unicornpublishing.org

ISBN 978-1-917458-29-0
10 9 8 7 6 5 4 3 2 1

Designed by Big Orange Door
Printed in Turkey by Fine Tone